Jewellery in context

A multidisciplinary framework for the study of jewellery

Dissertation
to obtain
the degree of Doctor at Leiden University,
on the authority of the Rector Magnificus Prof. P.F. van der Heijden,
in accordance with the decision of the Doctoral Degree Board,
to be defended in public on Wednesday, 17 March 2010
at 15.00 hours.

by
Marianne Unger-de Boer,
born in 1946 in Bussum, the Netherlands.

arnoldsche

Foreword

You hold in your hands the English translation of Marjan Unger's dissertation. In my opinion, this essay is one of her purest. Among all the other texts I know on adornment and jewellery, it stands out as an absolute elementary standard work, and I consider it a 'must-read' for every jewellery student. But also for professionals, it will certainly open new perspectives and widen horizons. For interested laymen, it is a perfect introduction to the field of jewellery and adornment.

Until now, 'Jewellery in Context – A multidisciplinary framework for the study of jewellery' was available in Dutch only. I often asked Marjan to also publish this text in English in order to make it available beyond the Dutch-speaking borders. But knowing that she did't have much time left, she kept telling me that she preferred to do 'new' writing and asked me to be patient – again and again. Just before she passed away, she gave me the right to publish the English version of her dissertation and asked me to take care of it. In consultation with Gerard Unger and Chequita Nahar, I conceived this book as a co-publication with many other jewellery institutions, schools, entrepreneurs and interested individuals. we considered this to be mostly in Marjan's spirit.

My sincere thanks go to Suzanne van Leeuwen, Chequita Nahar, Dirk Allgaier, Wolfgang Lösche and all the co-publishers for making this possible.

Dr. Marjan Unger passed away in 2018 – a grave loss, not only for our field. Her work and heritage however, will continue to inspire and educate generations of jewellery lovers worldwide. Holding the Englisch version of Marjan Unger's dissertation in my hands makes me happy. I wish you the same while reading this book!

August 2019,
Theo Smeets

Doctoral Committee

Promotors:
Prof. Dr. T. M. Eliëns, Leiden University
Prof. Dr. C. W. Fock, Leiden University

Other members:
Prof. Dr. K. Zijlmans, Leiden University
Prof. Dr. A. Bergmans, University of Ghent
Prof. Dr. J. R. ter Molen, Radboud University Nijmegen
Dr. M. Groot, Leiden University

Theorems

1 A term such as 'modern jewellery' refers more to a certain period within the twentieth century than to a distinction with jewellery from the preceding periods.

2 Jewellery is essentially nothing less than wearable money; all the same, it can be more than wearable money.

3 The goldsmith's trade is a shining example of a design discipline in which recycling has always been the norm.

4 Symbolism in jewellery is rooted in the motifs that underlie its wearing. These motifs are based not only on social, cultural and moral norms that often have a great deal of continuity, but also on the personal and time-bound points of view of the maker, the client and the wearer.

5 The term 'art' should not be used as a quality standard with regard to design products, including jewellery.

6 It is amazing to think that many of the natural materials used in jewellery come from 'the underworld': ores from deep underground, stones that are mined, treasures from the sea and the raw materials used to make synthetic materials. The things from 'the upper world' serve more as inspiration and model. This observation can serve as a metaphor for analysing the many forms of symbolism associated with jewellery.

7 The fact that jewellery primarily has an affirmative function within social groups, that each group lives with its own codes and that the lower classes or subcultures can also influence the preferences of other social groups, are recent notions from the human sciences that are of great value for the study of jewellery.

8 Craft does not exclude thinking.

9 An art historian cannot live on masterpieces alone

10 Neither the possession of a pearl necklace nor the wearing of a it constitute an essential obstacle to the scientific approach to a cultural phenomenon such as jewellery.

Table of contents

1 Introduction

Pieces of jewellery are expressions of the fundamental human need for decoration and ornamentation. They symbolise people's enjoyment of life and respond to their need to make themselves known to each other and to face the world around them with their head held high.

In primeval times people would already satisfy this need with a beautiful shell, a delicate stone, a few flowers or the teeth of a defeated wild animal. Pieces of jewellery belong to people and are probably as old as mankind.

The human body determines the size of jewellery. Being small objects, essentially, they can carry an incredible number of meanings. (1) Over the centuries, all human pleasures and challenges have been represented in jewellery: eroticism, power display, pragmatism, the conjuration of the supernatural as much as the love for the natural, the love for a certain person, sadness and the pure pursuit of beauty. Each era generates its own messages, usually as variations on these universal meanings.

Jewellery items are not always immediately visible. They have a certain intimacy, because they are close to the skin and they can generally be appreciated only from up close. In our culture we are not inclined to violate this intimacy too much.

What fascinates is the tension between the intimacy of jewellery and the scope of the messages conveyed by jewellery. (2) The concentration of meanings in small objects like rings, necklaces, bracelets, belts and headdresses is outright fascinating. The limited size invites not only precision and excellence, or the highest levels of craftsmanship, but also spontaneity, as ornaments may be worn for a few hours only.

Masterpieces of goldsmithing, composed of durable materials, have often withstood the times best, and they tend to be well documented as well. They are attractive to beholders largely for the monetary value they represent, and over time they have given jewellery the dubious aura of status symbol.

However, the value of an ornament is not only determined by its material value or market value. Jewellery generates an endless variety of temptations. As an art historian specialising in design, I like to be seduced by jewellery, but I also want to understand why people wear jewellery and what messages they thus communicate (at present and in the past) in order to arrive at more insight into what determines the value of jewellery.

For *Het Nederlandse sieraad in de twintigste eeuw* (Dutch jewellery in the twentieth century), a study published in 2004, I spent ten years researching jewellery made and worn in the Netherlands, with a specific focus on the underlying mentality which in several respects differs from uses and customs in the neighbouring countries. The most important difference is the particular reticence regarding outward display, which appears to be deeply anchored in Dutch culture.

This research addressed not only cultural highlights of the jewellery trade or jewellery worn by the upper classes, but also jewellery worn by the rank and file, such as regional jewellery, war and liberation jewellery and, for example, the discreet return of men's jewellery at the end of the twentieth century. I traced many unknown works from before 1968 and placed them in a cultural-historical context. I considered the post 1968 period, about which much more is known, according to the same principles and criteria: not only the highlights from applied art and design, but also popular and widely disseminated forms of jewellery. If for the period until 1968 I could address most developments in detail, for the period after that I had to be much more selective.

My quest for a comprehensive picture spanning an entire century complicated the effort to sketch the broad outlines in a number of ways. It proved hard in particular to develop a multidisciplinary approach to the study of jewellery in great detail, as all the information complicated the design of such approach. (3) Because many more jewellery items and texts on the jewellery trade are available on the period after 1968, I gave much attention to putting the so-called revolution in Dutch jewellery design of around 1970 into perspective. This approach was also a response to the unbalanced and limited view on jewellery, which in the study of jewellery has been the norm rather than the exception. (4)

For this reason, *Het Nederlandse sieraad* (Dutch jewellery) is perhaps best regarded as a collection of detailed studies, instead of as a consistent treatise on jewellery as a cultural phenomenon. Today, however, I would still forcefully defend the organisation of the book and the way in which it describes jewellery as part of Dutch culture throughout that most exciting century. The questions I explored as an art historian for each sub-topic are still relevant. My direct approach, one of a critical yet benevolent observer and wearer of jewellery, is quite appropriate for the study of jewellery. Wearing a piece of jewellery, after all, is and will continue to be the ultimate test to assess its effect. (5)

What a piece of jewellery is, is rarely or never defined in publications about jewellery. This also became evident in my follow-up research about which I report in this essay. (6) Jewellery is such a universal phenomenon that a definition seems superfluous, but the ways in which it is looked at are constantly changing. This was very much the case in the course of the twentieth century, for example, partly in response to particular societal and economic developments. In the western world, more people than ever gained access to luxury goods. At the same time, jewellery became more and more the exclusive domain of women. Strict divisions also arose in the jewellery trade: value judgements with regard to design and materials began to shift, certainly within the upper echelons of the cultural domain.

It is common for all kinds of opinions and arguments to be linked to the concept of jewellery, but when it is not possible to trace them back to a definition or other point of reference, they are hardly verifiable, if at all.

In all honesty, I should add that I myself did not solidly define jewellery as a concept in *Dutch jewellery*, even though I implicitly or partially may have done so when discussing specific sub-areas. In articles which I subsequently published about jewellery, I omitted providing such definition as well. In this essay I rectify this omission and I also develop a foundation for a multidisciplinary scholarly approach to jewellery. The scope of my research is limited neither to a time period nor to the work of Dutch makers. The latter will certainly please those amongst my friends and critics who are true lovers of jewellery. They always felt that my strong focus on Dutch jewellery and the modest approach underlying it went at the expense of a broader and more international perspective on jewellery. (7) This essay, then, is about jewellery in all its various meanings and manifestations.

The study of jewellery as a cultural good deserves a sound theoretical framework. This essay aims to develop such frame. I zoom in on more comprehensive and widely disseminated literature on jewellery and provide a thorough analysis of the underlying perspectives and personal motivations of various authors who have written about jewellery. I also discuss well-founded sub-studies which fell outside the scope of *Dutch jewellery*.

Since the publication of *Dutch jewellery* in 2004, my views on jewellery have been sharpened by attending symposia, giving lectures and writing a number of articles. (8) The many trips I was able to make were a great stimulus. I have enjoyed exhibitions in Paris and Brussels, which unembarrassedly spotlighted precious jewellery. It turned out that I was greatly attracted to the sturdy and colourful jewellery of the Naga, a people living in the eastern mountainous parts of India. These are also worn by men and nowadays can be found in cities like Istanbul, Paris, Brussels, Shanghai and Amsterdam – a contemporary sign of the ease with which jewellery can travel around the world. Africa continues to fascinate, with its nomadic peoples wearing their possessions in the form of jewellery on their bodies and with cities and regions whose economy is based on barter trade in jewellery and beads. Fortunately, there are still countries and cultures that have let themselves be guided by western notions of economy, culture and society less strongly, and that have different patterns of behaviour for men and women than the ones we live by. These western notions have prevented many critics of jewellery not only from placing it in a broad perspective but also from substantiating their claims about this comprehensive cultural phenomenon.

The development of understanding of culturally determined patterns of thought and behaviour which are not inherent to the current, western oriented awareness of standards proved to provide useful building blocks for the creation of a theoretical framework for the study of jewellery. It was crucial to recognise that most jewellery symbols by far are symbols of coherence within social groups, rather than elitist signs of power worn by high-ranking people to impress lower-ranking people. The current preoccupation with individuality in particular cultural circles also needs to be put into perspective. From such angle, it is possible to replace the hierarchical and chronological normative awareness of traditional art history by a more nuanced approach, featuring not only artistic qualities but also other values. In this way this study fits in with the current tendency within the arts and cultural history to consider all sorts of artefacts, tools and utensils much more in the context of their use and to analyse and map their social and economic dimensions.

2 Definitions and classifications

2.1 Definitions

Most publications on jewellery lack a definition of jewellery. Instead, authors first rely on standard dictionaries in their own language. The main Dutch dictionary, *Van Dale's Groot Woordenboek der Nederlandse Taal*, indicates that 'jewellery' refers to 'something that enhances the beauty of a person, of the whole to which it belongs, of his environment'. A second meaning given is: 'object made of precious metal, precious stone set in metal, etc. with which one adorns oneself'. To mention enhancement of beauty as the only purpose of jewellery and then to pin down the choice of materials to precious metals and gemstones twice involves an unnecessary restriction, one that is bound to be counterproductive to any sound study of jewellery.

Jewellery pertains to people's self-image and the ways in which they relate to each other; a jewellery item is like a piece of a jigsaw puzzle in how people demarcate their identity and reveal themselves to others. Pieces of jewellery are wearable objects and as such pre-eminently suitable as signs of affirming one's position within a society. They may thereby stress mutual similarities as well as differences amongst individuals. Additionally, they are vehicles for mitigating fears, they testify to the human joy of decoration or they help to keep memories alive.

Beauty is just one of the elements that play a role in people's interpersonal contacts. Beauty refers to something exceptional; it is a rather elusive norm which is set as example within a certain time and culture. By not further defining beauty and considering it the only purpose of jewellery, pieces of jewellery are reduced from the outset to being toys for fuzzy creatures, who are, yes, likely to be female. Although the Dutch dictionary does not suggest that jewellery is mainly about women, it is another rather fixed and typically western prejudice that men do not actually wear jewellery. This assumption does not seem limited to the Dutch language area (cf. section 4.4 below).

More useful is the description of jewellery found in another conventional Dutch source, the *Winkler Prins* encyclopaedia: 'objects to decorate body and/or clothing, made of (precious) metal, wood, ivory, jade, glass, mother of pearl, plastics, etc., whether or not provided with precious stones, semi-precious stones or imitation precious stones; the term jewellery is usually restricted in speech to jewellery in which (precious) stones are incorporated. The French term bijou (= trinket) is used as a synonym for jewellery'. This source only mentions ornamentation as purpose of jewellery, which is basically true of course. Moreover, the list of potential materials is much larger, while single pieces of jewellery are linked to jewellery in general.

The term 'jewel' is closely related to the term jewellery, as is true of the term 'bijou'. In *Dutch jewellery* I described this term as follows: 'A jewel is a precious adornment, basically one of precious metal in which one or more stones are incorporated'. (9) There is no misunderstanding about the term 'jewel', not even in the international literature: it is a category within jewellery. Sometimes the word 'jewel' is used to refer only to a stone that is placed as decoration on an object or a garment. The word 'bijou' was still frequently used in the Netherlands in the 1960s, but has meanwhile fallen into disuse in Dutch. (10)

The word 'jewel' is etymologically related to the Latin iocus, meaning 'sketch', 'play' or 'small diversion'. (11) This origin can still be recognised in several languages. In the English language area, jewellery refers to both bijou and 'high' jewellery. In French, joaillery and bijoux are used side by side, in German Juwelen is used alongside the more general term Schmuck, and in Italian gioiello is the most common term. For many people, then, a piece of jewellery is something that provides enjoyment, a fact that has rightly been used by many an author about jewellery to explain his fascination with jewellery. This sympathetic yet onesided explanation should not be a reason to close one's eyes to all the unsavoury practices associated with the extraction, processing and marketing of the typical materials for making jewellery – precious metals and precious stones.

Terms also relevant for the study of jewellery are 'decoration', 'ornament' and 'adornment'. Decoration means embellishment or distinction, and there is no doubt that a piece of jewellery can be described as a decoration of people's outward appearance. The concept of ornament has a more nuanced meaning. In everyday language ornament is used as a synonym for jewellery, embellishment or decoration, but within art history ornament stands for a specific motif, a decorative addition to works of visual art, architecture or particular utensils. In this essay the term 'ornament' is used in this way. 'Adornment' is synonymous with embellishment and decoration. In this essay, 'adornment' refers to all decorative elements on and around the body, not only jewellery but also accessories and body decorations such as tattoos and piercings. In connection with decorative elements on clothing, adornment can be highly complex; in this sense, a piece of jewellery is part of adornment.

In many languages, the word 'jewellery' is also used metaphorically. However, this essay is exclusively about jewellery as referring to concrete objects.

Proposal for a definition of 'piece of jewellery':
A piece of jewellery is an object that is worn on the human body, as a decorative and symbolic addition to its outward appearance.

A number of aspects of this definition deserve brief explanation:

1 Materials for making jewellery can vary widely – from metals, stones and other minerals to animal, vegetable and synthetic materials. Because there are hardly any restrictions as to the materials that can be used to make jewellery, it is not necessary to specify them in a definition.

2 The term 'accessory' is often mentioned in one and the same breath with jewellery. This definition also applies when referring to an addition to clothing or outward appearance. In terms of professional practice, the manufacture of clothing accessories is usually seen as part of fashion. The design, production and marketing of jewellery is a separate discipline and the making of 'high' jewellery is at most considered a specialisation within goldsmithing. There is also a grey area in which the distinction between jewellery and accessories appears to fade. Partly because 'accessory' is a broader term (cf. interior accessories, car accessories and so on), the distinction between jewellery and fashion accessories rarely causes problems in everyday language.

3 Pieces of jewellery which serve as autonomous objects are distinguished from body-related decorations such as tattoos, body alterations or mutilations and hairstyle. As far as their cultural and social aspects are concerned, the latter arise from similar motives as jewellery, but as 'immovable properties' they do not have the transferability and therefore the exchange value so strongly characterising jewellery. They do not survive their owner, while their making or craftsmanship markedly differs from that of the jewellery trade.

4 It is essential for a piece of jewellery that it can be worn on the human body. As such the person is both measure and yardstick: a piece of jewellery is only a piece of jewellery if you can somehow wear it on the body. The motivation for wearing it is a decidedly human affair as well. Whether this motivation is perhaps more important than the intentions of the maker is an open-ended issue. Metaphorically speaking, a wearer can make or break a piece of jewellery without changing or damaging anything. Furthermore, the maker is bound to include statements in his work about the way in which it can be worn and why. Even if he does not, inevitably he is still making a statement about this aspect.

5 This definition includes the reasons for why jewellery is worn at all in the two adjectives 'decorative' and 'symbolic'. The verbs 'decorate' and 'adorn' partly overlap, while 'decorating' also comes with the association of 'decor' or stage (for a theatre play) – in itself a beautiful metaphor for wearing jewellery. More importantly, 'decorative' is a common term in art history. Decorative art is a synonym for applied art or what is nowadays called 'design'. 'Symbolic' refers to an infinite array of meanings potentially comprised in jewellery as attribute. If 'decorative' as adjective basically refers to the effect of jewellery, 'symbolic' refers to the meanings of a piece of jewellery, including the reasons for wearing it. The decorative effect of a piece of jewellery may be more important than its symbolic value, and vice versa, but the two are not mutually exclusive.

6 By calling a piece of jewellery an addition to a person's outward appearance, it is distinguished from clothing, which covers or can cover the body. Jewellery represents an added value, which should be seen however in relation to clothing and other aspects of the way in which people show themselves to the world.

7 The notion of 'outward appearance' emphasises that the human body is not a static given, but a complex form that is potentially subject to being shaped quite a bit. This notion of 'outward appearance' actually comprises all aspects of the question of why people want to wear jewellery on their bodies and how and when they do so.

8 The definition of Winkler Prins makes the distinction that jewellery can be worn on the body and on clothing. This is a useful differentiation within the jewellery trade. In the definition formulated above, neither is excluded, while the actual naming of the decorative and symbolic aspects of jewellery as primary motives for its wearing is much more important. The fact that jewellery can be worn on clothing may indicate the original function of a piece of jewellery: to keep a piece of clothing in place or to fasten it.

2.2 Classifications

In dealing with such a universal and rich phenomenon as jewellery it is only natural to ask whether a sensible subdivision into categories can be made. Jewellery is worn all over the world, there is a great variety of materials from which it is made and it is worn for various reasons by people from all walks of life. Moreover, jewellery has an incredibly long history, which even was considerably expanded in recent years. After the publication of *Dutch jewellery*, data became available on archaeological finds of beads, which stretched the history of jewellery back in time with as many as 100,000 years. This prompted me to write an article about the jewellery discipline's long history, entitled 'Wat niet verandert' (What doesn't change). (12) While writing it, it became clear to me that many a motif for wearing jewellery has not changed substantially compared to 100, 1000, 10,000 and perhaps even 100,000 years ago. Times have changed, techniques have been developed and refined, new leads for symbolism have emerged, but there seems to be a hard core that does not change. This awareness has been an important reason for me to do more research on jewellery, this time as a universal phenomenon.

In a strictly historical sense, there is little certainty about the meanings linked to the earliest jewellery preserved, due to a lack of written sources from these early days. Therefore, it is not possible to determine exactly from which moment jewels were worn as a means to keep out the evil eye, for example, or to indicate rank. But in conjunction with other sources of information, archaeologists can make reasonable estimates.

The Australian art historian Anne Richter states in the introduction to *The Jewellery of Southeast Asia* (2000) that as a result of the western custom of considering pieces of jewellery as luxurious vehicles for human vanity, the notion that jewellery has spiritual power and a protective effect for many has often been neglected. (13) The body ornaments from prehistoric times found so far consist of shells, teeth, ivory, antlers and stones. These materials suggest that they acted as trophies, that they were given a medicinal value or that they were a means to ward off threatening natural phenomena, leaving aside whether that threat came from outside or was caused by pain and unrest in one's own body. The use of animal material indicates magical powers and a protective or medicinal effect attributed to them. Animals as motifs and symbols that refer to the sun, moon and stars are common all over the world, even in the earliest metal jewellery we know. These items also point to a conjuring function. (14)

The pleasure found in decorating one's body must have been a major motivation for making many a jewel. These may have been ephemeral decorations that have left little or no trace. Historians can only describe the early history of jewellery on the basis of time-resistant ornaments made of hard materials. These can be subdivided into artefacts serving as signs of a social or religious position and personal pieces that for the wearer represent a memory, for example, of the moment when they were acquired.

The most beautiful, well-preserved pieces from before the Renaissance are largely among those reflecting a certain status. Most of these items are grave finds. All over the world jewellery has been given to the deceased, in order to establish their earthly position in the afterlife as well. (15) They also seem to be made with their effect on some external dimension in mind; often they are made of materials clearly representing monetary value – like gold, stones, shells and glass beads – and one will find incredible feats of technical ability. Other extensive finds were buried in secret repositories; probably they were hidden and never collected spoils of war. Among them, too, one will find beautiful pieces, many of which nowadays are used to illuminate books or museum presentations. (16)

Much less is known about the history of jewellery which derived its value primarily from the private life of the wearer and which may have rather inconspicuous meanings. Yet the shelves of museum depots and research institutes are loaded with loose beads, shells and other parts of jewellery that will have symbolised some aspect of the mutual relationships between people within a family or community. After one or two generations of wearing, their specific meaning got lost, unless the jewellery was linked to historical figures or facts. Sometimes such a personal meaning is recorded in a different way, for example in family portraits or wedding gifts. The value of such items of jewellery need not lie in the value of the materials of which they are made. Their history tends to be poorly documented, especially the time-periods before the rise of photography and public media. The role of adornment among the lower classes before the nineteenth century has barely been the subject of serious research so far, not even on the basis of written sources. (17)

Another differentiation is whether jewellery had a function for fastening clothes or whether it was worn purely as decoration. Brooches and pins are basically derived from such functional jewellery, and necklaces may once have had such a function. The transition from the Gothic era to the Renaissance is sometimes indicated as an important moment in this development, and sometimes the transition from the eighteenth to the nineteenth century as well, when men started wearing less and less jewellery. In men's jewellery this functional aspect has been preserved for a long time, for example in tie pins, buttons and watch chains. In female adornment, jewellery became purely a decorative element at that point, to which precisely during the nineteenth century many emotional and symbolic meanings began to be attributed.

In the case of a historical collection, it is obvious to opt for a chronological classification, possibly broken down by country, city or region. In ethnographic collections, the place of origin generally weighs more heavily than the chronology and this order can be reversed: first origin, then chronology. When the makers are known, which is the case in particular in twentieth and twenty-first century collections of jewellery, a classification by designer, maker or producer makes sense.

Another obvious system is a classification based on monetary value, which can be determined fairly accurately for most jewellery. This often happens implicitly, by choosing the most precious pieces from all the available material for an exhibition or by photographing the most impressive jewels for a publication. The monetary value is initially determined by the materials used. This is why many a book about jewellery has a classification based on gold, silver and other precious metals, as well as on the application of the most precious stones, whereby diamonds come first, followed by rubies, emeralds and sapphires, after which various other stones may follow. In the Far East, jade represents an important value as well.

In an important study from 1997 on traditional jewellery in India, the Finnish jewellery expert Oppi Untracht played it safe and incorporated the results of his extensive research by relying on different ordering principles. India is a country with five thousand years of uninterrupted tradition in jewellery, which has served as an integral dimension of quite diverse cultural units. Untracht chose an approach based on chronology, with smooth transitions from one culture to another, involving the design of jewellery in terms of religion, economy, politics, regional customs and raw materials.

For jewellery made by the Naga people, he indicates how it is an integral part of their identity. He describes the folk character and the direct messages in these jewels, as well as, for example, the fascination that shells exert on the various Naga tribes, which are living far from the ocean in remote, hard to access mountain areas and basically survive on a subsistence economy. Untracht also discusses specific categories, for example by devoting a separate chapter to bridal adornment for men and women.

To emphasise the physical aspect of the jewellery and not to skip anything, he also covers the main variations in jewellery items from head to toe, starting with crowns and other headdresses, and ending with tinkling ankle straps and toe rings. In the chapters on materials and techniques, he explicitly takes into account the preferences of the population – and thus also those of the individual wearer – and he finally deals with the images of jewellery in miniatures and India's trade relations with the rest of the world. It is questionable whether this approach is ideal, yet it is fascinating at any rate that a Finnish researcher – together with his wife, jewellery designer Saara Hopea-Untracht – managed to uncover so much about this incredibly rich jewellery tradition in India and to address so many aspects of it in his book.

When it comes to jewellery as a personal collection intended to be worn, practical considerations may give rise to a particular classification. The most expensive pieces go into the safe, while all the others are likely to end up in a bedside table. If it concerns a large collection of jewellery, this may imply that there is one drawer for brooches, one for necklaces, one for bracelets and two suitable storage systems for rings and earrings. Of course, it is also possible that the tie pins, cufflinks and a few extra watches fit in one box, together with a few smaller boxes for rings. Only those in charge of taking care of royal jewellery collections have to worry about where to leave the tiaras and all the badges with matching ribbons.

A logical classification for an individual wearer is to group jewellery in sets that fit together well: the rubies with the rubies and blue beads with matching earrings and bracelets. Another possible classificatory logic starts from specific uses or occasions of use, and this may even function as a formal classification system: the bridal gown that rarely makes an appearance on the top shelf (including the jewellery for festive occasions), the ornaments for everyday use within easy reach and the funeral jewellery at the bottom of the closet. These kinds of practical considerations seem of little importance for the study of jewellery, but still they inevitably reveal interesting dimensions involved.

Another classification of jewellery that deserves further attention in this essay is a subdivision into categories that correspond to the most important segments of the current jewellery market. This is determined by the circumstances of production, distribution and use of items of jewellery as they evolved.

Apart from 'high' jewellery, which has long received most attention, the range of jewellery began to change dramatically in the course of the nineteenth century, based on mechanisation, industrialisation and societal developments. A growing portion of the production of gold and silver jewellery was developed into series or even mass goods. The same process also took place in the production and distribution of fashion and clothing. The new social groups which arose in the west in the wake of the Industrial Revolution wanted to show their newly acquired status. With the emergence of the fashion industry, a new commercial system was created, in which jewellery featured as well. If jewellery items have long functioned as part of particular fashion or clothing styles, in the course of the nineteenth century and certainly in the twentieth century they were also produced and marketed as products in their own right, and as such they complemented the craft products sold by jewellers and self-employed goldsmiths.

All of this implies that in the western world, especially from the second half of the twentieth century onwards, there are a number of categories or even blood groups in the jewellery trade, each of which has its own expertise, as well as its own scene and media. The classification provided below does not meet any scientific or scholarly criteria, however, because it is not sufficiently systematic. Moreover, it has little or nothing to do with the way in which jewellery is worn and with the various decorative and symbolic values that can be attributed to it. (18) The categories involved can be described as follows:

Precious jewellery – These items function as symbols of a specific social status, which serves as a measure for wealth and preferably also for the good taste of the wearer. They can be seen as a form of property or capital, though their production reflects all kinds of degrees of value, up to the most expensive one. They vary from unique items to mass products and are worn by members of many social groups, depending on their level of income. But only the very rich can afford the really expensive pieces of jewellery. Their artistic value is usually derived only from the craftmanship of the maker.

Jewellery as personal expression of the maker – These items are a reflection of contemporary culture and their value is mainly determined by their artistic quality. They will have been made in all kinds of times and countries but were only identified as such in the second half of the nineteenth century, in the wake of the Arts & Crafts movement. These jewels can be made of all sorts of materials, varying from precious to ephemeral. In principle they are unique items or designs made in small series. They serve as an indicator of the cultural refinement of both the maker and the wearer; they have their own clientele which is mainly limited to the wealthy bourgeoisie. A subcategory is 'artistic jewellery'. These items are designed by visual artists (varying from Hans Holbein to Pablo Picasso), as an integral part or a by-product of their oeuvre. Sometimes they are presented as an independent category of jewellery; however, there are no specialised sales venues or specialised media for such jewellery.

Fashion jewellery – These pieces of jewellery are produced and marketed within the framework of the fashion industry or in relation to fashion accessories. These pieces tend to comprise few precious materials, which does not automatically imply that they are not valuable or pricey. They may vary from items by renowned designers (created for a specific fashion show) to colourful bulk-produced items. Fashion jewellery is worn by the young and the old, and the rich and the poor. Colour, style and atmosphere are the characteristics that count for the public interested in fashion. There is another subcategory of fashion jewellery:

jewellery from leading fashion brands. These tend to be made of precious metals and stones, and come with the halo of the fashion house involved. At the end of the twentieth century, these jewellery items became important instruments to emphasise the luxurious character of major fashion brands.

Ephemeral ornaments – Jewellery as wearable signs of a particular worldview. They do not represent any monetary value, but can be incredibly powerful as a sign. As a trend or craze, these signs can have a huge distribution, and then they will also respond to the need to conform or to want to belong to something, a need which tends to be strong among adolescents. These pieces of jewellery are mainly studied as part of mass culture.

Heritage and antiques – Pieces of jewellery which survived their first owner. This is a substantial category. They can range from precious jewellery to favourite earrings with glass stones or a small religious symbol. The best pieces represent a respectable commercial value and are interesting for museums and auction houses. The other pieces will often find their way through all kinds of channels to the next owner, nowadays also via the internet. Jewellery is given an important place in archaeology because it may offer keys to a better understanding of cultures and periods of which little is known. This is why they may serve as museum pieces, though probably quite a few of them are privately owned as well.

Ethnic jewellery – non-western jewellery. These items may be the most beautiful pieces of jewellery, such as bead necklaces made of glass and shells, or necklaces made of splendidly coloured feathers from the Amazon region. Within fashion, they belong to the category of folklore, and as jewellery they are mainly considered part of the discipline of anthropology. The clientele for ethnic jewellery ranges from teenagers looking for an exotic accent to stylish collectors with an exquisite collection.

In my study on Dutch jewellery, I described pieces of jewellery, the personal expression of the maker, fashion jewellery and ephemeral ornaments side by side and in relation to each other. Antique and inherited pieces of jewellery are only relevant if their form or use lives on in the work of individual designers, jewellers or designers of fashion jewellery. This applies, amongst other things, to jewellery that belongs to traditional costume, as described in chapter 1 of the abovementioned study, and for example to the 'entourage ring' with rose diamonds, described in chapter 5 of the same study. Ethnic jewellery does not seem to be important at first sight in a treatise on Dutch jewellery, but for a trading nation like the Netherlands it is common to see ample reference to forms and materials from many corners of the world. In chapter 2, attention is paid to influences from the former Dutch East Indies and in chapter 6 a section is devoted to ethnic jewellery and the phenomenon of fair trade. (19)

Conclusion

A definition of jewellery must describe its function and provide points of reference for the many meanings that can be associated with jewellery. Furthermore, it is important to make a factual distinction between jewellery as an autonomous artefact and body-related decorations, and between jewellery and clothing. Jewellery can be classified in many ways, from practical to systematic, and based on time, origin, type or occasion. If they all have their own merits, inevitably each classification covers merely one or two dimensions at best.

3 Art history as foundation for the study of jewellery

3.1 A useful basis

Jewellery items have been the subject of serious attention for their decorative, symbolic and material value, as is true in much the same way of manuscripts, paintings and sculptures. Makers, traders, buyers, wearers, collectors, notaries, archaeologists and historians have always expressed value judgments on this subject, in whatever form.

Furthermore, jewellery has always acted as a means to symbolise or perpetuate relationships. In this function, particular pieces were also described and documented, an aspect that has generated many fine anecdotes.

In the twentieth century, the study of jewellery as an independent object of study ended up within art history. On good grounds, to be sure. From the outset, the discipline of art history has been based on the description and interpretation of objects. It mainly focuses on identifying the artistic quality of these objects and creating a historical framework.

Art history is a profession with a built-in duality. Its subject involves images. It doesn't matter if they are made of paint on canvas, carved from marble, printed as a photo, played on a screen, or composed of precious metal or leftover textile – it is always about things you can see. The profession consists of ways of looking at these images and putting them into context. Looking, however, is hardly an objective act. Neurologically, our eyes are directly connected to the brain and all our countless experiences and insights stored in it. Essentially, these are all personal.

There are art historians who claim to practice an objective science and who mainly work with texts in which everchanging ways of looking are recorded and new contexts are identified. I myself am rather one of the passionate ones, those who enjoy to keep looking at the things themselves, always searching for more aspects or other artefacts to consider than the ones studied already. They want to be able to fathom art in all its material dimensions and connect their findings with earlier insights and experiences. In the past they were called 'amateurs' – in the sense of enthusiasts – or 'connoisseurs', if they had managed to acquire a lot of knowledge about a certain subarea or subject.

Art historians inevitably operate in the dynamic field located between objectivity and subjectivity. Only on the basis of solid documentation, linking various insights and well-founded arguments can a contribution be made within that field at a scholarly level. Fortunately, art history is a fairly young branch of academic research, certainly in relation to for example the natural sciences and philosophy, and since the years of Bernard Berenson and Aby Warburg the profession has always managed to retain its dynamics. As a discipline, art history originated in fondness of the arts and the urge to analyse and describe the most important developments in visual art, architecture and other artistic expressions. It developed because more and more works were described and thus a framework emerged to which new and different insights could be added.

In principle, items of jewellery can be described in the same way as works of art or, for example, pieces of furniture and ceramics. As part of important archaeological finds, items of jewellery have even been key in some cases to a better understanding of other products from the same period or people. A case in point is the Scythians. Jack Ogden, an archaeologist, describes in *Ancient Jewellery* (1992) how jewellery from archaeological excavations can be compared to literary sources or murals.

Gold continues to be the best-preserved precious metal. During poorly managed excavations in the past, objects made of gold – usually jewellery – were immediately picked up with a view to quick profit. Fortunately, archaeology has developed into a more ethical discipline, but in the past many important excavations were carried out and documented badly. As a result, traces of silver jewellery or other more ephemeral materials are likely to have been lost, confirming the image that jewellery was usually made of gold and intended to impres.s (20)

Art history is also a form of historiography of course. As far as jewellery is concerned, especially the noble elites – who had the means for lavish adornment, who in their time were also portrayed in their full glory and whose lives are well documented – served as welcome starting points for descriptions of jewellery. (21) This is amply demonstrated by Joan Evans in *A History of Jewellery 1100-1870* published in 1953. In the foreword to the first edition, she states that jewellery from before 1100 consists mainly of burial finds, while the pieces she treats are to be regarded as personal belongings, which have often been preserved purely by chance. An important source of information for her was the art of portraiture from 1470 to 1910. The text and images in Evans' study show a clear preference for elaborate jewellery amongst members of Europe's high nobility.

As Evans herself claims, she only deals with 'important examples', as is evident from the last chapters of her book. She strongly opposes the rise of industrially produced jewellery and the fashions of the second half of the nineteenth century. After a description of the jewellery worn by Empress Eugénie of France at the time of the World Exhibition of 1867 in Paris, she comes to the following conclusion: 'Such ornaments, in which the legendary techniques that had made jewellery a kind of sculpture in miniature were brought to nothing, were a prelude to a new and debased age of jewels'. In other words, it was only in court jewellery that the highest level of jewellery could be achieved, which set the standard for all other types of jewellery. (22)

The direct predecessor of my study on Dutch jewellery was *Juwelen en mensen* (Jewels and people) by M.H. Gans (1961). This study also deals with jewellery owned by those in power and the well-to-do, and is mainly based on inventories and portraits. As a result, Gans pays a lot of attention as well to jewellery as symbols of power. The elitist approach of Evans and Gans was also practised by other authors on jewellery in the twentieth century. The art historical interpretation of jewellery is therefore indebted to general historiography, in which kings and rulers have traditionally held a key position.

Much less is known about the history of jewellery made from less precious materials or as used by the lower classes. As confirmed by the Austrian art historian Gerhard Eggert in his publication *Bürgerlicher Schmuck* (Bourgeois Jewellery - 1984), the study of jewellery within art history has mainly emphasised goldsmithing skills and precious stones. The main focus was always on dating objects and artistic qualities of decoration found amongst the high nobility. Eggert also argues that much jewellery is not around for long, as the tiny items are often lost, stolen or demolished, and this makes it hard to gain a representative overview of a particular time or genre. (23)

Within general history, many attempts have been made over the past twenty or thirty years to approach history from a less exalted perspective, but the study of jewellery has scarcely benefited from this shift. Eggert is one of the very few who has explicitly chosen jewellery from the bourgeois middle and upper classes in Europe as a subject. Although his study was also published in English in 1988, he has so far found little following amongst art historians. Within the context of material culture, however, such research is increasingly initiated nowadays (see section 5.1.3 below).

Within art history, the history of style is the most important framework for dating and interpreting jewellery. The history of style has a compelling chronology: a new style is seen as a logical consequence of previous styles and from the sixteenth century onwards they are often linked to rulers who, with their opulent lifestyle, set the tone for their time. A style is determined on the basis of the visual characteristics of artistic highlights from architecture, the visual arts and the applied arts. Initially, this was done mainly on the basis of western artistic expressions, but during the course of the twentieth century, interest in other cultures arose as well. Ornaments hold a key position in the history of style, which makes them a wonderful starting point for the interpretation of jewellery items, especially when one considers them as wearable ornaments.

For my study of Dutch jewellery in the twentieth century, a focus on western stylistic history sufficed, except for jewellery and other goldsmithing work from the former Dutch colonies. From the above, it is obvious that for an overview of the developments in jewellery, a different, socially broader, approach is needed. It also goes without saying that a comprehensive stylistic history is needed for a broad study of jewellery. Furthermore, precisely in the case of a subject such as jewellery, which is based on human desires and fears, the reiteration or reinterpretation of existing conceptions and forms must always be kept in mind. The constants deserve as much attention as the innovations.

Over the course of the twentieth century, art historians have gradually developed an arsenal of relevant concepts and studies on the work of artists and designers enabling future generations of researchers to build on them. Crucial in this construction phase was the visual material that scholars and art critics could work with. Until the last quarter of the twentieth century, there were major limitations in the number and quality of the available images, which led to many misguided assumptions and interpretations.

But in recent years we have become spoilt indeed with better printing techniques, fast and sharp photography, the increase in print media and the ever-improving quality of images in it, and on top of that, the Internet and all the blessings of digital media. Although nowadays there is much more to discover from images than in the past, this may still lead to incorrect assumptions. During the research for my study of Dutch jewellery I regularly came across names of jewellery makers from before 1970 that seemed interesting, but of which I could trace at most one or two small images. And even with respect to the leading jewellery designers of the last three decades of the twentieth century, it turns out that the same pieces tend to be shown over and over again, causing the other work that might shed a different light on their oeuvre to be neglected.

In my study on Dutch jewellery I described and highlighted several pieces of jewellery in order to give an impression of characteristic pieces from the period at hand. I did so on the assumption that readers are unlikely to have an idea of this themselves, even though the information is important for linking the general introduction to the specific image of the time involved. These short texts can be seen as finger practices of an art historian, but by placing jewellery from leading designers alongside ordinary pieces, their interpretation acquired a specific tone and scope, which usually goes much further than the down-to-earth descriptions of the traditional art historian. (24)

3.2 Obstacles within the art historical approach to jewellery

Although the framework of art history provides a good basis for the study of jewellery, this framework also comes with drawbacks, several of which are tied to the discipline as such. In order to understand the current position of jewellery as a subject for theoretical study, it is necessary to go back to the sixteenth century and look at the development of views about valuable objects and their collection.

In the sixteenth century, major royal collectors, ecclesiastical prelates, members of the high nobility and art traders made a distinction between ,artificialia', or man-made objects, and 'naturalia', referring to objects of natural origin. Both groups of artefacts ended up together in art collections and curiosity cabinets, as part of a comprehensive collection.

In the eighteenth century, a hierarchy of the arts was established, whereby painting and sculpture, on the basis of their artistic content, were considered to be higher arts, just like music and poetry. Partly as a result, these large collections were gradually divided into two categories. The visual arts were put on a pedestal, while the applied arts were considered to be in the domain of the crafts. In the course of the nineteenth century, the applied arts actually became increasingly disconnected from the visual arts. In large museums, where objects of visual art, together with the most prestigious, traditionally manufactured products, were increasingly collected and exhibited as national treasures and from an educational perspective, jewellery – involving fairly small objects – increasingly lost out against the large collections of paintings, classical sculptures, precious furniture and larger silversmithing objects. This implied a certain degradation of pieces of jewellery.

Together with the development of science, it became a challenge to distinguish and define objects as clearly as possible. This caused the division between artificialia and naturalia to be stressed. If jewellery is man-made, at the same time it may rely on most beautiful elements derived from nature. In the course of the nineteenth and twentieth centuries, precious stones and their applications were moved to the new natural history museums, where they are still found today. But items of jewellery conceived as wearable objects with cultural meanings based on refined craftsmanship do not belong there. Museums and royal palaces in many European cities created a separate 'treasury' for pieces of jewellery made of the finest materials and largest historical value, comparable to the treasuries found in temples, churches and much older worldly collections. Once again, all emphasis was placed on jewellery as a high-value object. (25)

Other obstacles within the study of jewellery have their origin in the jewellery trade. In the nineteenth century the profession underwent many changes. Under the influence of the Napoleonic laws of around 1800, the system of guilds in many European countries was abolished. In many countries, goldsmithing continued to be subject to government regulations, such as the 'law on guarantees' in the Netherlands. (26) Governments did not want to lose control over a profession that in its dealing with expensive materials such as silver and gold was a cornerstone of the economy.

Mechanisation and industrialisation developed only gradually within the jewellery field, in which quality was based on refined craftsmanship, but the progression of these processes was inevitable. In the wake of the upper classes, growing groups of prosperous citizens began to be interested in jewellery and interrelated items of value. Consequently, the industry gained a tighter hold on the production of jewellery. Margaret Flower has analysed this development in her book on Victorian jewellery, involving for instance the rise of Birmingham as a centre for industrially produced jewellery. (27)

New distribution channels such as department stores were essential to reach the new groups of customers. In this way, the world of jewellery became linked more and more with the production and distribution of fashion and clothing, which blurred the difference between jewellery and fashion accessories such as corsages, ribbons and bows. The reaction to this process within the Arts & Crafts movement has been well mapped by art historians. Jewellery constituted an integral part of this development from the outset. The role of goldsmiths, possibly assisted by a few assistants, continued to be closely linked up with the concept of craft, as was true for self-employed ceramists, textile artists and furniture makers. They still had their craftsmanship in common with the visual artists of their day and age, and their ideas were nourished by evolving social and cultural developments. In many countries there were associations or collaborative organisations that included both artists and designers. Although in the course of the twentieth century only few art historians concentrated on the role of crafts and design, their attention safeguarded the place of goldsmiths and jewellery designers within art history. The clientele for their products mainly consisted of those among the wealthy bourgeoisie who were interested in contemporary expressions of culture, which has always remained a fairly small group.

Another reaction to the process of industrialisation within the jewellery trade, which took place at the same time as the Arts & Crafts movement, is rarely addressed explicitly in art historical literature: those in the upper strata of society also demanded the highest quality in design, technique and stones. They were the ones to purchase the most gorgeous jewellery, as they had always done, and around 1900 they still decided on issues of style and served as role model for the social groups ranking immediately below them, as has been analysed by sociologists such as Thorstein Veblen and Georg Simmel. (28)

In the confusion that arose after the abolition of the guilds, a number of jewellers in Europe's main cities developed into major centres of expertise on jewellery, with an exquisite staff of experts serving an equally exquisite clientele. (29) Like the craft-minded goldsmiths, they distanced themselves from the factory-produced items. These jewellers also had to distinguish themselves from each other, and it would depend on the personal taste and creative abilities of those in charge whether they made it to the top. They added a personal signature to their jewellery items, as well as their own name and these were also recognised as such. They ran well-equipped studios of their own, where many items of jewellery or parts thereof were still fabricated according to traditional methods.

The books by Henri Vever have mapped the various jewellers with a business location in France. Fine pieces by Émile Froment Meurice, Alexis Félize, Alphonse and Georges Fouquet, Lucien Gaillard, René Lalique and Louis Cartier serve as undisputed attractions in major museum jewellery collections. Paris was the veritable centre of culture, fashion and taste around 1900, with the 1900 World Fair serving as apotheosis. In the nineteenth century, London also had a number of its own jewellery houses, including John Brogden and Hancocks' & Co. The Italian jeweller Carlo Giuliano settled in London, and in 1902 Cartier also opened a business there. Archibald Knox's jewellery was sold under his own name at Liberty's & Co. Carl Fabergé became a famous name operating from St. Petersburg and Moscow. In the second half of the nineteenth century, the Castellanis had built up a great reputation from Rome for their artistic work, which was clearly influenced by the classics and excavations in Pompeii and Herculaneum. Louis Comfort Tiffany in New York should also be mentioned here; he earned a name for himself as influential artist not only with his jewellery but also with his glassware. In Belgium, Philippe Wolfers became an important name in this field, while I should also mention two Dutch houses with a good reputation and a long track record: Bonebakker in Amsterdam and Steltman in The Hague. (30)

The work of these jewellery houses now makes up the heart of most important museum collections of jewellery in the world. The artistic value goes undisputed and they are considered to represent an integral creative force within Jugendstil or Art Nouveau and Art Deco. However, during the last decades of the twentieth century, this high-quality jewellery disappeared from the view of most art historians, with the exception of a few curators of historical collections and employees of auction houses. The handful of art historians concerned with contemporary jewellery turned against jewellery as a combination of precious metal and precious stones, and thus as a status symbol (in accordance with the standards of their time), and focused mainly on the work of individual jewellery designers within the emergent scene around galleries, art centres and specific museum exhibitions.

A number of these jewellery houses still exist today. Some attract interesting designers and bring out jewellery with their own signature, such as Cartier, Tiffany and newer names such as Bulgari, Henry Winston and others. The large fashion houses also occasionally attract top designers for their jewellery collections, such as currently Victoire de Castellane for Dior. Those in the so-called avant-garde of jewellery design tend to dismiss these names as belonging to a world only concerned with gold and money, and most amateurs or critics with a background in art history share this view. This is particularly the case in the northern European countries. But in Parisian museums and in Italy, for example, more positive attention is paid to this contemporary tradition in jewellery. Many of the authors who have devoted themselves to the description of this part of the profession are antique dealers or staff employed by auction houses. (31)

3.3 Conflicting classifications

Around 1900 there was another development in the trade of goldsmithing and jewellery design. Up to that time, it was primarily a profession for men. In the Netherlands, too, men managed to monopolise the manufacture of jewellery until the beginning of the twentieth century. In the second half of the twentieth century, however, the field of jewellery design shifted towards women. Their active presence in this field has increased sharply. The profession of jewellery designer offered them attractive prospects at a time when wearing jewellery was also more and more considered to be the exclusive domain of women. Being a small entrepreneur in the arts sector also turned out to be a perfect fit for them.

In her study *Vrouwen in de vormgeving in Nederland 1880–1940* (Women in design in the Netherlands between 1880 and 1940, 2007), Marjan Groot mapped the position of women in this field extensively for the first time. Highlighting ornamental aspects, she analysed the gender dimension and a number of characteristics of the work of female designers from this period. (32) Throughout the twentieth century, however, concepts such as rationalism and functionalism have been used as the most important standard in considerations of the applied arts and design. The rational and the functional were generally considered masculine in this period, while the ornamental was usually seen as feminine. This is one of the reasons why more has been written about the work of male designers of this period than that of their female colleagues. (33)

The changes in the jewellery profession during the first decades of the twentieth century resulted in further shifts in the study of jewellery. Items of jewellery as tokens of status and craftsmanship and as objects of historical importance were given more and more attention as artefacts aimed at individual and artistic values, while within jewellery design women also started to play their part.

Within the history of art, however, jewellery would remain an unpopular specialty, because decorative and ornamental aspects of design in general were under heavy pressure during this period. Under the influence of Modernism, there was growing resistance to ornamentation and embellishment of products and buildings and also to ornaments worn by human beings. Craftsmanship and ornamental art played a minor role in art appreciation already, but now, as a result, the prestige of an art historical approach of jewellery would decline even further.

At the time, the hierarchy within art history, which foregrounded the visual arts as supreme artistic expression, could no longer be called into question. Architecture was recognised as a separate discipline, partly on the basis of the constructional expertise necessary for its proper assessment. It literally united all the arts under one roof and also offered the clearest support for the history of style. The applied arts, however, were 'contaminated', so to speak, with requirements other than purely artistic ones. Furniture and other products for domestic interiors, such as textiles and ceramics, actually fitted under the umbrella of architecture as part of interior design, but this was not the case for products related to the human body, such as fashion and jewellery. In the last four decades of the twentieth century, this subordinate role was increasingly experienced as a punishment by the various practitioners of the applied arts. In this same period, however, the study of jewellery as part of the art historical discipline also began to gain ground, albeit slowly at first.

In retrospect it is puzzling perhaps why Modernism, with its purist resistance to any use of decorative elements and repetitive patterns in interiors, on products, on our clothes and on our skin, has managed to exert such enormous influence in the western world. Earlier, the history of architecture, the visual arts and the applied arts had been closely linked up with concepts such as style and ornamentation. The most frequently cited culprit is the Viennese architect Adolf Loos, who in 1908 wrote an essay with the catchy title *Ornament und Verbrechen* (Ornament and crime). His militant yet nuanced argument is based on the abundance of ornamentation that he saw all over Vienna, a legacy of nineteenth century neo-styles and, on top of that, Jugendstil. The future he outlined in this essay was based on a drastic break with history and the conservative expectations of the wealthy bourgeoisie. In the course of the twentieth century, the title of his text has repeatedly been turned into ,ornament is crime' and as such has functioned as one of the cornerstones of Modernism. If the influence of Loos on his own time may have been limited, later on he certainly began to feature as one of the flamboyant exponents of a mentality shared by many an architect, artist, designer and critic.

There are many definitions of Modernism, but the main pillars on which this concept was founded in the twentieth century are the idea of progress, functionalism and social equality (or socialism). In the 1920s and 1930s, the sincere pursuit of the new – and implicitly the rejection of what is 'bourgeois' and traditional – resulted in a number of very beautiful and clearly structured buildings with a great deal of glass, as well as a number of clearly defined products that were added as highlights of twentieth century design. Still, anyone who takes stock of Modernism at the beginning of the twenty-first century must conclude that there is no social or cultural base for its grand ideas anymore.

For historians, doubts have rightly arisen about the idea of progress and about linear chronology as a compelling norm for explaining the succession of developments in cultural history. The desire for something new or different is understandable, but history teaches us that the introduction of the new takes place in a leapfrog fashion and that there are almost always unexpected events or dynamics at play. Nor is the argument that each new development will turn the world into a better place to live viable any longer. As far as Functionalism is concerned, the undecorated, cleanly shaped products that are regarded as highlights of Modernism almost without exception place high demands on the materials used, while their production costs are high, they are vulnerable in terms of maintenance and – one has to be realistic – rarely they are truly functional. The assumption that geometric forms are universal is true, but so are flowers and other forms of naturalism. And the greatest failure of Modernism is that the promise of a better society did not materialise. If this is perhaps too much to ask from a cultural movement, these claims and promises were certainly made by its main representatives.

It is because of Modernism that the very human need for ornamentation and ornamental elements in the west came to be despised widely. Modernism gained a dominance that can still be felt today, certainly in the Netherlands, through illustrious examples such as De Stijl and New Objectivity – movements which initially enjoyed only marginal recognition – and through the politically and socially disruptive experience of the Second World War. The study of jewellery as a wearable ornament has clearly suffered as a result, as can be seen from the somewhat defensive attitude that most authors have adopted towards jewellery. As pointed out by Joan Evans in the first chapter of *A History of Jewellery*: 'Jewels, indeed, though they may seem alien to an age of austere functionalism, still play a living part in our civilisation'. (34)

Interestingly, some of the basic principles of Modernism can also be used as a negative standard in the quality assessment of jewellery. The first generations of modernists did not get along very well with jewellery. The Centraal Museum in Utrecht, for example, owns several pieces of jewellery made by Gerrit Rietveld for Mrs Schröder. They are unsightly pieces of tinker, clumsily put together and in no way do they bear witness to a sense of form. This renowned furniture maker and architect must have become so entangled in the conflict between wanting to please his lover and his learned aversion to ornamentation that he failed to make something of value at all.

To my knowledge, other modernist leaders did not make any jewellery in this period, but such objects may be stored away in archives and depots of course. One of the few Bauhaüsler who successfully focused his talent on jewellery and made interesting jewellery is Naum Slutzki. The French designer Jean Desprez has been guided in his formal language by the austere formal language of Modernism, but in terms of mentality he cannot really be called a modernist. In principle, it was only the third generation of modernists who from the late 1960s onwards created beautiful work that is indebted to the modernists' formal idiom and ideas. In the United States and Canada, the situation is more nuanced. In the 1940s and 1950s, a generation of interesting jewellery designers was able to work relatively undisturbed by World War Two and its disastrous effects. (35)

As a result of the more prominent position of independent jewellery designers with a distinctive signature, and out of dissatisfaction with the subordinate position of jewellery in art history, a handful of jewellery designers, curators and journalists introduced the concept of 'modern jewellery' around 1970, with the aim of distinguishing the work designated as such from the work of conventional jewellers, and in particular from the more common work in gold and other precious metals. The word ,modern' was a clear attempt to connect with the concept of modern art, which had been in use for a long time and now had gained an unmistakable status. They also emphatically distanced themselves from fashion jewellery and accessories, which they hardly considered to be of interest. In the 1970s, this new way of thinking about jewellery also gave rise to a new sales venue: the jewellery gallery. Over the years, gallery owners increasingly gained a key position in the new network of creators, customers and cultural institutions that began to exhibit and collect modern jewellery. ,Modern jewellery' became a nickname for the work of individual jewellery designers who preferably had been enrolled in an applied arts school, a teacher training college or an academy curriculum. This was often the case in the Netherlands indeed, but a similar development took place in other Western countries as well.

Art historians with a preoccupation for the artistic level of jewellery have mainly followed the trail of the individual silversmiths and jewellery designers. They interpreted the developments in jewellery design as a new style history, distilled from the common visual characteristics and the successive works of the group of makers involved. On the basis of their independent position, they could be fully committed to their work and its artistic statements. This was a group with which the art historians felt affinity in a social sense as well. The only side street they eagerly took in their account pertained to the jewellery by renowned visual artists such as Picasso, Braque, Dalí and Calder. In a nice publication, titled *Nur für ihre Frauen*, about jewellery made in the first half of the twentieth century by members of 'Die Brücke' in Germany, several authors state that these early examples of artists' jewellery were barely related to larger artistic developments and had little or no influence on the jewellery trade. The same applies to the jewellery of the abovementioned artists from the decades after the Second World War. (36)

This approach to modern jewellery – jewellery as a medium of personal expression that reaches a small clientele through a select circle of specialised galleries – became a connecting factor for individual jewellery designers in various parts of the world, creating an international network, with centres such as Munich, Barcelona, Philadelphia, London, Tallinn and Amsterdam. These are cities with educational institutes of importance to jewellery designers, gallery owners, art experts and collectors alike. (37)

Incidentally, those involved did not merely seek to claim a place for jewellery in the domain of the visual arts on the basis of its cultural value. This was also done within material-related fields such as textiles, ceramics and glass, and right now it is again a striking development within the design of furniture and other interior products – albeit on other grounds.

Because of the need within cultural circles to acknowledge modern jewellery as a medium for personal expression, there has been a sustained urge to define the character of this kind of jewellery, especially in relation to fashion jewellery and commercial jewellery. (38) A recent term used to isolate this type of jewellery from the general jewellery market is 'author's jewellery'. As a gallery owner, jewellery designer and publicist Paul Derrez, in *New directions in jewellery* (2005), defines the jewellery he wants to discuss as 'art jewellery', or, better still, as 'author's jewellery'. He defines this work as jewellery of which the author is the only one to determine the concept and execution. (39)

In the catalogue *Sieradiën ... een noodzakelijke zotheid* (Jewellaria ... a vital folly, 2006), Liesbeth den Besten also argues in favour of reserving the term 'author's jewellery' for this *inner circle* of contemporary jewellery production. She attributes the origin of this term to the southern European countries, notably Italy: *gioielli d'autore*. After first observing that unsightly and inconspicuous jewellery may well represent a complete story for the wearer, she states: 'The addition "author" is not an empty one but has a specific meaning. It indicates a creative process, an individual style and content. A piece of jewellery by an author – unlike a pearl necklace or a fashion item – triggers questions.

(...) It is obvious that such piece has something to say, that it has an autonomy of its own, and that it does not merely serve to entertain, seduce or please. It wants to be less foolish than jewellery, more self-directed than fashion jewellery and bolder than jeweller's jewellery, but if all goes well it is a pleasure for the mind and a feast for the eye' (40) It is clear that a distinct status is claimed here for author's jewellery as being different from more conventional kinds of jewellery.

These author's jewels, which tell stories and open up new worlds, take on an extra dimension when they are worn: 'The wearer is needed to perfect the piece of jewellery, as it were'. That is to put the cart before the horse: jewellery is there to be worn by people, of course, and the reasons for doing so are entirely up to the wearer. It is also possible for designers to add considerations related to its wearing to their piece of jewellery, but the introduction of the concept of autonomy confirms that in the case of author's jewellery the maker's world of experience is the one standard that counts and that he or she, significantly, pursues a specific role for jewellery within the domain of the visual arts.

Florian Hufnagl, head curator of the Pinakothek der Moderne in Munich, takes the issue even further by stating in his introduction to the catalogue to the jewellery exhibition *Des Wahnsinns fette Beute* (The fat booty of madness, 2008) that only jewellery which is recognised as belonging to an autonomous genre and no longer has anything to do with 'the historical objects of a traditional arts and crafts museum' will be considered for his museum collection. (41)

In the same publication, the Frenchman Thierry de Duve explains the concept of *contemporary jewellery*, which has been used for several decades in English-speaking countries to refer to the work of individual and contemporary jewellery designers. He blames the lack of a clear terminology for 'this very specific art form' with reference to the fact that most authors address an audience which already belongs to the insiders. 'Contemporary jewellery would be, according to that view, a matter so elitist that rendering the phenomena associated with it in terms of language, that explanations and interpretations, have hitherto not reached a broader public. Another explanation might be that the authors and their expert public definitely do not compete on what the jewellery of the present really is.' (42) He goes on to state in no uncertain terms: 'Jewellery is an applied art. It is art that is worn on the body and has the function of distinguishing the wearer from others, of adding something to him or her, something that he or she may not need but that is only valid in connection with him or her'. Once again, he hits the mark by labelling contemporary jewellery a distinctive niche. (43)

In her book on Gijs Bakker's jewellery, Ida van Zijl unequivocally places his work among the visual arts: 'It is (...) time to judge avant-garde jewellery according to the same standards as other disciplines in the visual arts. Hardly ever, a design is produced in an edition or even industrially, and this can be compared to the multiples from the 1970s, which mostly originated in that period as well, but this is no reason to have the scales tip towards the design. Innovation, craftsmanship and ideas are the criteria against which a work of art is tested, based on the specific characteristics of the discipline. In essence jewellery can be distinguished from other disciplines in the visual arts only by its relationship to the body or the wearer. Just as space is essential for sculpture, its being worn is a fundamental aspect of jewellery'. In this argument, too, the wearer is reduced to a spatial form and a reason is given for considering Bakker's work as art: 'Gijs Bakker is undoubtedly the most important Dutch jewellery designer from the second half of the twentieth century, because his work has given a decisive impulse, both nationally and internationally, to the new positioning of jewellery. His best pieces are not only strong in terms of originality of the concept and in the execution of the design, but they also grant a new interpretation to the function of the piece in general. They push the boundaries of the range of instruments available to the jewellery designer as an artist'. In short, he is the best among his peers. (44)

All of this appears to be a question of terminology, which, incidentally, plays a slightly less important role in the Netherlands than in other countries. In the Netherlands, jewellery is considered part of design, an area in which this country now enjoys great prestige. In contemporary reflection, 'design' has replaced such terms as applied arts and decorative art; these have fallen increasingly into disuse. In the English-speaking world, however, the work of individual jewellery designers is still regarded in terms of *crafts*, while in the German language one will even refer to *Kunsthandwerk* (craftsmanship). These are now loaded concepts which hardly shake off the suspicion of old-fashionedness. Nevertheless, the supporters of the concept of author's jewellery refer to qualities that are also typical of crafts and craftsmanship, by emphasising the individual's complete mastery of his self-acquired skills and creative processes. This seems suggestive of the romanticism associated with being an artist, while the most successful artists of our time are in fact reluctant to do so and take all kinds of paths in order to relate their work to the real world. They make installations by using utensils, they cook, sew clothes, tattoo and even regard providing services as an expression of art.

In our new media era, in which all kinds of information can be retrieved from the internet, in which people seem to be more concerned with taking pictures than with looking closely, and in which editing, remixing and sampling are part of everyday life, true authorship exerts an unmistakable fascination. This is why in my opinion the term 'author's jewellery' is only interesting if placed in a broader context and if compared with other disciplines in which authorship is currently under discussion, such as music, science, literature and graphic design. But this is precisely what is not happening.

As a form of personal expression and exquisite craftsmanship, jewellery has an aura of authenticity that represents a market value, no matter how vulnerable it may be. Nowadays, fashion is witnessing a development in which craft aspects and an individual signature are seen as a new form of luxury and *crafts* serve as a special distinction. But advocates of author's jewellery are opposed to fashion and its systems of presentation and distribution, which are as complex as they are seductive. (45)

Even as a present-day means of distinction, I do not appreciate the term author's jewellery, because throughout the history of jewellery, individual silversmiths have left a personal mark on their work. Nor can this term be used to indicate a level of quality, to distinguish the good from the 'less good', because the latter often comes with a personal signature as well. Jewellery designers can derive their position in the world of culture only from the qualities of their work, namely whether or not they are able to create something in terms of design which is relevant to their time and recognised by others and which is shared to the extent that people are willing to buy and wear their jewellery. The creation of a new term contributes little to this, unless it represents something new in terms of content.

The effort on the part of jewellery designers with a personal signature to hook up with the visual arts has produced beautiful objects and interesting work, including the jewellery gallery as a new sales venue and a large number of publications, lovingly written by a small group of art historians, journalists and others. But even though jewellery makers adopt the working methods and mentality of visual artists, and rely on their own world of experience as standard, by taking little or no account of the acceptance of their work and the way in which people would like to wear it, their product is still an object of applied art or design. Because of this attitude, their work forms a niche within the jewellery trade, but on the basis of its function, jewellery will never become an autonomous visual art, even though the boundary between the two may be blurred, as in the case of performances, installations or video works that have jewellery as their subject matter.

I hereby do not wish to express a negative value judgment on the group of jewellery designers in question. On the contrary, they enrich the world with their sparkling and versatile work – its personal dimension and often narrative aspect invite reflection. It is clear that items of jewellery, as autonomous artefacts, should also be looked at in the context of the intentions with which it is made, as far as these can be traced. The reason for a critical analysis of this terminology lies in the fact that many art historians and other serious authors largely concentrate on this one sector of contemporary jewellery production and ignore most other sectors.

On the basis of the above argument, it can be plainly stated that the hierarchy used within the discipline of art history, in which the applied arts are given a subordinate position, in combination with the modernist influences and the abovementioned developments within the jewellery trade have led to an uncomfortable position of jewellery within the history of art.

With the exception of a number of valuable studies on ornamentation and articles in trade journals, the study of jewellery from a cultural and historical perspective took off only by the 1950s, with a clear flourishing in the 1960s. (46) After the publication of a number of surveys on the history of jewellery, almost all of which suffer from limited perspectives and other prejudices, such as with regard to jewellery for men, the groundwork was put in place for a more specific approach to various aspects of jewellery. As part of a general medialisation in the world of art and culture, the number and size of catalogues for contemporary jewellery exhibitions increased as well.

The fairly few art historians who work on jewellery have, in most cases, committed themselves to a specific part of the profession. Their attention goes either to antiques and jewellery, which clearly represent a commercial value, or to the work of contemporary designers who manifest themselves within artistic circles and who rub shoulders with the world of the visual arts.

The media which publish about the different types of jewellery have all adopted a tone and way of photographing of their own. Fashion has generated the most beautiful jewellery photography, the jewellers have their trade journals in which a lot of attention is paid to watches, the auction industry publishes catalogues with bare and razor-sharp photos of the goods on offer, and the world of ethnography is most colourful and has an eye for the context in which jewellery is worn. Yet these different media seem hardly related to each other. This situation of divide and rule is not productive for a broader study of jewellery, and art historians have contributed to this situation as well.

In the meantime, jewellery in its various manifestations will always be around. It is and remains a primeval phenomenon. People will continue to wear jewellery, be it pieces inherited from their forebears or ethnic jewellery, while the market for fashion jewellery and accessories has become larger than ever in the past decade. With its incredible range of decorative, emotional and social aspects, jewellery is omnipresent. Yet the same cannot be said about the study of jewellery, which is in need of more incentive indeed.

Conclusions

Research into jewellery as a cultural phenomenon is a matter of finding an acceptable balance between objectivity and subjectivity. On the basis of the data available, the facts and claims believed to be true have to be continually reconsidered. Art history offers a plausible framework for the study of jewellery, partly because of the focus on the visual qualities and the historical value of independent objects. Style history, as one of the cornerstones of art history, provides a credible framework for dating jewellery.

The art historical study of jewellery is indebted to general historiography. The focus on the great jewels of those in power and the upper strata of society, as in the studies by Evans and Gans, will have to be replaced by a broader social approach within a new theoretical framework for the study of jewellery.

The hierarchy that arose in the course of the eighteenth century in the arts, in which the art of goldsmithing was classified as a craft, has had a detrimental effect on the objective study of jewellery. Partly under the influence of Modernism, jewellery has not been very popular as an object of study among art historians for a long time. This applies not only to jewellery, but also to other artefacts studied and documented in art history. It is only since the 1950s and 1960s that jewellery began to be mapped from a cultural and historical perspective.

The fuss that a number of renowned critics are making today about terms such as modern jewellery, contemporary jewellery or author's jewellery, which are contrasted with jewellery, fashion jewellery and terms such as applied art, crafts and handicrafts, should not be allowed to dominate our search for a theoretical framework for the study of jewellery. Without calling author's jewellery or contemporary jewellery dead, superfluous and autistic – as Gert Staal did in an ironic manifesto in his book about the Dutch jewellery designer Ted Noten – this new tradition can be viewed as an elitist niche within jewellery based on it its emphasis on autonomy in both concept and execution. (47) Interestingly, a dialogue is conducted about an extremely lively part of the jewellery trade, even though it is still true that jewellery is there to be worn – instead of it merely being a form of autonomous art.

4 Man as measure

4.1 Body

The cause of the minor and sometimes unclear position of jewellery within art history cannot be attributed unilaterally to the nature and development of the art historical discipline. The main cause lies in the very essence of jewellery, which is marked by a number of important aspects that can be better approached from other disciplines.

As I suggested in section 2.1, it is essential for a piece of jewellery to be worn on the human body. Man is the measure in this context. (48) In the traditional, art historical approach to jewellery as an autonomous object, most attention is paid to the maker and sometimes to the person who commissioned it. The background information may include information about a wearer, but this is usually of minor importance. When portraits are involved in the study of a piece of jewellery, the wearer is automatically included in the picture, but the piece of jewellery is centre-stage. In the case of historical pieces from before the nineteenth century, however, the wearer is more likely to be known than the maker. The fact that man literally serves as measure for jewellery is obvious, even in a quite dry description of the jewellery depicted. The places where jewellery is worn determine the size, main shape and generic name. The ring – which is worn on the fingers and sometimes on the toes; the bracelet – worn on the wrist or possibly higher on the arm; necklace – worn on the neck; earrings or ear jewellery – worn on the ears, headdress – somehow attached to or on the head; the belt – concerns the waist or hips. And then there are for example anklets and toe rings. In addition, there is the brooch or decorative pin that is attached to the clothing. Brooches, belts and necklaces may originally have had a function of holding garments in place, especially in the primal forms of clothing as wrapping garments, but in the extremely long history of jewellery their decorative and symbolic effect has prevailed.

As autonomous objects, jewellery items are worn in prominent places on the body, such as the frame of the face and the moving, slender parts of the body. This is where the decorative effect is most effective and where they can best be attached to these slender body parts. These leads are the same all over the world. Tattoos, paintings and decorative scars can also be applied to the skin of other parts of the body as body-specific decorations. The relationship between jewellery, clothing, accessories and body decorations such as tattoos and piercings can therefore be highly complex. In the west, some types of jewellery are less popular nowadays, such as jewellery in the nose, on the forehead and around the ankles or toes. These are the exceptions that confirm the rule and they may return any moment. For example, the ankle bracelet has become increasingly popular again within the contemporary culture of sunbathing and summer holidays.

Sometimes items of jewellery may actually be hidden, very intimately, such as beneath clothing. The effect is then only intended for the people who are allowed to share this intimacy. There have been moments in the history of jewellery that this aspect was deliberately played with. The armoured bodies of the court costume from the first half of the sixteenth century were adorned with necklaces which disappeared between the flattened breasts, thus drawing attention to the hidden curves. This can be nicely seen in the portraits that Holbein made of a number of ladies at the court of Henry VIII of England. Contemporary jewellery designers also play with the intimacy of jewellery; the interaction between seeing something and thus leading the eye to what cannot be seen is endlessly varied and captivating.

It is not only the shape of the body that determines the design of jewellery; the colour of the skin also influences the colour scheme of jewellery. This applies, for example, to the colour of gold, of which there are many variations, ranging from white to yellow gold and even darker shades, which are often referred to as 'pink' and 'red' gold. In tropical countries there is a clear preference for deep shades of gold. There is also a difference in the preference for pearls amongst white peoples. Jewellers nowadays keep in their shopping accounts the fact that northern European women, including Dutch women, prefer white pearls with possibly a bluish or greenish sheen, while in southern Europe many more creamy and pink pearls are sold. It goes without saying that dark skin provides a beautiful base for white shells and colourful beads, which can be too harsh on a white skin.

How a piece of jewellery relates to the human body is primarily an issue of importance to the wearer. The same applies to the tactile qualities of a piece of jewellery. Size, shape, weight, colour and finish of parts that make contact with the skin can make a lot of difference to an individual wearer. Size is crucial for rings and stiff bracelets that have to be slid over the wrist but which also should not be so wide that they can easily slip off the wrist. For necklaces it may also be necessary to customise their length.

Historians and critics who venture into the history of jewellery often make grateful use of the fact that the way jewellery is worn has much to do with developments in fashion and clothing. They use the changing forms of clothing as a timeline and relate these to more general cultural developments, without going into too much detail about the underlying questions regarding the processes and motives that play a role in fashion and clothing. This may be quite enlightening. During the late Middle Ages, when head and neck were covered, people mainly wore necklaces on their clothing as a clearly visible sign of power. But when neck and hair were released during the early Renaissance, neck and ear jewellery grew equally popular with ladies and many ornaments were woven into one's hair dress. In Italian women's portraits en profile from the early Renaissance, one can see how the fact that women's hair was allowed to be shown again, after having been covered for centuries, was celebrated by lavishly adorning it. Men were also able to show their necks in clothing from that time, and men's portraits from that time often show necklaces.

Such relationships between showing body parts and wearing jewellery therefore provide interesting information about jewellery and the way in which it accentuates the human body. Hugh Tait's study of seven thousand years of jewellery explains why women in China have worn so many hair ornaments: he assumes that this was due to the properties of the hair itself. Chinese women from the centre of this Heavenly Empire had smooth and dark hair that formed the perfect basis for beautiful jewellery. He also looked for evidence for this proposition in Chinese poetry singing the beauty of women in terms of their hair. (49)

The listing of the main forms of jewellery shows that originality in jewellery design is virtually impossible in this respect, however much contemporary designers would like to claim it. A brooch made from a new material or in a new technique remains a brooch and it should somehow be possible to pin it onto a garment. A ring must somehow fit on a finger. Apart from the philosophical question of whether something completely new can be seen and recognised as such, jewellery design is a discipline with incredibly strong conventions, which in all probability go back to times of which the history has not been recorded. (50)

4.2 Appearance

In the definition of jewellery in Section 2.1, jewellery is referred to not only as an object that people can wear on their bodies, but also as an addition to their appearance. Wearing jewellery is thus part of people's self-image and the way in which they prefer to face the world. By wearing jewellery, people can radiate sexual availability, exercise power, be accepted by their own kind or, on the contrary, be expelled and even condemned for manifesting undesirable symbolism and sympathies.

The many blatant remarks and moral rejections that exist with regard to jewellery are a confirmation of these forces. Condemnation only makes sense if there is a force to be taken into account. These critical refusals are all the more proof that jewellery is a subject of importance. Much of this criticism is justified by the way; as stated in the introduction, all human burdens and sufferings are represented in jewellery, including all the less beautiful aspects of being human.

People are seldom satisfied with the external characteristics given to them at birth. It does not happen often that these are in accordance with the standards and customs that are taught to them in their upbringing and education. In addition, it is unlikely that the ideals that they cherish at a certain stage of their life will correspond well with the realities involved in having made their own body and personality. This is part of a discussion that nowadays is being conducted in many areas.

The human body is a complex shape that can still be shaped. The English fashion expert Ted Polhemus (originally an anthropologist) describes this process very accurately and concisely in the exhibition catalogue on Florian Ladstaetter's jewellery from 2007: 'Like every other natural object – only more so – the human body ceased to be a thing in itself and became a symbol of everything beyond itself. Not content with transforming how we think about, understand, experience and even feel our bodies, our ancestors immediately also set about transforming the appearance of the human body with paint, scars, tattoos, piercings, clothing and ornament. And this from the very beginning of human development. (...) Symbolic, decorated, the human body was thus forever torn from its "natural" state'. He further argues that sexual desires are subject to visual and symbolic codes, rather than being the result of a so-called natural process. (51)

How people deal with their body and appreciate the body of others is determined by their culture. Notions about the naked body are often determined by ideals of beauty that exist at a certain time and not so much by an anatomically correct representation or a medically responsible approach to the body. This is evident from the depiction of nudes in the visual arts, amongst other things. At a time when fashion prescribes a narrow waist, nudes are also given such an exaggeratedly narrow waistline, while in the 1920s, for example, when a straight and boyish silhouette dominated women's fashion, female nudes did not appear to have a waist either.

Moreover, a body is not static; it can move, it has to be cared for and fed, it can adopt a posture and that people can express something with their body goes so far that we speak of body language.

Jewels can be sensual. The flowing movement of a hand gliding along beautifully finished links can be very pleasant. Movements of the body can be accentuated by the shine or sound of jewellery. A good example are the *tremblantes* or brooches with beautiful parts placed on metal springs. These jewels were worn in the late nineteenth century on tightly corseted upper bodies of evening dresses. They moved with the breathing of the wearer – who could only breathe from the top side of her lungs because of that corset – and while trembling drew extra attention to her upward pushed bosom.

Jewellery is also a rewarding object for indulging in neuroses, such as twisting a ring and fiddling an earring. Necklaces with a high gold content take over the body temperature perfectly and almost become part of a body; this is also possible with other materials. As soon as jewellery is worn on the skin, it can also become part of sexual acts. Where sexual drives may lead to goes far beyond this study, but the boundary between jewellery, accessory and erotic toys is sometimes difficult to draw.

The notions of what may or may not be shown of bodies are always in motion, even in this day and age in our western culture. In the western world it seems as if everything can be seen nowadays, but this is not really the case. In daily interactions, the pubic parts and also the secondary sexual characteristics remain covered. It is interesting to note that western men have been able to show more and more of their neck and chest in the last fifteen to twenty years. This has improved the sales of necklaces for men; the turnover in jewellery for men has increased considerably in this period. (52) Western women sometimes show more of their upper body and sometimes more of their legs. This has implications for the jewellery they wear; for example, a bare neck invites them to wear necklaces. On the basis of social and religious views, other women cover their bodies as completely as possible and also their hair, which also obstructs the view of their jewellery. In such cases, seeing a few bracelets around the wrist can already have an incredible erotic effect. When considering jewellery in its purest form, western notions of physicality should under no circumstances be used as a self-evident norm.

Another point that deserves attention is that jewellery is not worn constantly. In a decent collection of jewellery, most pieces are more often not worn than worn. Laying off jewellery is an act that implies that one is at home and for example goes to bed. That can have an erotic charge; in literature and films the removal of earrings is almost equal to the full-fledged sexual act, which within a story is only really interesting when it is the first time or when it is about adultery. (53) The putting on and laying down of jewels can also have to do with a ceremonial function, such as religious ornaments and chains of mayors, which are only worn in function.

In the Dutch language, decorating (versieren) has a double meaning: 'decorating' someone also means seducing someone. Jewellery is an extremely suitable accessory for accentuating physical attractions. This can vary from refined eroticism to offensive accents. But jewellery accentuates the face and, for example, the hands and wrists rather than the primary genitals. In the case of African peoples, ornaments are often used to draw attention to the back of the woman. (54) Breasts, as a secondary sexual characteristic of the woman, have a beautiful position at the front of the body, just below the face and near a narrow body part like the neck: an ideal position for wearing jewellery. But that does not necessarily mean that necklaces for women always have an erotic effect. The interplay between jewellery and clothing, accessories, make-up, movement and behaviour provides the best indication of whether a piece of jewellery is about accentuating sexual attractions. A necklace with a pendant can be a sign of prudery or good citizenship in one woman and a tempting signal in another woman. The context in which a piece of jewellery is worn also determines the effect, and this does not only apply to the erotic effect.

For the beholder of jewellery and for a jewellery designer looking for inspiration, the erotic aspects of jewellery have useful sides. Eroticism has been studied from other perspectives than jewellery. Eroticism has also been depicted in interesting ways, which proved to be useful for the study of the decorative aspects of jewellery. Information about jewellery from the Renaissance and, for example, the first half of the twentieth century, was obtained by studying nudes in painting. (55) A nude is only considered truly erotic when this object of desire still wears a few pieces of jewellery, a hat or shoes.

With regard to the relationship between jewellery and the human body, medicine offers a number of angles that may be important for the study of jewellery.

The beneficial and less beneficial effects of metals and stones are the subject of a great deal of speculation, which has been recorded by authors at various times. Such texts – by no means the least minds – often go back to very ancient wisdom. In his *History of Life and Death* from 1638, the British philosopher Francis Bacon included advice on how to dissolve gold and ground pearls in liquids and drink them as a cure. The renowned French medievalist Le Goff recalls that the symbolism of stones for the Middle Ages culminated in the attribution of healing and harmful properties to them. Red stones were supposed to cure bleeding, yellow stones jaundice and green stones liver diseases, purely because of the colour association. Oppi Untracht argues that in India, too, the colours of stones have symbolic meanings that connect man to the cosmos, and that ground stones and pearls are drunk as medicine. (56)

For the supposed effect of stones, the signs of the zodiac are often used as a guideline. (57) Stones which are hoped to have a beneficial effect on the mental and physical health of the wearer should preferably be worn on the skin. This places specific demands on the shape and material of a piece of jewellery and the way in which the stones in question are processed. Gold and platinum derive their value from the fact that, like medical steel, they do not react in any way with the body. Silver, copper and other metals and their alloys do; the question of whether they can be used consciously is relevant in connection with the current development to administer medicines gradually by means of plasters.

There are also jewels without stones to which a healing effect is attributed. Sometimes there are more or less scientific grounds for this, such as the fact that metal bracelets can have a magnetic field. (58) But most of the time magical powers are involved which for example are attributed to animal materials or religious symbols. The idea that a certain type of stone, a metal or another material may be beneficial to one's health and can heal the wearer or protect him from evil, is in many cultures a stronger motive than many western observers would like to admit.

A fascinating collection of objects related to people's health and appearance is the one Henry Wellcome (1853–1936) has collected all over the world. Wellcome was a rich entrepreneur with a great interest in medical science, archaeology and anthropology. He put a considerable part of his capital at the service of medical science. Medicine Man, the book published by the British Museum in 2003, includes objects from his collection that were intended to contribute to a better understanding of the functioning of the body and all kinds of aids that came in handy with it. Wellcome was also fascinated by objects related to the end of life. The accompanying exhibition included pretty mourning jewellery, memento moris, a fine collection of artificial eyes and limbs, masks, fertility symbols, birth tongs, sexual aids and wearable amulets in the form of animal figures such as salamanders and turtles, proof that he was prepared to include jewellery among the medical aids. The most diverse expressions of the relationship between jewellery and human health have been brought together in this collection.

In some cases, it is only a small step from an object that can be carried on the body to an orthopaedic accessory. There have been attempts to make hearing aids more attractive and to elevate them to jewellery, which means that they are hidden in or behind a piece of jewellery as well as possible. Jewellery can be useful in concealing wrinkles or scars in the neck. In recent years, spectacles have been turned into a hybrid product, somewhere between a functional tool and a piece of jewellery or fashion accessory. Especially sunglasses are subject to all kinds of fashionable standards.

Human beings seem to be willing to do a lot to model their body to the desired appearance. Consideration of jewellery as well as fashion shows that people are willing to go very far when it comes to their appearance. Take, for instance, all possible measures to obtain a narrow waistline, going as far as destroying inner organs and surgically removing the floating ribs. The boundary between medical and cosmetic products and procedures is vague, especially in our time, when cosmetic procedures have become an entire industry and young girls in the United States may receive such operation as a birthday gift from their parents

Insights into genetics are still very fresh, especially in relation to the incredibly long history of human ornamentation. Genetic research and the resulting opportunities to create 'designer babies' will become an increasingly important focus of attention in the near future. Are these purely medical matters – such as the prevention of serious illnesses – or are they also aesthetic values that have to do more with people's desired appearance? From a medical point of view, there is still much to be expected in terms of people's desired appearance, more than the most sceptical observer could have imagined a few decades ago.

4.4 Men, women, children

When it comes to man as measure, it's about men, women and children. In jewellery, women tend to be mentioned first because it is usually assumed that women wear most jewellery, that men hardly wear any kind of jewellery (beyond a wedding ring), and that children should not be burdened with it. These are contemporary, western notions, which can be very decisive and therefore also hinder the study of jewellery.

As Graham Hughes, renowned jewellery expert and organiser of one of the most important jewellery exhibitions of the twentieth century, *Modern Jewellery* from 1961, has claimed: 'It is often said that jewels are useless, that unlike chairs or saucepans they have no practical function, which is why their designs can be such fun. This is certainly true, but if jewels do not have a function, they do have a job, and a very important one: the beautification of woman, the conversion from desirable to irresistible, the promotion of the smart to the tremendous.' (59) In her description of the history of jewellery from the same year, Giltay-Nijssen was more neutral in her description of the shift in fashion and social conventions that caused jewellery and other ornaments to become more and more the domain of women. Giltay-Nijssen starts her historiography with the time of Louis XIV, a fervent jewellery enthusiast himself. In the second half of the eighteenth century the competition between men's and women's clothing came to an end and although the same fabrics were still used for both, man's clothing gradually began to simplify. As regards to wearing jewellery, women also became more important than men. At the end of her book she provides the following advice: 'Jewellery should accentuate a woman's beauty, rather than overshadow it' (60).

Men have always worn jewellery, to be sure. Precious jewels, or large jewels, were even mainly worn by men, as an external characteristic of their power. The lustre of their jewels was very functional at a time when there were no newspapers or other news media. Especially in cultures where women lived in seclusion or otherwise played a subordinate role, it was the male rulers who adorned themselves most elaborately. This applied to the court of the Russian czar, especially in the times before Catherine the Great, and also to other kings and empires, such as Persia, India and China. (61) How this pattern manifested itself in lower social strata needs to be investigated in more detail. For ancient African peoples and Indian tribes in North, Central and South America the same principle applied: men had most adornment on their body. This phenomenon, when addressed for instance in sociological or anthropological studies, will invariably prompt a comparison with the animal kingdom, including references to lion manes, the colours of bird feathers and macho behaviour.

As of the early 1800s, men in the west began to wear less and less jewellery, even though in 1810, when Napoleon married Marie-Louise, the daughter of the Emperor of Austria, as a parvenu emperor he was almost more richly adorned than his bride. (62) The slow emergence of the soberly tinted, three-piece suit is nicely described in the exhibition catalogue *The ideal man* from 2008. (63) Until well into the twentieth century, however, men still wore watch chains (often draped prominently over their bellies), rings, tie pins and fine buttons, including cufflinks, precious metal buttons and diamonds on the vest of their tailcoat or dress suit. It was actually only a very short period that men in the western world wore little or no jewellery, except for their wedding ring or a functional product such as a watch. This mainly concerned the decades after the Second World War, which was precisely the period in which ground-breaking studies about jewellery as part of art history were published. Hippies, drug dealers and other striking male representatives of subversive groups in the western world did wear jewellery, and at the end of the twentieth century men's interest in jewellery increased again.

It is therefore remarkable that in such a comparatively short period of time, the notion has been taken up that it is mainly women who wear jewellery and that, in principle, they do so in order to increase their beauty, purely as decoration. However, like men, women wear jewellery as signs of their power or social position, or to highlight their physical qualities, while also using intimate ornaments and signs of personal relationships and memories. It is an undeniable fact that the status of women is often related to their physical attraction, but men's vanity should certainly not be underestimated. The reasons why men wore jewellery in the past may have been largely due to its symbolic value, but the effect was also decorative, as in most cases the jewellery was intended to impress and be seen from a considerable distance. One may therefore say that powerful men probably paid more attention to the decorative effect of their jewellery than many women.

Much less is known about the history of jewellery made from base metals, textiles, porcelain or less precious raw materials derived from nature, such as amber, shells, bones, fossils, wood or feathers, than about the history of precious jewellery. It is likely that people attributed all kinds of forces to these materials. Whether they were worn more by men or women is unknown.

There is actually little hard evidence about the difference between men and women when it comes to wearing jewellery. The physical differences between the two can be described concretely, but both men and women have worn necklaces, rings and earrings. They have both worn signs of their religious beliefs and ornaments to ward off evil forces. That jewellery for men has generally been heavier and stronger than that for women is an assumption that seems plausible on the basis of the available studies, but, like women, men have worn hats with feathers on them, to give an example of a light ornament. That certain forms of jewellery look typically masculine or feminine largely seems a matter of views associated with the different social and economic roles of men and women over time.

Children are more vulnerable than adults; their personality has yet to develop to a significant extent and their welfare is the responsibility of their parents or caretakers in almost every culture. That children should not wear jewellery because it impedes their freedom of movement is a contemporary notion. For centuries, babies were bandaged. Moreover, children have always been vulnerable because of high rates of infant mortality. In particular cultures, children were given all kinds of amulets and materials with a protective or medicinal effect to wear. (64) Often, children will also serve as an extension of their parents' social position. The large degree to which children nowadays are fitted with accessories from expensive brands proves that this habit is still alive and kicking.

One of the most dramatic events in any life is the transition from childhood to adulthood. This, of course, has everything to do with fertility and sexuality. If in one culture this will be celebrated extensively with initiation rites and all kinds of physical signs, in another culture this may be addressed in much more subtle ways, for instance because people prefer to pay attention to achieving social maturity and the interrelated responsibilities and attributes such as a pearl necklace, a signet ring or a beautiful watch. The intermediate period of adolescence with its hormonal fluctuations may therefore be seen as a somewhat more problematic stage in these cultures.

Being young as an appealing standard has been prominent in western countries since the 1960s. Adults have adopted or imitated young people's habits and clothing and accessories in many different ways. It is interesting how, exactly, this has influenced our outlook on jewellery and other accessories. Nowadays there are quite a few children's jewels on the market which are also intended to be worn by adults, such as charm bracelets and pendants in the form of toy animals, but the supply of adult jewellery has not decreased as a result.

In other times or other cultures, the transition towards adulthood was something to be proud of and was also reflected in body decorations. But these should not be seen as tied to our current preoccupation with a youthful appearance.

Conclusions

The main shapes of pieces of jewellery are determined by where on the body they are worn. As a result, the design of jewellery is based in strong conventions, which show little variation across time and from one region to another. This is why a piece of jewellery should always be judged in terms of its shape and size in relation to the human body.

Jewellery can be directly visible in daily interactions, but may also feature more intimately, as ornaments mainly intended for the wearer. By linking jewellery to people's self-image and, for example, their health, a number of scholarly perspectives present themselves, including the role of suggestive powers and pure magic. The notion that stones, animal material and symbolic forms can influence both the mental and physical health of people may be controversial, but this is an important motive for wearing jewellery in many cultures.

On the basis of the above analysis, one persistent prejudice in the study of jewellery should be denounced. The rise of the idea that jewellery is in principle intended for women and should be described as such coincides with the rise of the field of art history and the study of jewellery within the overall field of art, architecture and design. Pioneers in the historiography and contemplation of jewellery from the 1950s and 1960s, such as Flower, Evans, Hughes, Gans, Giltay-Nijssen and Gregorietti, have set the tone in this respect, while subsequent authors have given little or no thought to this issue. The contemporary production of jewellery has been strongly geared at women as well; at best, catalogues of exhibitions with contemporary work speculate on the possibility that men could also wear the works on display.

But this situation is gradually changing. In my study on Dutch jewellery I paid explicit attention to men's growing interest in jewellery and their willingness to wear it during the last period of the twentieth century, a trend which – if still marginal – appears to last. (65) The idea of jewellery as chiefly intended for women, as persistent as it is incorrect, can therefore be traced back to a convergence of developments in the practice of art history, in the historiography of jewellery and in slowly evolving – and rather unfortunate – notions within western society. Because anthropologists are less afflicted by this prejudice, if at all, anthropological studies of jewellery and other forms of body adornment may have a useful corrective role. This chapter on the intimate relationship between jewellery and the human body perhaps underscores that historical examples of jewellery display mainly involve rulers and members of the high nobility and that in the western context still very little attention has been paid to the role of jewellery for other social groups.

5 Perspectives from other disciplines

5.1 Humanities

With the shift of attention to man as measure, a crucial question emerges: *why do people wear jewellery?* I have already indicated several motives: marking a social position, enjoying decoration, mitigating fears or cherishing memories. The question of how in this respect man functions as a yardstick with regard to jewellery, however, should be investigated more systematically. In the human sciences, motives for wearing clothing, jewellery and other body ornaments have been analysed, as well as their effect on mutual relationships between people. This is rarely, if ever, referred to by authors who focus their attention on jewellery. As a result, an important link in the study of jewellery is lacking.

That link can be found in the study of clothing and fashion. Clothing and fashion have been researched much more fundamentally than jewellery, especially in psychology and sociology. Within anthropology, it is customary to place jewellery in a social and cultural context, just like other body decorations and clothing. In much of the literature on the history of jewellery, authors consider jewellery in the context of clothing, as part of an overall image and as a reference for a specific timeframe, but underlying motives relating to the wearing of clothing and changes in fashion are hardly addressed. If in my study on Dutch Jewellery I implicitly did so, this will be further elaborated and substantiated in this essay.

5.1.1 Psychology

In 1930, John Carl Flügel published *The Psychology of Clothes*, the result of his research into the fundamental question of why people wear clothes. He came up with 'modesty, decoration and protection'. Flügel saw modesty as the opposite of the most important reason for wearing clothes, namely the need to adorn one's own body. According to him, protection was much less important than the duality between adornment and reticence or even chastity. With this, as a psychoanalyst, Flügel opened a specific door for the contemplation of jewellery that, as far as I'm concerned, should never be closed again. (66)

Many anthropologists and historians of dress have used and elaborated on the study by Flügel. The Danish art historian Rudolf

 Broby-Johansen uses insights from anthropology, psychology and sociology for his quite polemical and lavishly illustrated history of dress, titled *Body and Clothes* (1966). He also argues that it is incorrect to assume that wearing clothing is primarily motivated by the need for protection against the cold and other external influences. In his view, the main reason for clothing and physical adornment is linked to exerting sexual attraction. (67) The prominent and productive English historian of dress, James Laver, argues in *Modesty in Dress* (1969) that in the nineteenth and early twentieth century modesty was seen as the most common motive for wearing clothes, but that insights from psychology and anthropology have discredited this notion. He, too, argues that protection does not suffice as primary motivation; instead, in his view, it is the desire to attract the opposite sex. (68)

The consensus that has grown over the years means that the main motives for wearing clothes are the pursuit of status, decoration and protection. In this respect, status should be seen as a bipolar concept, because it is used to distinguish oneself from others, but at the same time to confirm that one belongs to a certain group. Since the 1960s and 1970s, following the wave of democratisation, critics of fashion and clothing have introduced a new dichotomy, namely between vertical and horizontal social relations. In fashion, even diagonal proportions are recognised. With his Système de la Mode (1963), Roland Barthes has provided a much-appreciated foundation for this approach. Other authors, such as Rudolf Broby-Johansen, Anne Hollander, Giles Lipovetsky, Alison Lurie, Ted Polhemus and Bernard Rudofski, amongst others, have developed this point in various ways. In chapter 5.2, a number of these authors are mentioned in more detail.

The desire to adorn the body, however, is regarded as the undisputed primal impulse for wearing clothes and ornaments, whether it is to mark status, to want to belong to something or to exert sexual attraction. This serves as a perfect stepping stone towards a theory of jewellery indeed, and it is curious that jewellery researchers rarely, if ever, refer to these studies, although some of them do address these motives in one way or another and also rather timidly include them in their arguments.

All the various motivations for wearing jewellery are expressed in the design of jewellery items and the way in which they are worn. A lot has already been said about the decorative aspect of jewellery in section 4.1, but these motives are also expressed in the symbolism of jewellery. This refers to jewellery as an attribute, to characteristics that belong to the essence of jewellery, as described below in chapter 6 on symbolism in jewellery.

Developments in psychology have their own dynamics and there are probably more amateur psychologists than professional psychologists. This is why we can be brief about psychology as an angle for the study of jewellery: this field has provided important building blocks and as such it may well serve as source of further insight into jewellery and body adornment.

The contribution of the human sciences to the study of jewellery is of fundamental importance for interpreting the function of jewellery as a means of marking one's own identity. This is a basic need of people, but it is also a complex matter, especially in our era of globalisation and mass media. The way in which academic disciplines such as psychology, sociology, ethnology and cultural studies are interwoven today can be regarded as an effect of this current need for identity and the need to interpret all the means by which such identity can be marked.

5.1.2 Sociology

A study by the American economist and sociologist Thorstein Veblen, *The Theory of the Leisure Class*, constitutes a cornerstone for the development of theories about clothing and fashion.
In 1899, Veblen laid the foundations for a critical approach to consumerism. He considered the process of fashion, the constant urge to innovate in clothing, as an expression of money culture and introduced the concept of *conspicuous consumption and the principle of conspicuous waste*, amongst other things. A wealthy

upper class was able to dress and decorate so finely that at a single glance it was clear that its members did not have to do any physical work. If socially and financially slightly lower ranked people had adopted the most important characteristics of the clothing and ornaments of this group, they could afford to use their tailors and couturiers, including their jewellers, hairdressers, hatters and cobblers, to create a new image of clothing and thus respond to the essence of fashion. This principle had already been beautifully expressed by Hans Christian Andersen in the middle of the nineteenth century in his fairy tale 'The Emperor's New Clothes'. As a sociologist and economist, Veblen has further developed and substantiated this fact.

As an economist, Veblen refuted the notion that people always want value for money. He argued that irrational motives, such as the desire for luxury and expensive things that increase status, are of great importance for a country's economy. An interesting point for the study of jewellery is that Veblen pointed out that in his day and age men had already delegated the need to dress expensively, wastefully and uncomfortably largely to their wives, although by present standards the edges of their shirts, the tying of the right tie and jewellery such as tie pins and cardigans with diamonds could still be regarded as part of that need. Yet this was modest indeed when compared to the vicarious ostentation that chic women exhibited at the time in a fluent combination of their clothing – worked up with lace, embroidery and trimmings – and an overloaded quantity of jewellery.

At the same time as Veblen, the German philosopher and sociologist Georg Simmel studied the principles behind the changes in fashion. He focused his attention on the advancing money economy. He also analysed the underlying motives of fashion, such as the human urge to distinguish oneself in clothing and at the same time to visibly join the social group to which a person belongs or wants to belong – in short, the game of distinction and imitation. (69)

Today's social relations are very different from those in the days of Veblen and Simmel, and their theories have now been subjected to quite a bit of criticism. What they are accused of is that they worked out the exemplary function of the highest positions mainly in a vertical direction, like a sinking cultural good that moves from the higher to the lower classes in society. Clothing and body style are also an important instrument in horizontal contacts between people and that the lower classes or subcultures can influence the preferences of completely different social groups are notions which could perhaps not be expected of mindful representatives of their time.

Fortunately, they were not the only ones to analyse the changes in the appearance of people on the basis of sociological, philosophical and economic insights. As a versatile art historian and artist, Quentin Bell was fascinated by people's sometimes peculiar behaviour. In his study *On Human Finery* (1976), he extended the theory of Veblen to the twentieth century clothing industry and added concepts such as conspicuous leisure and conspicuous outrage. The latter is about consciously wearing things that are considered tasteless and thus cultivating bad taste. (70) At such an expression of protest, jewellery can once again be of good service. The will to offend can give fascinating impulses to fashion and jewellery. Punks and a number of pop stars are good examples of this phenomenon. The current popularity of heavy necklaces around the neck – especially for men, but also for women – can be traced back to the conspicuous outrage in the decoration of black drug dealers. Workwear such as jeans has undergone a status increase in recent decades as a hallmark of an active and youthful appearance, with various consequences for the wearing of jewellery, ranging from no jewellery at all, the craze for buttons, a preference for ethnic and pearl necklaces and real jewellery as a deliberate contrast.

Every community has hierarchies and codes of conduct that cover the wearing of jewellery. It is therefore logical that developments in time and changes in social relationships become visible in their design and the way in which and by whom they are worn, as well as they are expressed in clothing, literature or architecture. For this reason, striking uses and changes in the way people dress can be a good reason to analyse social mobility within a certain time or group. (71)

The merit of Veblen and his followers is that they have shown that people need examples to connect their own identity to. Social science must provide insight into the standards of conduct that are considered normal within a social group. Nowadays, sociology and other behavioural sciences are recognising that the primary need of the vast majority of people is to conform themselves rather than to be an exception. Their behaviour is determined by the culture in which they grew up and the first reaction of people to a deviation from the known patterns, such as a renewal or provocation, is more defence than desire. Aligning one's own cultural pattern with the behaviour and decorations of the higher ranked only works if the distance is not too great, otherwise such behaviour from both sides will immediately be experienced as affected and unreal. (72) Much has been said about the way in which social relations are expressed in the wearing of jewellery in studies on the history of jewellery, and little of it is well-founded. In his otherwise valuable survey of jewellery over the centuries, Gregorietti states in his conclusions that the most important developments in the history of jewellery are of a social nature. According to him, the use of jewellery until the eighteenth century was limited to court life. With the Industrial Revolution, the old class system was broken and jewellery and other ornaments became available to broader segments of the population.

Perhaps the unspoken difference between adornment and high jewellery plays a role here, but still I do not agree with his assertion that until the eighteenth century, citizens did not wear jewellery and other precious ornaments. Just take the way in which the more or less well-to-do bourgeoisie were portrayed with pearls and diamonds in sixteenth and seventeenth century Dutch painting, leaving aside the question of whether all those pearls were real. The lace they wore often represented a nice fortune as well. The number of gold necklaces with which the wealthy bourgeoisie were portrayed at the end of the fifteenth and the beginning of the sixteenth century is overwhelming, particularly in the German-language region. In principle, Gregorietti is quite right when he links developments in society inextricably to developments in design and manner of wearing jewellery, but he proves once again that much more research can be done into the jewellery of the wealthy bourgeoisie and the lower classes (73).

In the course of history, the adaptation of dressing behaviour and decoration to the social and cultural group to which one belongs and the accompanying rules of conduct with regard to upper and lower places has led to geographically determined characteristics of jewellery and the way in which they are worn. Research into Dutch jewellery in the twentieth century has shown that the typically Dutch mentality with regard to outward display is an important connecting factor. This was expressed not only in the jewellery of the wealthy, but also in jewellery that was worn by broad segments of the Dutch population.

The extent to which social conventions play a role with regard to the wearing of jewellery is evident from the habits relating to the moments when jewellery is worn. This requires a delicate sense of finesse in regulated societies. Western prescriptions of roughly the last century and a half determined that the elegant and well-mannered married woman was not allowed to wear her rings with diamonds and other high-quality gemstones in the morning. The question of what she wears when she visits in the afternoon, what she wears during dinner and what she wears at gala venues, was subject to equally strict rules. These formed an excellent social barrier for all too eager social climbers.

This difference between jewellery for the day and the evening is traced back by Giltay-Nijssen to the difference in fabrics; the brilliance of the evening jewellery would be too opaque for cloth, taffeta and muslin, which were worn during the day. A shaky excuse in my opinion. A better explanation lies in the rules for the cleavage. In the course of the nineteenth century the custom grew that women were only expected to expose their necks in evening wear, a good example of the concept of 'giving opportunity'. (74) Cabochon cut stones and types like garnet, quartz, turquoise, agate and amber were worn during the day, faceted gemstones like diamond, sapphire, ruby and emerald were reserved for the evening. Nowadays such rules are applied much more loosely, but they still work in certain circles.

The rules for wearing crowns, tiaras and badges during royal receptions have been fixed for centuries, although they may have changed at some point. The idiom of the adornment of the European royal houses has recently been documented in the catalogue accompanying the exhibition *Schitterend Europa* (Dazzling Europe) from 2007. It also contains a number of miniatures of rulers, which are encased in diamonds or otherwise processed in jewellery. (75) Wearing these jewels belonged to the privileges of members of royal and imperial families and of their closest confidants. Only the rulers concerned could grant that privilege as they saw fit, as a token of a special bond. In principle, the gentlemen and the ladies were the same for this social convention. However, the custom of including portraits of loved ones in jewellery goes far beyond this royal privilege, as Marta Gandy Fales, amongst others, has demonstrated in her book on jewellery in America. (76)

Looking beyond the Western European conventions, we know what people were supposed to wear at the Russian tsarist court, at Indian royal houses and, for example, at the imperial courts in China and Japan. As far as the United States is concerned, as a powerful and rich country without a royal family, it was a bit of a help, but this was soon compensated by its own standards. (77) Interesting is the traffic between all kinds of cultures and courts. What did envoys wear, what was brought with them as gifts, and did new fashions emerge from them? A good example of a free interpretation of all etiquette regarding the wearing of jewellery are Hollywood films, certainly those from the thirties and forties, when the ostentatious wearing of jewellery in real life was curtailed by economic crisis and war.

Addressing the question of good manners with regard to wearing jewellery, during the last two centuries this issue has been more about when one should *not* wear one's most beautiful jewellery, rather than about when one should wear it. Especially in the Netherlands this was only done in private circles and the less privileged were not pestered in daily traffic. For representatives of the highest social classes in western countries the most important thing was to know that they owned such jewels. So, for example, if one was travelling one did not have to wear them; copies were sufficient as a reference to the original pieces. This was a form of snobbery and potential swindle, for instance if the real jewels had to be sold in a financial setback and the copies continued to be worn. (78)

Then there is the widespread rule that marriageable young women were not allowed to wear jewellery, a simple necklace excepted at most, unless it was difficult to bring them the right man. A loved one was not allowed to give jewels to a young woman, only an engagement ring as proof of his serious intentions. This was made up for on the wedding day in many countries by gifts from benevolent parents and other family members and especially by the *corbeille*, a basket of jewels that was offered as a wedding gift by the groom to his bride. (79) In some cultures, it is common for the jewellery intended to be worn by a bride to be made available and managed by the family or a community.

Mourning has always been expressed in clothing and decorations. In well-educated, western circles the rule was that in a period of mourning black and white could be worn, which for jewellery means that pearls and diamonds could be worn and on everyday occasions also black ornaments of jet and onyx. (80) At the time of mourning in the eighteenth and nineteenth centuries many jewels were also worn in which hair of the deceased was incorporated. These western views are now firmly diluted, although in certain circles they are still taken into account. In other cultures, very different colours may be considered for mourning.

In contrast to cultures with such social limitations in terms of wearing jewellery, there are cultures in which simply everything one possesses is worn on the body, as in the case of nomadic peoples. They must be able to move around freely and take their entire possessions with them from one moment to the next. In her book *Parures ethniques* (2001), archaeologist and art historian Bérénice Geoffroy-Schneiter adds that nomads in North Africa move in regions where banks are scarce: 'the parure offers a mode of idealisation at the same time as a means of displaying it to all its riches'. (81) Practical considerations, as well as the pride of certain cultural groups and their modest social status, underlie this decorative desire.

The difference between the urban population and the inhabitants of the countryside also plays a role in other parts of the world when considering what people are and are not expected to wear. In my study on Dutch jewellery I described the social control in the countryside, which in the beginning of the twentieth century was stronger than in the city. Farmers knew exactly how many cows they owned and they were able to assess whether their wives were wearing head jewellery and bead necklaces that matched their position, while they also took into account their own valuable items, such as precious buttons and other precious metal items of clothing. (82)

5.1.3 Anthropology, ethnology and material culture

All over the world, jewellery has been worn in an infinite variety of shapes, colours and materials, but most of it fits within the basic forms related to the human body, such as necklaces, headdresses, bracelets, rings, belts, etc. It is almost impossible for jewellery scholars to study variations in body style from all kinds of cultures other than those with which they are most familiar. It is always important to recognise the relationship between the form of this decoration, the available raw materials and the social and religious customs within another culture, in the first place as a test of ingrained notions from one's own culture. The fact that in certain places this body style can be so fascinating and rich that one can completely lose oneself in the study of it is another matter.

Anthropology is concerned with the nature and way of life of peoples. Jewellery is studied in this field as autonomous objects, but also in relation to other body decorations, such as tattoos, haircuts and body changes or mutilations. It follows that the study of such bodily decorations can once again provide insight into the motives why people wear jewellery. Or at least that anthropology can be used to put too limited and time-bound ideas about jewellery into perspective and thus to create a broader framework for the study of jewellery.

In *Body and Clothes* by Broby-Johansen, the motifs for body decorations and mutilations are directly related to the history of fashion. He shows plainly in word and image that the body decorations and mutilations of so-called primitive peoples can be equated with western notions and customs: 'The tightly laced stays and bindings worn by Europeans and Indians, from the Bronze age right up to the present day have resulted in deformities even more shocking than those known among primitive cultures'. (83) As claimed by Broby-Johansen in his introduction, one must know what the underlying motives for wearing clothes are in order to be able to understand what clothing is. According to him, the meaning of clothing and other body decorations can only be understood if one always considers the relationship with the body. This is exactly what has to be done in studies of jewellery. (84)

His implicit criticism of the current approach to books on fashion and clothing also applies to most books on the history of jewellery. The study of fashion has now been enriched with a much broader theoretical basis than was the case in his day, but the approach to jewellery is still characterised by the fact that cross-references between different times or cultures are seldom made. (85) A point of criticism is that he has seldom supported his firm statements with empirical evidence. They derive their credibility mainly from the combination of unconventional yet logical thinking and a few well-chosen images. However, many of his statements have been confirmed by other publications. (86)

Angela Fisher's beautiful books seduce the viewer with their magnificent photography and at the same time create a distance; they are so exotic that they can be compared to a visit to the zoo rather than inviting us to critically examine ingrained notions of body style. *Africa Adorned* from 1984 was the first publication to make an indelible impression on anyone interested in jewellery and the ethnographic. The quality lies in the combination of geographical and ethnographic information and the beautiful photography, with a great deal of attention to detail. In this way Fisher shows that the human body and all the ornamentation released onto it can grow together into a fascinating unity, and that pieces of jewellery should not be seen separately from the body and other forms of body decoration.

Anthropology is a very rich discipline, but it is not easy to highlight the main points of view for the study of jewellery and information on the nature and manufacture of jewellery. Anthropological studies are classified according to geographical grounds and classified according to continents, countries, peoples and tribes. This can make it difficult to gather the right information to make a comparison between jewellery from different cultures and to distil connections from them or to gain a deeper insight into certain motifs and their symbolic value. Almost without exception, the presentations of museums of ethnology are also classified on the basis of geography.

Interestingly, jewellery and other body-related objects and decorations in ethnographic museums are usually displayed according to the context of the peoples concerned, their physical appearance and the way in which they live. This can go very far if entire houses and even villages are rebuilt. However, even if jewellery or other consumer goods and, for example, weapons are displayed as separate objects, information about how they are worn and used is usually provided in these museums.

Those eager to look beyond the borders of their own country or even their own continent will have to find their way within anthropology in order to extract the relevant information for the study of jewellery. The French historian and archaeologist

Bérénice Geoffroy-Schneiter is one of the authors who took human adornment as a subject and who, on the basis of comparative research, came to interesting conclusions. She also deals with jewellery in her book on ethnic decoration in connection with body distortions and tattoos. According to her, much of the symbolism in these traditional ornaments can no longer be traced, for example in the rich formal language of the face statues of the Maoris. (87) She pays a lot of attention to the magical powers that are attributed to jewellery in many places in the world and she recognises a number of universal motifs, such as the sun and the moon. If one motif is most suitable for jewellery, it is the snake in her view, for it can swing itself so nicely around an arm, the neck or a finger.

Anthropologists themselves recognise the need to distil information from the results of all kinds of research of different cultures or regions when it comes to achieving greater depth in their knowledge. The authors mentioned above, such as Broby-Johansen and Fisher, called themselves anthropologists, but ethnology, which has roots in the study of folk art, is a common term here as well. Ethnologists deal with the cultural practice of peoples, including western ones, and they examine the meanings attributed to objects by their users and what it means for a culture if certain objects are widely used. This focus differs from the one in art history, which is much more geared to the artistic quality of those products.

A more recent approach that is gaining momentum is the study of what is called material culture. It focuses on the meanings that objects can have for people within a certain group or culture and how they relate to similar objects and, for example, the materials they are made of and the numbers in which they are produced.

As with archaeology, this research is based on all the available material, without first eating the best bits, as is the case in art historical study. Much-needed research into decoration amongst broader layers of the population in western countries can be best expected from this angle. In the Netherlands, Anton Schuurman has done pioneering work in this area by including jewellery in his studies of the material culture of the Dutch rural population in the nineteenth century. He approached this subject from an inventory of consumer durables. Key concepts in his findings are identity and solidarity, concepts that feature regularly in theoretical frameworks for jewellery. Schuurman split up his findings for socio-professional groups, on the kind of goods and, in the case of jewellery, even on the use of materials (blood coral, cornaline and garnet). His research shows that men's jewellery was still well-represented amongst objects in precious metals owned by the Dutch rural population at the time, and that the property of peasants was more focused on external appearance than that of the wealthy bourgeoisie, who also owned objects in precious metals for use in the home, such as silver cutlery. (88)

Oppi Untracht has done exemplary work for jewellery in India with regard to this broad approach. He not only treats the precious stones and the refined techniques of the best goldsmiths, but also the glass ring bracelets as a universal wedding dress. (89) Fortunately, more and more studies on jewellery from non-western cultures and their meanings – such as *The Jewellery of Southeast Asia* (2000) by Anne Richter, *Parures Ethniques* (2001) by Bérénice Geoffroy-Schneiter and *Bijoux ethniques: Afrique, Asie et Îles du Pacifique* (2002) by Michiel Elsevier Stokmans on the collection of René van der Star – which offer timely reflection on western notions about jewellery. In any case, they provide a considerable extension of the meanings and forces that can be attributed to jewellery.

Conclusions

By identifying perspectives from the human sciences, a number of useful elements can be listed for the study of jewellery, with an emphasis on the recognition of the human need to decorate oneself and those to whom one committed oneself in life. What is crucial is the bipolar, social need for distinction and affirmation, in all sorts of variations, as well as the need for people to serve as role models. The notion that only those in power can serve as such has already been rectified as far as fashion is concerned, but this still has to be done for jewellery. Codes of behaviour and body decoration are usually attuned to like-minded people within a social group, but influence can take place in all kinds of directions. Even those who expressly dissociate themselves in their ornaments from applicable norms can be set as an example by others at unexpected moments and places.

Protection as a motive for wearing jewellery should mainly be seen as symbolic protection – as a sign of trust in supernatural powers and in magic, with which many people live.

In addition to an at times overwhelming richness in jewellery, anthropology offers a valuable touch and helps to put rusty notions from one's own culture and one's own time into perspective. With attention for the cultural and social context of artefacts, careful observations by social groups and attention for signs of distinction and coherence within these groups, both anthropology and newer disciplines such as ethnology and material culture can serve as examples for the study of jewellery as a universal cultural phenomenon. Within this approach, research into jewellery provides useful information for the understanding of other cultural and social developments and phenomena.

5.2 Relationship between the study of jewellery and the study of fashion and clothing

The worlds of fashion and clothing and the worlds of jewellery are often seen as two different worlds, which barely touch each other and sometimes are even depicted as each other's rivals. But it is perhaps more useful to explore how they can be productively related to each other.

Fashion is movement. 'Fashion is a passing thing – thing of fancy, fantasy, and feeling', said Diana Vreeland, who lived in the world of fashion and in her role as fashion editor for American *Vogue* and *Harper's Bazaar*, was able to analyse the changes in fashion like no other and communicate them to her readers. (90)

Fashion, understood as expressing the urge for change by means of clothing and decoration in order to make a social order visible, is usually considered to be a western phenomenon. A precondition for the emergence of fashion is a highly differentiated society that offers room for social mobility. Since the nineteenth century, fashion has also been the ideal means of keeping a wide-ranging industry going. (91)

Fashion is not so much about skirts and pants or beautiful dresses. Even if one can buy and wear a beautiful dress, the satisfaction is short-lived and the possession of that dress is the seed of the desire for something else, for something that one does not yet own. (92) Fashion is essentially immaterial. This is why it is not easy to understand fashion, which requires a combination of insights from many different angles. Or as Ted Polhemus and Lynn Proctor put it in *Fashion and Anti-Fashion*, their ground-breaking anthropology of fashion, clothing and ornaments from 1987: 'Fashion is an advertisement for the ideology of social mobility, change and progress, a message which is symbolised by the fashion system's own mechanism of constant change'. The following sentence also applies to the study of jewellery: 'This has often been made difficult to appreciate by those who have seen change, progress and revolution simply in terms of the rich upper class or of the bourgeois middle class'. (93)

Clothing is material and practical; clothing is body covering that is, can be or has been fashionable. When defining clothing, aspects such as wearability and protection are quickly raised, although a clothing image as well as a fashion image can just as easily be interpreted from a cultural and social point of view.

Jewellery is even more important than clothing in terms of ownership, material value and memories of moments and persons. A ring that you have received from someone you really care about is worn regardless of the fashion of the moment. Yet jewellery, just like fashion, can be an expression of their time, of the desire to create something that wasn't there yet. Despite all the meanings that designers put into their jewellery, they usually do not acquire their meaning for the wearer until the ring is put on the finger or the necklace is put on the neck. As a result, jewellery is, in principle, much more resistant to the passage of time than fashion.

In this polarity lies the at times rather uncomfortable relationship between jewellery and fashion. As far as designers, producers and makers are concerned, this is often a matter of clashing egos as well. A fashion designer does not want the attention of his clothing to be distracted by the jewellery, unless he needs an accent for a particular model and can market such a piece of jewellery or accessory under his own name. (94) The clothing accessories closest to a piece of jewellery in terms of the way they are worn are the corsage – a flower, real or not, spelled on a shoulder or lapels – and scarves worn as collars. Jewellery such as brooches and pendants are often worn on a ribbon around the neck, whereby jewellery and accessories can be considered as a whole. In the eighteenth-century court dress, the distinction between jewellery and ribbons, bows, ruffles, false locks and other accessories was almost entirely lost in the rich overall picture. (95) Jewellery of many non-western peoples can sometimes hardly be distinguished from the other body decorations; it is the overall picture that counts.

It is the wearers who can combine clothing and jewellery on their own bodies to create a harmonious or interesting overall picture. Today, stylists play a similar role in department stores and fashion magazines. However, I have often been able to recognise a division of spirits even in the case of wearers. In recent decades, I have seen many valuable and stylish jewellery worn on clothing that can be labelled as stiff and conventional, while beautiful, fashionable suits with the signature of a leading designer are often combined with meaningless chains of fake gold by their proud owner.

The relationship between fashion and jewellery and the way in which jewellery is combined with clothing quickly leads us to the concept of taste. The fact that taste cannot be disputed is a stupid platitude. The fact is that it happens a lot, and why not? A dialogue or even a difference of opinion is a good way of clarifying certain matters. The difficult thing about taste is that it is a collection of values: partly aesthetic, partly ethical, partly cultural, partly tied to a particular time. The issue contested here pertains to the remaining part, which is personal taste. This is the part which belongs to someone's individual integrity and which should not be disputed.

Style is as much a linking concept as taste. In study of cultural phenomena – particularly of design and fashion – style is often presented as a personal characteristic in the work of its makers, but within art history style is the pre-eminent standard for classifying works of architecture and applied art. Style then stands for the connecting characteristics within a period of time, a social group or a country. (96)

For the study of jewellery one could roughly say that style is rather something that relates to the art historical interpretation of the work and to the personal qualities of a maker, while taste has more to do with the manner of wearing and the combination of jewellery with clothing, accessories and, for example, make-up, haircuts and tattoos. Taste is also a criterion for the viewer, who looks at the effect of the piece of jewellery and attaches his own value judgement to it. It is safe to say that in such an emotionally charged phenomenon as jewellery, which has such a long history and a very wide variety of appearances, every viewer is guided in his choice and approach by his own taste.

The use of opposites is a tried and tested way to get a grip on difficult concepts. Within art history, concepts such as style and taste have been given relief by means of classifications such as the Apollonian and the Dionysian, the sacred and the profane, romance and logic, functionality and decoration, etc. For the study of both fashion and jewellery, the extremes of the primary motifs for wearing jewellery and clothing, such as the polarity between the desire to stand out and the search for safety by conforming, can very well be presented.

5.2.1 Study of fashion is a few steps ahead

During her installation in 2005 as a lecturer in fashion theory at the ARTEZ University of the Arts in Arnhem, the Netherlands, José Teunissen dealt with the changes in the view of fashion over the last hundred years on the basis of the theories of a few pioneers. In it she described the usual distrust of fashion as the subject of serious study – fashion as an escape valve for vain souls and fashion as an outgrowth of capitalism – but ended her argument with the optimistic observation that an enormous amount of fashion research has been initiated in recent decades. (97)

Until about three decades ago, observers of fashion had great difficulty in shaking off the aura of superficiality attached to fashion. If fashion was taken seriously by scientific disciplines, this was often done from an economic perspective, for example as an outgrowth of capitalism. Fortunately, this reasoning can also be reversed: since the rise of industrialisation and the rise of capitalism, fashion is the best way to show that people can achieve something in their lives if they are open to social impulses and interesting cultural developments from their own time. Clothing, as a less charged concept, has never suffered much from critical approaches, because the convention requires us to dress as soon as we show up among other people. Furthermore, the notion of 'costume' and 'costume history' also helped to remove the sharp edges in the distinction between fashion and clothing.

Since the end of the 1970s, philosophy, semiotics, postmodernism and even deconstructivism have brought the interpretation of clothing and fashion into line. Clothing as a purely functional means of protecting the body has even been accorded the high status of anti-fashion by fashion critics. José Teunissen states in her inaugural speech: 'Having taste – knowing how to dress – is a vital status symbol of our modern, visual culture, in which class and status are no longer bound to origin by definition, but are constantly redefined in the everchanging sign system of fashion'. She argues that it is not possible to avoid this, because that too has its place within the system. Even the intellectual in the baggy sweater who believes thus to ignore fashion has a place in the spectrum of fashion. He too is part of the system because others like him wear a similar sweater; it makes him belong to his group. We all communicate our identity and personality through our appearance. (98)

The link between the history of jewellery and developments in both fashion and clothing is an important ingredient in the literature on jewellery. Many a piece of jewellery formed an integral part of a fashion image by accentuating an important aspect of that image and confirming the characteristics of that image in terms of colour and style. This starting point is the main guideline for Margaret Flower's treatise on Victorian jewellery from 1951, because at that time she could not fall back on a history of jewellery. Joan Evans, M.H. Gans, Graham Hughes and other early authors on the history of jewellery were also right to look for a foothold in the history of fashion, as it had been researched and described in much more detail already. In her 1961 booklet on jewellery, Giltay-Nijssen states neatly: 'Because jewellery is, or should be, the shining star of an outfit, it is closely linked to, and often dependent on, fashion'. (99) In this way she wanted to examine how our dress influences the shape of jewellery. Considering the time in which her booklet appeared, this view is rather representative. Giltay-Nijssen, like Joan Evans in *A History of Jewellery*, pays particular attention to the decoration of the highest classes, qualifying the design of jewellery through quick and interesting references to style and fashion, as well as political and social developments. In her account women ultimately feature as most important wearer of jewellery, whereby she singles out vanity and the striving for beauty as cornerstones of her discourse, also in relation to earlier periods.

Graham Hughes did the same in his book *Modern Jewellery* from 1963, although in a very English way he is more nuanced, while as art director of the Worshipful Company of Goldsmiths in the City of London he could also share more in-depth knowledge of the profession of goldsmith and jewellery designer. Other books from these years, such as *Juwelen en Mensen* (Jewellery and People) by M.H. Gans from 1961, and *Jewellery through the Ages* by Guido Gregorietti from 1969, basically follow the same pattern by linking jewellery to changing clothing images. In this way they provided a valuable yet onesided basis for overviews by later jewellery experts such as Clare Philips and Christianne Weber-Stöber.

Hugh Tait related jewellery more to traditions and customs. His survey of seven thousand years of jewellery history is based on the British Museum's collection and was produced with the input of other experts associated with the museum, including specialists from the Middle East and the Far East. (100) As a result, the difference between fashion and clothing is largely eliminated in this publication, for that is typically a Western European preoccupation. Of course, countries such as the United Emirates or China and Japan are now also captivated by western consumerism, but this is not the norm by which jewellery from those cultures is studied. In general, ethnology does not distinguish between fashion and clothing. This can be seen as a simplification, because there must have been a similar distinction in non-western cultures in the past, especially in court circles. But it can also be considered a benefit, because the relationship between jewellery and the accompanying clothing is thus kept transparent.

The great revolution in fashion that became apparent in the late 1960s and early 1970s was that different styles of fashion emerged side by side. In the course of the seventies and eighties, fashion became a complex combination of trends, colour indications and more constant silhouettes and styles. It was a reflection of all kinds of changes in social relations, sexual morality and the growing importance of the media, now including television. Given the dynamic process of changes in the 1960s and 1970s, it is usually referred to as a cultural revolution. Before that time, developments in fashion were linear. In principle, there was one dominant style whose standards were determined by the upper classes, and this would function as a model for other classes.

These developments in fashion from the late 1960s onwards provided a framework within which individual jewellery designers could create their own world full of personal statements and stylistic characteristics. That is why the history of jewellery up to that point, based on the history of style, can be well linked to fashion and other cultural expressions, but after 1970 this becomes a lot more difficult.

The authors who mainly focused on the generations of jewellery designers who have set the tone in their profession since the 1960s, such as Peter Dormer and gallery owners such as Ralph Turner, Helen Drutt and Paul Derrez, paid little or no attention to the relationship between fashion and jewellery. They concentrated on creativity within the jewellery trade and in so doing set the tone for the decades ahead. Their approach represents a breaking point in the study of jewellery as linked directly to the development of fashion. In this case, the connection between the two is shown precisely by the denial of such connection.

In the 1980s the attack on fixed hierarchies in culture and society prompted many philosophers and cultural critics to question the nature and causes of these developments and new cultural conditions, which are often referred to as postmodernism. Many of them looked to fashion as a discipline that is close to the skin and whose new expressions are immediately visible in the media. As a result, fashion became a serious subject of study and was particularly understood as a system of signs.

An early and exceptional example of a contemplative text in which the piece of jewellery was involved in the changes that took place in fashion at the time is *Des joyaux aux bijoux* (1961) by Roland Barthes. First, he describes jewels as lifeless trinkets, made of 'cold' materials taken from the gloomy depths of the earth which still managed to be seductive. They are symbols of power and masculinity. He rightly wonders why they are mainly associated with women in his time and argues that this is because men have delegated the task of displaying their wealth and power to their wives. In this way, woman herself was turned into a 'cold jewel'. He observes that this is fortunately changing in his own time. As part of fashion, jewellery items or bijoux were also made of wood, glass, non-precious metals and fake stones. In this way, jewellery grew less sacred and more democratic. Taste became more important than money and like a vivid detail in a statue the piece of jewellery is freed from its lifeless coolness. It had become a meaningful indication of style and was incorporated into the language of fashion.

In 1961, Barthes used this text to pinpoint a change in jewellery design and the way in which it was incorporated into everyday clothing images as a stylish detail. In 1963 Barthes published his doctoral thesis *Système de la mode*, in which he describes fashion as a complex system of signs with which people communicate with each other and provide information. In doing so, he provided the foundations for the semiotics of fashion and thus a basis for many theorists after him who studied the phenomenon of fashion. (101)

Initially, however, jewellery benefited from this interest of first-rate theorists marginally at best. It is telling that 1961 was also the year in which Graham Hughes presented his startling exhibition 'Modern Jewellery' in London, which for several years travelled to many European cities. This exhibition can be seen as a sign of the new developments in the jewellery field. The wave of democratisation in the 1960s and 1970s deeply affected how jewellery was made, presented and worn (as also amply addressed in my study on Dutch Jewellery).

Contradictory to what Barthes observed in 1961, a striking part of contemporary jewellery production distanced itself from fashion during the 1970s and 1980s. Individual jewellery designers sought little or no sympathy or economic support from the dynamics of fashion. The handful of authors who spoke and wrote about their work did not say much about the relationship between contemporary jewellery and fashion, a phenomenon I analysed in 1987 in an article for the Dutch magazine Bijvoorbeeld (For example), entitled 'Jewellery cannot release itself from a dangerous triangular relationship' (the third point of the triangle being the world of jewellery).

An interesting study on fashion and clothing that should be mentioned here is Alison Lurie's *The Language of Clothes* (1981).

Without losing herself too much in semiotics, she describes clothing as a language with its own vocabulary and grammar. People communicate with each other through their appearance before they have spoken a word: 'The vocabulary of dress includes not only items of clothing, but also hair styles, accessories, jewellery, make-up and body decoration. Theoretically at least this vocabulary is as large as or larger than any spoken tongue, since it includes every garment, hairstyle, and type of body decoration ever invented. In practice, of course, the sartorial resources of an individual may be very restricted'. She thus leaves at least some room for jewellery. (102)

When considering fashion, a popular statement is that the right clothes, and thus the right appearance, can provide a sense of security that no other religious conviction can match. (103) Jewellery, as an integral part of people's outward appearance, contributes to their self-awareness. It has been used at all times to guide the eye to certain parts of the body, whether or not covered with clothing. Significantly, then, most jewellery for women has always been found on or near the face and on the chest, while men have often worn precious attributes on the chest and belly, in accordance with macho behaviour. Take the watch chain that draped across men's vests, often around a robust belly; when they would pull out their watch it pointed to the underside of their belly. Both men and women have always worn rings, emphasising the movement of the hand in relation to their dressed body.

It is also pleasing to note that nowadays the Netherlands is making a useful contribution to the development of theories about fashion. Under the editorship of the Arnhem Fashion Lectorate, books are regularly published, including *Mode en Accessoires* (Fashion and accessories, 2007), in which a great deal of attention is paid to jewellery in relation to fashion. The contributions by the French philosopher Gilles Lipovetsky on the concept of luxury are particularly useful for the study of jewellery (see section 5.5.1).

Our understanding of jewellery can only go up by involving the most important achievements of the study of fashion. Three stages can be distinguished in the study of fashion: the pioneers who analysed fashion from the perspective of sociology and psychology; the costume historians who chose the history of fashion as a subject, processed their insights and went on to investigate interesting sub-topics in which anthropology was also involved; and the third wave of philosophers, fashion specialists and other viewers who saw their analyses of fashion as an opportunity to map developments in society, and in doing so often owed a great deal of attention to semiotics and post-modernism. Their insights form an integral part of ongoing historical reflections and contemporary analyses of fashion. Since the late eighteenth century, actual changes in fashion have also been recorded in all kinds of public media. This wealth of information, linked to art historical artefacts, has constituted the basis for detailed insight into forms, materials and customs with regard to fashion and clothing.

The study of jewellery is still lagging behind; it can be said to have reached the second stage. The first stage for jewellery is based almost exclusively on art history, including the history of fashion and clothing, and on a number of professional publications. Gradually, other angles are now being taken into account. In my study on Dutch jewellery I combined and integrated approaches from many different disciplines, including the study of fashion and clothing.

Developments in fashion and clothing provide a suitable context for studying developments in the design of jewellery. The relationship between jewellery and clothing images also determines the symbolism or social meanings that can be associated with a piece of jewellery. After the cultural revolution of the 1960s and 1970s, the relationship between developments in contemporary jewellery and those in fashion was neglected in the study of jewellery. This often went so far as to make fashion a negative standard for assessing the work of individual jewellery designers.

5.3 Literature

It should not be necessary to recognise language proficiency as an important tool for the study of jewellery and creating a theoretical framework for it. The ability to describe the work of visual artists, architects or designers in such a way that the reader becomes fascinated and wants to know more about it is important for each discipline. A number of movements in the history of art and design have greatly benefited from the verbalisation of their ideas, such as Futurism, Surrealism and Deconstructivism.

Much of the specialist literature on jewellery, however, consists of a somewhat leisurely combination of descriptions of pieces that are available for example in the context of an exhibition. In the case of historical material, these descriptions pertain to pieces of jewellery that happen to be preserved, and this inevitably involves an unrepresentative selection which will rarely be a balanced one as well. Such texts are then elaborated with some historical factual knowledge, but often they are more about interpretations than hard facts. Historical anecdotes are often mixed with the author's assumptions and his or her particular pleasantries or unpleasantries.

The foregoing highlighted the importance of different academic approaches to the study of jewellery. A completely different and surprisingly rich source of insights into jewellery is found in literary texts. The most beautiful references to jewellery can be found in literature from all eras and in all languages. Often, these references will be deployed for their metaphorical value. As part of a story they have a specific function: they may define characters, symbolise mutual relationships between them, connote wealth or social background or serve as a key motif. These references suggest the infinite number of symbolic values linked up with jewellery. If this information does not necessarily have to be historically accurate, it does reflect how jewellery was thought about in a certain period of time and in what contexts it may have played a role. It is a bonus of course when these references are beautifully expressed in a story whose characters, and the circumstances in which they live, are convincingly developed.

Jewellery may also refer to literature, however. The sentimental symbolism linked to jewellery from the late Middle Ages and the early Renaissance will have been influenced by the stories people told each other during those years. (104) The popularity of figurative elements in Art Nouveau jewellery can be traced back to symbolism in literature and the visual arts. (105)

The relationship between literature and jewellery becomes even more intimate when novels on the subject of jewellery are involved. The mysterious diamond necklace that was intended for Queen Marie Antoinette of France has captured the imagination of many a novelist. There are also authors who have cast their knowledge of jewellery in a literary form, such as Tobias Hill in *The Love of Stones* (2001).

Historical novels and biographies nicely reflect the intersection of history and literature. Here, too, there is a sliding scale, of course, with historical facts on one side and the artistic freedom of literature on the other. Yet the two discourses will often serve as an interesting source of information about how items of jewellery were purchased or commissioned and how they were worn, by whom and when, and what meanings were attached to them.

One of the nice and underexposed effects of wearing jewellery is the sound they can make. In the middle of the nineteenth century one might recognise a lady of standing by the noise of her silk petticoats – a sound which petticoats made of wool or cotton fabrics could never produce.

In *Georgy Porgy*, a short story by Roald Dahl, the dominant character of the mother of a growing boy is typified by the sound that her ringing bracelets make and that he can hear anywhere in the house. (106) This aspect of jewellery is hardly ever addressed in books about jewellery, proving all the more that the artefacts themselves should serve as starting point, rather than how they are worn. In literature such sensory experiences are frequently described. In *Il Gattopardo* (1958), the famous novel by G. Tomasi di Lampedusa, the embrace of Princess Maria Stella with her handsome future niece is described. The princess pressed the girl so energetically to her own bosom that the impression of her famous necklace with rubies was left on the girl's skin. (107) This is a beautiful rendering of the symbolism of the transfer of family jewels, and an effect like this can never be discerned from a piece of jewellery as such.

When it comes to the social dimensions of jewellery, L.N. Tolstoy is a good source. The main character in his novella *The Kreuzer Sonata* (1891) expresses his views explicitly in a monologue on the changing market mechanisms of the second half of the nineteenth century. He describes the key economic position of the department store and condemns the power of women who, with their penchant for luxury – including useless jewellery – make most of humanity work in slavish labour. (108) Gabriel García Márquez, in *Love in the Time of Cholera* (1986), manages to characterise in just a few sentences the difference between well-to-do men and women who have lunch in the countryside: while the men are wearing their daily suit, it is as if the women dress up for a party, wearing evening dresses adorned by fine jewellery with precious stones. (109) Jewellery is often used symbolically, to underline the festive nature of some event. As such, it often proves to symbolise the opposite as well, when the author links some item of jewellery with a sense of disillusion or misguided expectations, as is the case in Irène Némirovsky's novel *The Ball* from 1930. (110)

The misjudgement by Mr. and Mrs. Richebois as parents of a nice young girl in a short story by Dutch author F. Bordewijk from 1953 is extremely tragic. The parents judge a woman by her jewels, amongst other things, and Bordewijk refers to them in detail. According to Mrs. Richebois, there were 'not many, but precious, certainly real'. And as she adds: 'I'd like to have that one ring of hers myself, or that pin'. (111) The American novelist Edith Wharton, in *The Custom of the Country* (1913), indicates that there are certain jewels that you shouldn't wear. The main character, a spoilt American woman, is blown to pieces by her father when she is wearing a pearl necklace given to her not by her husband but by some other man. Her father urges her to return it immediately. (112) Jewellery fulfils an attractive and at the same time mysterious role in a novella by Guy de Maupassant, *Les Bijoux* (1883). It is about the pleasure jewellery can give. In a few unexpected closing sentences, the author convinces the reader that a life without pleasure can make a person deeply unhappy. (113)

In literature, jewellery features frequently in quick characterizations. It is astonishing how mercilessly a man can be rejected by mentioning a pink ring with a large stone on his left hand. In one of the volumes of the Maigret detective series, Georges Simenon describes a group of brothel keepers as 'five self-assured gentlemen, in expensive clothes, with fingers full of rings, who had come in a twelve-cylinder'. (114) In *The Beautiful and Damned* (1922) by F. Scott Fitzgerald, a film producer turns out to be more socially acceptable because he dressed more quietly and had left at home the two heavy rings he was used to carrying on his right hand. (115)

To extent to which men affirm their position by wearing jewellery is clear from *The Love of Stones* (2001) by Tobias Hill. He describes John the Fearless, the second Duke of Burgundy who lived at the beginning of the fifteenth century, as a lover of large jewels: 'In John's lifetime, no commoner in Europe had ever worn a diamond. He lived in an age when jewels were the international currency of power. The display of stones had more to do with muscle than desire. A great ruby might be beautiful, but the beauty made it functional. It was the means to wage wars, after all, or the motive for waging them. The dowry to avert invasion, or the sacred mystery that justified it'. (116)

Jewellery as a means of recognition can be found in texts ranging from *The Merchant of Venice* by Shakespeare (late sixteenth century) to a popular Dutch children's book such as *Kruimeltje* (Little Crumb, 1923) by Chris van Abkoude. In the first case it involves a golden ring, in the second case a medallion with portraits. (117)

Of course, the great writers of crime stories have almost all made use of the possibilities offered by jewellery as a motive for murder or as a key to identifying the guilty party. Sir Arthur Conan Doyle lets Sherlock Holmes characterises the power of a stone in *The Adventure of the Blue Carbuncle* as follows: '"It's a bonny thing," said he. "Just see how it glints and sparkles. Of course it is a nucleus and focus of crime. Every good stone is"'. (118) He was right. Covetousness, greed and financial gain cause jewels to be stolen all the time. A recent example that attracted international attention is a well-organised and well-informed group of criminals who regularly rob large jewellery houses and are referred to as the 'Pink Panthers' in reference to the English films with Peter Sellers from the 1960s. (119)

There are also many examples in the world's literature of the role of jewellery as memento. At the end of the story, the main character in Aleksandr Koeprin's novella Olesya (1898) only has a cord of cheap red beads left as a tangible reminder of his beloved. (120) As far as religious symbols are concerned, Stefan Zweig's description in his biography of Maria Stuart is beautiful. At the end he describes how this Catholic queen of Scotland wore only three ornaments for her last public performance, her walk to the scaffold, which were meant to protect her from fear and to give her confidence in a life after her inevitable death: a golden crucifix around her neck, a jewel-covered paternoster necklace on her belt and an ivory cross in her hand. In the epilogue, Zweig also describes how a court lady of Elisabeth I patiently waits for her death, finally to remove the ring from her hand and have it dispatched to Edinburgh by courier, so that James VI of Scotland and son of Maria Stuart knows that he now was James I of England. This ride is actually a historical fact. (121)

These are merely a few examples from the collection of literary quotes about jewellery I gathered in the past year. (122) From their always unique cultural and historical background, highly different authors will refer to jewellery in their writings in lively and unexpected ways. Many of their descriptions are factual in evoking which value is attached to a particular jewel or how jewellery features as a reminder of a moment when life was enjoyed most purely. All these details and fragments culled from stories and novels will amount to a rich historical account of jewellery as both a playful and important motif in literature.

Conclusions

All in all, then, literary perspectives serve as a most welcome complement to data and insights from professional literature. The various ways in which jewellery is described in fiction and other works of literature do not have to be historically correct, but they do provide us with insight into how jewellery has been looked at and what people's motives have been for wearing it. Jewellery items can be quite 'time-resistant' and through literature one can experience their lasting role within a particular family or culture. Literature is thus a highly useful source of information for the study of jewellery, especially with regard to the personal values and social connotations associated with it.

Conversely, there are particular moments in the history of jewellery, such as tied to themes in the design of jewellery, which can be traced back to literature from that time. One example is the rise of sentimental jewellery during the late Middle Ages and early Renaissance. Another example pertains to particular kinds of symbolism used in jewellery of the late nineteenth and early twentieth century and which may be linked to their rise in literature and culture at large at that time.

5.4 Economy

5.4.1 Market value

One of the important and complicating factors in the study of jewellery is that individual pieces can be easily traded as a commodity. Jewellery made of precious metals or expensive materials has commercial value in particular. One might even refer to jewellery as 'wearable money'.

Of all the values ascribed to jewellery, this trade or exchange value is commonly used as the most important feature. This is true not only in our capitalist, western society, but also in the Middle East, India and Indonesia and amongst many African peoples. Jewellery made of precious metal is synonymous with money. For this reason, jewellery, with commonly a selling price set per gram, is considered an investment. (123) This means that jewels as forms of body decoration are inextricably linked up with the economic position of the owner and with a cornerstone of the world economy, which is the price of gold or the market value of diamonds and other precious stones. (124) Less valuable components of jewellery, such as shells and glass beads, may also function as a means of exchange and therefore they represent a specific monetary value as well.

A re-reading of a number of key texts about jewellery reveals the depth of respect for the precious nature of large pieces of jewellery. This applies not just to items worn or owned by pharaohs or Louis XIV, as the outward appearance of members of Europe's remaining royal houses or the most recent jewellery items purchased by Madonna tend to be closely watched by the public, at times almost to a sickening degree, as well. The market value of jewellery, then, is both a somewhat irritating feature and an inevitable aspect in the study of jewellery.

The material value of jewellery in precious metals and gemstones can be determined in great detail. This price, also known as the 'scrap value', fluctuates, because it depends on the daily prices of, for example, gold and diamonds. And given the current means of communication these rates are instantly known all over the world while the legal trade also adheres to them. A diamond dealer from Antwerp once assured me that he is more likely to notice the outbreak of riots or financial crises anywhere in the world sooner than most politicians and journalists.

In the course of history, many large jewellery houses have functioned as bankers and have even supported the exchequer if it was convenient for them. Lorenzo de Medici, an influential banker, had a point when shifting the tradition of wearing jewellery from noble rulers to his own person and class. Living at a time of great social and cultural changes, he himself was an important factor in those changes. Financially speaking, he could afford to pay for any jewel he wanted to have. In other countries, too, jewellers served as bankers. (125)

Those in power around the world have always tried to control the trade in gold and precious stones through exercising physical and economic power or through legislation. The same applies to the trade in glass beads in Africa. Social rules on wearing jewellery were an extension of this. Rulers will have more insight into the financial position of their closest associates if only those of high rank are allowed to wear valuable jewellery and if they are able to set the tone in this respect. Owning jewellery made of gold serves as a sign of financial reliability also amongst other classes in society. (126)

As far as the illegal trade in gold and precious stones is concerned, there is a great deal of mystery about it, but a great deal is known about it as well. All the various inhuman and fraudulent outgrowths of mining, processing and marketing precious metals and stones have been the subject of criticism. The recent term 'blood diamonds' refers to diamonds which are extracted and traded under appalling conditions in Africa to finance civil wars. No matter how hard the trade will try to get rid of these abuses, such as issuing certificates as a guarantee that the stones in question are 'clean', it will never be possible to do so completely. After all, all the different links in the longwinded process involved – from the dirty work of mining gold to the fine crafting of that singularly beautiful engagement ring – cannot be subsumed under a single control system. Gemstones as such are never marked because that would harm their perfection. (127)

For a proper study of jewellery, the most sensible starting point is the recognition that it is plausible that the darkest suspicions of injustice can be true (as greed can never be ruled out) and that it is right to undertake action against such abuses. In international politics there have been efforts to undermine criminal regimes in Africa by sabotaging the trade in blood diamonds from these countries. If all of this is complicated, it also underscores that there is more to jewellery than fun or pleasure.

5.4.2 Materials and technique

It is not just essential but also highly rewarding to study items of jewellery as much as possible as manageable objects from up close, holding them in your hands. This is crucial for a proper assessment of technique and use of materials. It also provides insight into how a piece of jewellery can be worn. The profession has its own expertise, including gemmology, or the knowledge of stones, traditional goldsmithing techniques and all the raw materials and techniques that continue to renew the field. Gold, platinum and silver are metals with special physical properties. In the right alloys, they can be hammered, floated and chiselled by hand into refined shapes which retain a great deal of tensile strength. These metals have shiny shades, which have fascinated mankind since time immemorial. Silver can oxidise and lose its shine to the air or on the skin, but gold and platinum do not. That these rare precious metals serve as basis for making jewellery and other luxury artefacts lies in the nature of these metals.

As mentioned in the introduction, jewellery invites precision and excellence due to its body-related size. This implies different levels of quality. Only by holding a piece of jewellery in your hand and by closely observing it, preferably through a magnifying glass, it is possible to distinguish the refined craftsmanship of a top jeweller from coarse work and poor mass production. Hallmarks in works of precious metal are often difficult to read, even with a magnifying glass. They are important keys, however, to determining the country of origin or dating of a jewellery item. If all is done according to legal standards, the maker's mark will provide a definite answer about the maker. These labels are often lacking in jewellery made of base materials, and especially in contemporary work from the artistic sector, which will render it difficult for later researchers to determine who the maker is, especially if no other visual materials or written sources are available. (128)

This implies that works of precious metal serve as the best basis for building a historical frame of reference for individual pieces of jewellery. This also fits in well with the importance attached by the first generations of art historians to precious pieces. In the course of the twentieth century, however, a great deal of research had to be performed with respect to hallmarks. Their registration by the Assay Office has not been completed yet even in a well-regulated country such as the Netherlands, and it remains to be seen whether this will ever be possible. For example, a substantial number of maker's marks of jewellers and silversmiths from Rotterdam and the surrounding area were lost during the bombardment of Rotterdam in May 1940. Karel Citroen's collection of Art Nouveau jewellery, which in the early 1960s was sold in two portions to the Hessian Landesmuseum in Darmstadt, Germany, was described by him with great care, but many of his attributions were made on stylistic grounds and turn out to be incorrect, which can be established on the basis of the current knowledge of hallmarks and the availability of many other well-documented and published reference materials. (129) Citroen himself has worked hard to achieve this throughout his working life. In the Netherlands, the Assay Office in Gouda is the body responsible for research into master marks and other signs of responsibility. It also publishes on this subject. (130)

Only when holding a piece of jewellery in your hand can you feel what it is like to wear a piece of jewellery or can you turn it back and forth and compare the back with the front. Splendid jewellery often has a beautiful clasp or invisible fastening and a delicately rendered backside. In fancy jewels much attention will have been paid to this in particular. The backside may come with decorations that cannot be seen while wearing it, and these purely serve as a secret pleasure for the wearer.

The central position of gems in common definitions of both high jewellery and more pedestrian jewellery is likely to have its origin in the profession itself. Stones are often used for jewellery, especially when involving large, particularly polished or tinted and therefore precious stones. The available stone, or a combination of stones, is an important starting point for the setting and therefore for the overall design of a jewel. When later on such a piece with precious stones is sold, the setting – of gold or another precious metal – rarely plays a role anymore, unless the name of a large jeweller's house is tied to it. Obviously, this hardly does justice to the craftsmanship of the jewellery maker. (131)

The choice for gold does not always mean that the financial value of a piece of jewellery should be visible to everyone. Willy Jansen, anthropologist and professor of women's studies at Catholic University Nijmegen, describes in her essay *Waar is het goud gebleven?* (Where did the gold go?, 1970) a particular development in the 1970s in the Netherlands: the popularity of white gold had increased amongst the well-to-do at the time because yellow gold had become commonplace. Only like-minded people could see whether jewellery was made of expensive white gold or of silver, which at first glance looks a lot like it. Annelies Moors describes a similar distinction regarding Italian gold amongst women in the Middle East. (132)

The profession of jewellery designer or goldsmith has always been attractive to people who like to make something with their hands and want to work directly in materials. Goldsmiths and jewellery designers think in terms of materials and techniques, whereby their hand and head are inextricably linked. Or, as Richard Sennett put it in his prologue to *The Craftsman* (2008): 'thinking and feeling are contained within the process of making' (133). Their capital partly consists of the insight and experiences they have gained while working. They can therefore best assess the effect of a design by organising and shifting the available materials on their workbenches. Moreover, the handiwork in their product constitutes a certain market value, it is a symbol for their craftsmanship. At the same time, it can guarantee a personal signature and thus the authenticity of their work.

When a work of art lacks a signature, it can sometimes be attributed to a particular maker on the basis of signed sketches or presentation drawings. Such drawings often provide insight into the creative process. In the case of jewellery, this is only possible if the archive of a jewellery house or an individual jewellery designer has been preserved, as well as a large number of the pieces made. This rarely happens, however, and even when it does, it appears that sketches of jewellery makers usually do not amount to more than reminders of the execution found in the material itself.

Still, drawings and prints are an important source of information on jewellery in the western world from the late Middle Ages to the end of the nineteenth century. Hugh Tait argues that Northern European princes wanted to keep abreast of developments in Italy, and that they and their goldsmiths used ornamental drawings and jewellery studies by important court painters, including Hans Holbein, for the design of their ostentatious ornaments. (134)

The most interesting drawings of jewellery from the late nineteenth and twentieth centuries are probably those based on available stones made by the large jewellery houses for their clients. Such a customer can make a final choice on the basis of detailed representations of various models and settings. Although such drawings provide insight into the creativity and artistic ability of these jewellers' houses, they emphasise that the availability of particular stones is the determining factor for the design. (135)

The history of jewellery comprises many technical inventions which soon after their development enjoyed great popularity. Examples are cut steel and the ornaments in a new kind of stoneware from the ceramic manufacturer Joshua Wedgewood from the second half of the eighteenth century. Partly because of the colour differences in the stoneware, these ornaments with their embossed images strongly resemble cameos. The public's interest in such novelties will slowly fade again, but the pieces themselves remain in the picture as products from a bygone era. Experienced traders and valuers can quickly determine whether Wedgewood's brooch comes from the eighteenth, nineteenth or twentieth century, mainly on the basis of its setting. This is a determining factor for the price.

The rediscovery of certain high-quality techniques can give a new impetus to the profession. It took a long time, for instance, before it proved possible to match the beautiful Etruscan granulation work. Companies such as Castellani and Giuliano built their name on it in the second half of the nineteenth century, entirely in keeping with the historicism of their time, while a contemporary jewellery designer such as the Australian Robert Baines has studied this technique extensively and bases his current work on it. The development of all kinds of plastics in the twentieth century has led to completely new forms of mass production of jewellery. As far as the techniques for making jewellery are concerned, there are plenty of manuals. In the Netherlands, 'de Hammes' is the standard work. In the conclusion of my study on Dutch jewellery, a section is devoted to the consequences of the use of precious metals and precious stones in jewellery and the entire process of recycling in its wake. (136) This aspect is becoming increasingly important. It is and remains a question of great importance how the world handles raw materials, what quantities are available and how they are extracted, transported, processed and distributed. This applies to oil and food, but also to wood and metals. In the world of design, the recycling of materials and products is now a key concept, as a means to achieve interesting design and, more importantly, to save materials and energy.

In this context, a new phenomenon is the cradle-to-cradle principle. (137) The jewellery trade is a shining example of this. It is fair to say that gold and precious stones are the oldest 'recycling materials' in the world, because they have been reused throughout the history of mankind. Each golden piece of jewellery may contain a remnant of jewellery owned by Cleopatra or a Mayan priest. In early 2009, Dutch newspapers even raised the question of what happens to the gold that is released in crematoria and who will receive the proceeds. (138) Regardless, for many environmental experts, it is too farfetched to consider jewellery a beacon of environmental conscience; as such this cultural heritage comes with too many negative connotations, as reflected in, as some would say, its superfluous and luxury nature and its ostentatious ornaments.

The jeweller's profession is based on craftsmanship which has always been characterised by precision and which has been passed on almost unchanged from generation to generation. This profession has seldom if ever been at the forefront when it comes to embracing new techniques and production methods. Nineteenth century techniques such as electroplating and embossing ornaments from sheet metal are seen as essential to the Industrial Revolution, and they have also proven their worth in the mechanical production of jewellery. But the profession of goldsmith or silversmith has always consisted of endless repetition of the same actions, especially for chain works, and long before the nineteenth century there was already talk of serial production. Hugh Tait's *7000 Years of Jewellery* includes an image of a painting by Allessandro Fei on the subject of a goldsmith's workshop. It was made between 1570 and 1575 for Grand Duke Francesco de Medici and clearly shows parts of jewellery made in series. (139) Even today, the production of jewellery still involves dull repetition of actions when one considers all the labour – and especially child labour – carried out in Asia in order to provide the western world each season with the bead necklaces necessary for the correct colour accent in a new fashion image.

As far as recent developments are concerned, it is striking how little influence digital techniques still have on the design and manufacture of jewellery. While the introduction of the computer, for example, has brought about a true revolution in graphic design, textile design and industrial design, both in terms of design and production techniques, the jewellery trade seems to be almost unaffected by the new techniques. The computer is mainly used by the current generation of jewellery designers to maintain their international contacts via the Internet.

Of course, there are exceptions, such as Gijs Bakker, who in his quest for perfect forms has used the computer to set the coordinates for a series of bracelets with the title *Shot* from 1997. In doing so, he consciously abandoned his artisanal training and the endless hammering, filing and polishing of the goldsmith. Dinie Besems worked for her series of jewellery from 2006 with a spatial grid that was developed to calculate the distance between random stars. The resulting rings displayed a nice tension between an arbitrary starting point and calculated lines and shapes. (140)

Slowly but surely, the first influences of CAD/cam techniques are becoming apparent in the jewellery trade as well. Young jewellery designers are increasingly experimenting with rapid prototyping during their training. However, as starting entrepreneurs in a vulnerable profession, they can rarely afford the necessary equipment and have to find ways to realise their work with the help of these new techniques. This is a growth market, just like laser-cutting, another technique that is increasingly being used by jewellery designers. (141)

In the jewellery industry, conventional techniques still prevail as well, yet one may invest in equipment to ensure a certain systematics, pure customization or perfection in finishing. But often, even within the industry, polishing is still done by hand, while the setting of precious stones is still a matter of individual craftsmanship. The need to come up with new solutions arises mainly when new techniques or materials have been developed outside of the profession, for which at some point an application in jewellery will be found. A new challenge nowadays are synthetic diamonds, for example the ones which under very high pressure can be pressed from the mortal remains of the deceased.

5.4.3 Single copies, serial production or bulk goods

When it comes to the market value of jewellery, the question also arises as to whether they are unique pieces or whether they are produced in series, which should, in principle, lead to a reduction of prices.

In contemporary fashion, this quickly becomes clear: unique garments are the exception. Even the couture houses make several pieces of one model, unless the first buyer purchases the exclusive right. But jewellery usually conceals whether it is unique, made in a small number of copies or bulk goods. In exhib itions with historical pieces and presentations of contemporary work, jewellery is almost without exception presented as single copies. Jewellery made in series is also supposed to accentuate a unique identity of its own. Large jewellers like to give the impression that their jewellery is the perfect way to emphasise a unique personality.

The question of whether a piece is unique, part of a small series or produced in bulk has to do first of all with the various parties within the jewellery trade, whereas the market value of a piece is only of secondary concern. Particularly in the Netherlands there are razor-sharp dividing lines between those who present their work as unique pieces in art centres, designers who make jewellery in small series and under their own management, and jewellery manufactured in limited editions. Nowadays there is a strong emphasis on brands. The products themselves can come from all corners of the world and certainly amongst the range of items sold by jewellers only very few are from the Netherlands. In the countries around us, this distinction in categories of jewellery is often applied less strictly, and in the case of an average jeweller, there is also some work in the shop window that, with some optimism, is called 'modern' – a qualification that rightly or wrongly suggests uniqueness.

Amongst the jewellery produced in editions and of which the brand is well known, 'fashion jewellery', or 'costume jewellery', constitutes a striking group. This has become the collective name for industrially manufactured fake jewellery, which shines as beautifully to the inexperienced eye as the real thing. Fake jewels are often larger and more colourful than jewellery made of gold and precious gemstones, because size is not a limitation when the raw materials are (comparatively) inexpensive. Over the past fifteen to twenty years, the fairly brief history of the most important brands active in this field has been studied and documented.

The most popular brands from Germany, the United States and France date from the first half of the twentieth century. Today, they have acquired their own position amongst dealers in antiques and they are the subject of special exhibitions. The fact that a longer history of fake jewellery precedes this development can be seen in the sad story of a necklace of fake diamonds, entitled *La Parure*, by Guy de Maupassant from 1884. (142) One should also have serious doubts about the number of pearls with which members of the wealthy Dutch bourgeoisie had themselves portrayed in the Golden Age. There were many glass beads or alabaster balls that were covered with a shiny layer. In the eighteenth century, fish silver was developed in France for this purpose, and its recipe was in fact preserved in Dutch professional literature. (143)

It would not be appropriate, however, to include only fake jewellery as ornaments produced and marketed within the system of fashion. It is fair to refer also to other industrially manufactured ornaments made of base materials and, even more broadly, to jewellery made from fairly inexpensive raw materials that were most fashionable at one point. Such jewellery has been made and worn for centuries. The cut steel from the second half of the eighteenth century was clearly part of the fashion of the time, characterised as it was by a strong preference for diamonds.

Another point is that fashion jewellery does not necessarily represent the greatest common denominator. It may also be a matter of decorative additions made in small series or even unique pieces. Particularly within fashion, exceptional and sometimes even frenzied pieces are created, with which a fashion designer can literally steal the show. Such extreme pieces, though, will often blur the boundary between jewellery and accessory, or even between jewellery and garment.

Because the study of jewellery often emphasises artistic value and the individual creator, it rarely does justice to the jewellery produced in series or even in large numbers and which responds to the need of people to conform to a prevailing taste. Not to mention the fads from the period after the Second World War: necklaces and bracelets of chicken rings; plastic beads with a bulge fitting in the hole of the next bead which were distributed with a detergent in the 1950s; the boom in buttons, sometimes purely decorative but usually with a catchy message; bracelets of a thin metal strip coated with plastic which curl around the arm because of the tension in the metal; the red AIDS ribbon which now comes in all sorts of variations and the coloured plastic bracelets with a humanitarian message. When writing my study on Dutch jewellery, I still managed to trace a number of popular forms of jewellery from the period of the Second World War, such as brooches made of ceramics from Tegelen (NL). (144) There must be many more examples of such bulk goods all over the world, which will tell us a lot about the time and place of their creation but which so far have not been well documented or included in considerations about jewellery. Such ornaments are only documented and exhibited under the heading of mass culture or social history. But they can just as much be seen as jewellery as precious jewels or unique pieces by individual jewellery designers.

High jewellery is perhaps the most visible group within the wide array of forms of jewellery in terms of its market value. Jewellers know who to seduce with their best products, namely the people with money. Since the second half of the nineteenth century, a number of jewellers have built up their own signature and a good reputation, giving their name as producers of status symbols a solid foundation. The affluent upper classes at the time distinguished themselves by wanting to have the same forms of decoration as the old nobility. In the twentieth century, film stars and prominent figures from the worlds of culture and politics were added. The designers who work and have worked for these houses are known by name, their greatest achievement being that they managed to create an image that was decisive for their time. To this day it is not difficult to see the difference between the work of the renowned jewellers' houses and the jewellers who serve a less affluent public with their machine-made and highly conforming design jewellery in gold and silver.

5.4.4 Pricing and consumption

Even if a distinction is made between unique, serial and mass products, there is little to say about the final price of jewellery. Nowadays it depends on many different factors how the price of a piece of jewellery is determined. This is partly an economic issue, but also partly a culturally determined fact.

One of the few authors who has written fairly much and meaningfully about the market value of jewellery, and especially of precious jewellery, and who linked this to the consequences for jewellery as a cultural good, is Graham Hughes. The first chapter of his pioneering *Modern Jewellery* (1968) is devoted to 'Value – the essence'. In it he rightly stated that design with a strong and time-based signature is subject to fluctuations in taste. This is why, in general, little or no risk is taken in the design of jewellery with truly precious stones: 'The most inspiring pieces are therefore not the most expensive: big stones lead to dull designs'. (145) However, Hughes observed a change in his time and argued that the monetary value of a piece of jewellery, in addition to its material value, was increasingly determined by its design and by the signature of a renowned jewellery designer or artist. He predicted that cultural values would increasingly be expressed in monetary terms, and he was right in that.

The generation of jewellery designers from the 1960s and 1970s who opposed common notions of jewellery and who started working with base materials such as aluminium, Perspex and, in the 1980s, even with textiles and paper, also strongly opposed the notion of jewellery as an investment. The latter implied a focus on the dependent, married woman who had to show the prosperity of her husband to the world. But the new generation emphatically focused on the artistic value of their work.

There can be quite a difference between a piece of jewellery's material value and its artistic value, yet both may strongly influence its price. At first glance, prices of gallery jewellery hardly seem to be related to the value of the material used, even though trust in gold and precious stones is deeply rooted and continues to play a role when purchasing a piece of jewellery in a gallery. Nowadays the prices for jewellery by renowned designers in the Dutch gallery scene are higher than much jewellery in precious metal for sale at Dutch jewellers. (146) The same phenomenon can be seen in other West European countries.

On the other hand, there are countries where the trade in fairly inexpensive jewellery is one of the few opportunities for men and women to earn a basic income, as in many regions in Asia and Africa. If such jewels are easily dismissed as inexpensive or even as cheap tourist items, they usually reflect long traditions in decoration and are linked to the primal need of people to command a certain level of social status by wearing a piece of jewellery, even if it would be largely a matter of self-respect only. The low market value of such jewellery should not make us ignore the fact that such items represent a real economic value for their makers, especially for women, and that this is an important social value.

Other dimensions which potentially influence the price of a piece of jewellery pertain to historical value or pedigree. Items associated with important moments in a country's history rarely enter the market, but when they do, they tend to be purchased by a museum and their price is usually not disclosed. The situation is different regarding jewellery owned by a famous woman, such as Jacqueline Kennedy, the Duchess of Windsor or Princess Margaret of England, and which has been put up for auction. The aura of a previous owner can have a dramatic effect on the price that buyers are willing to pay for such pieces, which may amount to multiple times their material value. (147)

As far as the economy of jewellery is concerned, a new phenomenon was added in 2008. The Brussels branch of the Pierre Bergé auction house began auctioning jewellery made by renowned designers and artists. Since the 1970s, this work had mainly become available through galleries and exhibitions. But the decision of the auction house implies a need for independent appraisals of 'author's jewellery' or similar works by contemporary jewellery designers. In time, this will establish whether bracelets made of Perspex or jewellery items made of textile or enamelled gold will retain their value, like jewellery made of precious metal, a category with which auctioneers have gained a lot of experience over the years. (148)

It is striking perhaps that the market value of jewellery has been a major factor in the attention for jewellery as well as its status and appeal, but that its role as consumer product has not yet been used as a starting point. In his introduction to *Aards geluk* (Earthly happiness, 1997), a collection of essays, Anton Schuurman states that in the 1990s consumption was still ignored by historians as a concept without a scholarly tradition. He argued in favour of more histories of everyday life, including people's everyday routines and the interconnections of meaning and power, culture and economy, identity and self-interest. In an earlier study, *Materiële cultuur en levenstijl* (Material culture and lifestyle, 1990) this same author had argued already that consumer behaviour is more than just a matter of satisfying needs and that it involves a language or discourse of its own. (149) This material culture approach follows in the footsteps of the French Annales school of general historiography. (150)

By starting from use or consumption as a central category – rather than production or supply – Schuurman and his co-authors deviate from the principle that an economy is based on the production of goods and that supply generates its own demand. By shifting attention to consumption, more emphasis is put on the reasons why people wear jewellery and what they are prepared to do for it. It is an approach that not only makes sense for our western society; it is also interesting for countries with a low standard of living, where jewellery and for example beads are an important factor in the economy, where wearing jewellery is an integral part of life and jewellery items find their way to a new owner each and every day through barter.

The challenge of employing consumption as a starting point for the study of jewellery is in finding the right data. There are all sorts of cultural and economic data available, but it is not easy to show how they are interrelated or may explain each other. As far as the Netherlands is concerned, the Federation of Gold and Silver keeps track of the annual turnover of all Dutch jewellers, but these figures do not say anything yet about sales by jewellery galleries and small studios or the proceeds from auctions and the trade in ethnographic items. Furthermore, many wealthy families will have substantial collections of jewellery stored away in their bank safes, but no one knows how valuable they are. Descriptions of inheritances and household furnishings will also comprise information about the history of jewellery, but these are less and less recorded in wills. Jewellery insurance figures are not available in the public domain and if they were known, it is doubtful whether people would list and insure their entire property. It is not easy, for example, to determine how much money people spend on jewellery each year, how this figure relates to their income, social position and the value of all their belongings. (151)

As far as the market share of jewellery in the world economy is concerned, data provided by De Beers, the world's largest trader of rough diamonds, serve as a good indication. But they only pertain to diamonds, while it is difficult to interpret them, for instance in terms of their breakdown for different social groups. Department stores may provide a breakdown of their turnover in fashion jewellery, fashion jewellery and other fashion accessories, but these data rarely correspond to other statistical materials.

This is why consumption is still largely an unexplored field within the study of jewellery. One of the unforeseen conclusions of my study on Dutch jewellery was that the common assumption about the marginal role of 'frivolous' jewellery in times of war was incorrect. The opposite turned out to be true. Precisely in times of war jewellery is used in exchange for more urgent needs or services, such as medication, identity cards, travel documents, food, information and protection. Moreover, specific items are remade and stones are given a new setting, also, probably, to conceal their origin. (152) In addition, precisely in stressful and difficult times people seem to want to pay attention to the way they dress and look, including a nice piece of jewellery as an expression of self-respect.

Conclusions

Jewellery cannot be dissociated from the monetary value it represents. If this value varies over time, the use of precious metals has always been an important factor in establishing a historical framework for jewellery, also because of the legally established and protected labels.

In terms of technology, the trade of goldsmiths and silversmiths still relies heavily on conventions. Although mechanisation, industrialisation and computer-controlled techniques have clearly affected the production of jewellery, the constants in the profession weigh heavily, which applies both to design features and people's motive for wearing jewellery. One should therefore refrain from adopting an exclusive focus on the role of innovation when studying jewellery.

More sustained attention needs to be paid to the fact that many pieces of jewellery are made in series, that their value lies in their recognition within a certain group and that on this basis they contribute to establishing the social and cultural identity of the wearer. This implies the significance of no longer seeing jewellery exclusively as a means of emphasising individuality.

Specifically, fashion jewellery deserves a wider critical approach. In the world of fashion, they are appreciated as effective accents as part of an overall fashion image and as an economic factor. Likewise, it may be productive to look more closely at industrially manufactured jewellery based on precious metals and at particular trends or crazes in jewellery, be it with or without a social message.

Following Schuurman, I would like to argue that jewellery, both in the historiography of jewellery and in the valuation of various types of jewellery, should be looked at more in the context of everyday life. This implies attention for the connections between economy and culture, power and meaning, identity and consumption, as well as the need for social conventions and recognition. Historical value, traditions and the self-esteem of makers and wearers alike are just as important in determining the value of a piece of jewellery as financial and artistic values.

The economic value of a piece of jewellery is and remains a tricky subject from all sorts of points of view. Especially the pieces made of precious metals and gemstones are often vilified as wearable signs of an elevated status or abuses associated with the extraction of the raw materials. Regardless of this moralistic approach's justification, the scarcity of these raw materials and the interrelated value are precisely their attraction to others. The economic conflict implied in the study of jewellery is based on this duality. The fact that shells, animal body parts or glass beads may just as well represent a high value in other cultures does not detract from this duality. On the one hand, precious raw materials and their processing may compel our admiration for economic reasons, even if this also means that the role of precious jewellery as a means of displaying naked power remains effective. On the other hand, we may feel abhorrence regarding the unbridled greed and the political and social excesses associated with this kind of jewellery. I would like to suggest, in other words, that it is impossible to escape the schizophrenia intrinsic to the valuation of jewellery, which means that this duality, as an essential characteristic of jewellery, must continue to be part of its study.

5.5 Morality

5.5.1 Philosophy

At many points in this essay, I presented moral standards as relevant criteria in the study of jewellery. Jewellery is always subject to prevailing morals and customs, whether derived from religions with all their rich stories, from social conventions or from more abstract approaches based on philosophy. Obviously, it is possible to enhance our understanding of jewellery on the basis of philosophy as well. One may argue that the objects themselves are not to blame, but that their context – their creation, their trade and the ways they are coveted and worn – does invite a critical approach indeed. Moreover, insights from philosophy can also be expected to provide interesting perspectives on themes such as power and human relations.

In his *Utopia* (1516), Thomas More draws attention to the strange role of precious metals in human society. Despite the fact that people have much more to gain from stronger metals, such as iron, they attach value to gold and silver, while nature has been wise enough to give us much more earth, water and, for example, iron ore, and very little of that shiny precious metal. But the value of precious metal is precisely derived from this rarity. In order to remove that aura, gold and silver are used in Utopia for the humblest of functions, so that they lose their value. More makes a similar argument about pearls and gems, when he lets his Utopians deal with them in the following way: 'They find pearls on their coasts, and diamonds and carbuncles on their rocks; they do not look after them, but, if they find them by chance, they polish them, and with them they adorn their children, who are delighted with them, and glory in them during their childhood; but when they grow to years, and see that none but children use such baubles, they of their own accord, without being bid by their parents, lay them aside, and would be as much ashamed to use them afterwards as children among us, when they come to years, are of their puppets and other toys.' (153) In his time More gave a good analysis of existing abuses, but the solutions he put forward were less effective. Of course, he could not eliminate the limited availability of gold, as well as its attractive lustre and tactile qualities, on the basis of his reasoning.

In his *Kritik der Urteilskraft* (Critique of judgement, 1790), Immanuel Kant attempted to grasp the paradoxical contradiction between the power that man can exercise, through all his mental faculties, and the powerlessness he is always faced with. This is a fine metaphor for the above-described schizophrenia of jewellery as both an artistic artefact and an object of economic value. (154)

An interesting expression by a philosopher about jewellery of a more recent date is found in a lecture given by Pravu Mazumdar in April 2008 during a jewellery symposium in Florence. He asked whether it was possible to interpret all art, including jewellery, as a statement not to die yet. Beauty would have no other purpose than to make life visible and to keep death at a distance. Because jewellery is inevitably related to the human body, in contrast to art, he asked himself what jewellery does to the body. As he argued: 'There is something innately fugitive about self-transformation in general and the use of jewellery in particular. (...) When we drape ourselves with gold, we mask ourselves in a medium, which was traditionally reputed for its supernatural value and appeared as something like a stronghold against death. When we drape ourselves in plastic or wood or some other material, which may not have been considered valuable in our personal or collective tradition, we also drape ourselves in value. But in addition we draw attention to the fact that we have had to create a value before draping ourselves in it. We had to ascribe to gold the value we later perceive in it, before bejewelling ourselves with it. Contemporary jewellery making, as twentieth century art in general, seems to understand itself as the act of drawing attention to the relation between matter and value'. In other words, by adorning themselves with ornaments and constantly searching for new values and forms, people create a dynamic that withdraws them from the void, the meaningless. The same can be said about fashion of course. Mazumdar thus relates an essential characteristic of jewellery to fashion and today's consumerism. (155)

Jewellery belongs to the category of luxurious goods. It may respond to a fundamental human need for ornamentation and has an undeniable value as a means of identity marking, but jewellery is not one of life's basic necessities. Although pieces of jewellery are made in all price ranges while people's attention for them mainly goes out to precious items, jewellery can be seen as a symbol par excellence of the inequality in the distribution of wealth and power in the world. For centuries, this has made it an easy target for condemnation on puritanical grounds.

In 'Consumption and modern society', an essay by Schuurman in the abovementioned collection *Aards geluk*, the author quotes the definition of luxury as recorded in the encyclopaedia of Diderot and d'Alembert from the middle of the eighteenth century: 'Luxury is the use one makes of wealth and of industry to give oneself a pleasant life. The first cause of luxury is the dissatisfaction with our situation; the desire for more, which is present and must be present in all people. That is the source of their passions, their virtues and vices. This desire inevitably leads them to seek and embrace riches. The main object of this desire must be luxury. Luxury can therefore be found in all states and societies: the savage has his hammock which he bought for some animal skins, the European his sofa or bed'. (156) This definition of luxury is also shortened to 'everything that is not necessary for a normal life', a definition that of course raises the question of what a normal life is. French philosophers who have recently shed light on the concept of luxury, such as Roland Barthes and Gilles Lipovetsky, still see it as the human need for sensual pleasure and for things that embellish life.

Reasons to de-moralise luxury goods are often of an economic nature. This approach, which is still being developed, only confirms the economic value of jewellery. It was the London-based, Dutch physician Bernard Mandeville who argued in 1705 that society benefits from vices and that without the desire for luxury the economy would collapse and that the arts and sciences would not make any progress if they were not accompanied by ambition. He packaged his philosophical and economic message in the form of a fable about a beehive, one half of which worked for the benefit of lust and vanity, while the other half squandered that profit. This insight has been taken up by many economists and, as mentioned, was also expressed in a poignant manner by L.N. Tolstoy. (157)

In his 2006 essay 'Luxury and the sixth sense', the French philosopher Gilles Lipovetsky states that a luxurious lifestyle in earlier times was a process 'in which, with a view to rebirth, one appropriates the forces of the hereafter. So the ability to fight the earthly existence'. Many preserved jewels from earlier times are burial finds, indeed intended to guarantee the deceased his rightful place in the afterlife. Lipovetsky further argues that luxury only exists today when transient consumer goods reach the level of a legend and become part of a timeless myth. Luxury is linked to continuity. As he claims: 'In a society where the pace of innovation has been unleashed and products and brands are ageing at an ever-increasing rate, a new need emerges, that of timelessness and sustainability'. He assumes that there is still something supernatural in our desire to enjoy the beautiful and rare things in life as the gods. So once again, in response to fashion, a useful idea comes our way, this time for interpreting jewellery within our contemporary culture. Lipovetsky's argument, for example, can be extended directly to the scarcity and physical and symbolic value of gold and precious stones. (158)

An interesting concept that Schuurman introduces in connection with luxury goods, such as expensive furniture, is good manners. An even more beautiful concept is, in my opinion, being courteous, because that is even more generous. This is an approach that also belongs under the market value of jewellery: how do you deal with precious jewellery, when are you going to wear which jewellery, do you want to outdo your fellow man or put him at ease? The question that actually precedes this is how people deal with the unequal distribution of wealth and social stratifications in a society. Such humane questions are rarely addressed in publications on the history of jewellery, at least not in catalogues and other contemporary publications on jewellery design.

In my study on Dutch jewellery, I afforded the concept of civility a central place. It can be traced back to the Humanism of the sixteenth century and it served as a core concept in the analysis of the traditional resistance in our country to showing prosperity on the body. This is in contrast to what is acceptable in the countries around us. Especially in chapter 3, about the period of the depression and the war years, the highly popular etiquette books of that era were used to support the prevailing mentality in our country with regard to wearing jewellery. (159)

With nomadic people it is customary, as mentioned, to wear the capital that is invested in jewellery on the body, by women, but also by men. For the women this often means that the more they wear, the richer they are and the more prestige they enjoy as a confidant of their husband. These are beautiful values that can be attributed to jewellery, but for westerners and certainly for Dutch people, such ornamentation quickly appears as a barbaric display. (160)

The financial value represented by the adornment of wealthy ladies in the past has given rise to some fine habits. In the Netherlands, as in many other countries, it was a tradition for mothers to leave their jewellery to their daughters, not only as a souvenir, but also as a nest egg. In the case of other forms of inheritance of jewellery, too, this often occurred in the female line, as a traditional form of 'female bonding'. The women who inherited could thus face the world well dressed and with the distinction of a family tradition. In the event of serious financial difficulties, they were able to sell their jewellery as reasonably stable units of value. (161) The fact that jewellery has a protective function for women from a financial point of view is a worldwide phenomenon. Geoffroy-Schneiter has described the way in which jewellery forms part of the marriage negotiations in Algeria, while Annemarie Moors has developed this theme for women in the Middle East. (162)

A ring often featured as symbol for the transfer from one ruler to another. (163) The lavish jewellery owned by the great rulers was basically passed on to their successors, which has generated quite a few exciting situations. Gérard Mabille, for example, described the ups and downs of the diamonds that once belonged to the French crown and how they were squandered in the nineteenth century. Similar histories can be told about almost every royal family or powerful dynasty, which is why books about royal jewellery collections constitute a genre of its own within the historiography of jewellery.

5.5.2 Beauty, a moral standard?

At this point, it is worth analysing the concept of beauty in more detail. The definition of jewellery derived from *Van Dale*, which I used at the beginning of my essay, presents increasing beauty as the most important goal of jewellery. This goal should certainly not be downplayed, on the contrary – it is a primal force. At the same time, it is only one aspect of people's need to adorn themselves.

The first problem is that beauty is so difficult to define. The concept is often used too quickly without first making it clear whether it is about external beauty, a visual value, or more abstract and inward-looking values. Andy Warhol has summed up the relativity of the concept of beauty in relation to jewellery by saying: 'Jewellery doesn't make a person more beautiful, but it makes a person feel more beautiful'. In doing so, he placed the emphasis on abstraction and, by the way, he also left open whether it is about men, women or children. (164)

The philosophical question underlying this duality is whether beauty is something specific to an object or a situation, an objective value, or whether it is considered beautiful for subjective reasons and beauty is 'in the eye of the beholder'. As a visual value, beauty in a piece of jewellery can be seen as a characteristic of the piece of jewellery itself (as elaborated in sections 7.1 and 7.2). But it can also be seen as a means of enhancing the beauty of the person who wears it. Even then the question remains whether it is about increasing the physical beauty of the human being (as addressed in chapter 4), or whether it is a much more complex concept that has to do with people's self-image and the way in which they are judged by others. However, beauty as a factor in human relationships should under no circumstances be regarded as synonymous with attractiveness. Pure beauty – both objective and subjective – compels admiration, but for many it also has a deterrent effect.

In addition to aesthetic standards, which can be more or less objectively established, the establishment of beauty may be even more about culturally and historically contingent notions, and as far as jewellery is concerned, it is about the way in which they are worn and about social standards. Such subjective norms can largely be traced back to moral values.

A nice look at the concept of beauty in relation to jewellery can be found in a booklet about the Gallery of Beauty of King Ludwig I of Bavaria. In the first half of the nineteenth century he had Joseph Karl Stieler paint a series of portraits – consistently the head and upper body only – of women from his empire who differed greatly in terms of physique, hair colour and origin. Ludwig I saw beauty as a symbol of the highest moral values and human integrity. Many of the women portrayed wear jewellery that perfectly matches the chosen clothing in terms of richness, colour, shape and traditions. What fascinates me is the simplicity and clarity of these portraits. For this king, beauty was symbolised by women in many variations, who wear jewellery that matches their position, the colour of their hair and their clothing. The most important standard in his view, however, was their moral standard. (165)

Apart from this elementary approach, there is the one of, for example, semioticist Umberto Eco, who, surrounded by a whole staff of scholars, has written a complex work on beauty. The cut-out of the portrait of Eleonora of Toledo by Bronzino on the dust jacket of the 2004 English translation is somewhat reminiscent of the women from Ludwig I's Gallery of Beauty, but that is where the resemblance ends. Eco has compiled a richly varied history of aesthetics. According to him, beauty, like Kant, is something that we admire and can enjoy without asking ourselves whether we want to own it in advance, because beauty is selfless and has no purpose. In this respect beauty creates distance. Beauty, then, is an autonomous value and is essentially independent of desire, despite all the passion, greed, envy and assertiveness that collectors can show. Eco explicitly includes natural phenomena in his contemplation and does not only focus on art.

However, Eco does not dwell on Kant's view that beauty would be disinterested. He argues in favour of involving contemporary statements in the study of historical objects, something that he and his staff have done to the full. With this, beauty is – rightly – labelled as something relational, something that is always in motion. This is how he treats the beauty of the ugly, of monsters and death. Throughout the book all kinds of moral norms and a range of relevant concepts are presented, including luxury. This is how Eco presents beauty as a very complex concept. He shows that beauty is not purely decorative, but that it is a symbol of opinions, theories and moral norms. Beauty is interwoven with power, social relations and morality; this is where the reasons for experiencing beauty have to be found. (166)

This view is echoed in my study on Dutch jewellery. In each chapter, the introductory sections on international developments in jewellery and fashion and the Dutch context summarise the social, political and economic developments of the period in question and explain their influence on moral and cultural norms with regard to people's appearance and their attitude towards jewellery.

The fact that nature and elements of nature are often elevated to the highest beauty standard has left deep traces in the jewellery trade, both in terms of choice of materials and language of form and sources of inspiration. Over the course of 100,000 years, a wide range of vegetable and animal materials have been used to make jewellery. Sometimes debris from nature is only made wearable, as is often the case with shells and beautiful pieces of coral. Sometimes teeth or rough stones are caught in metal, but precious stones are usually firmly worked to the colour and brilliance of their crystalline structure to express themselves. The fact that nature is also violated in order to be able to function as an ornament of people should not be forgotten. Like all other man-made things, the approach to jewellery is not free of double standards.

It is astonishing to think that many of the materials used for jewellery come from the deep, such as ores from deep underground, stones that are mined, treasures of the sea and raw materials that are used to make plastics. The things from above the ground serve more as inspiration and model. Flowers, animal figures, the sun, the moon and the stars, they are all elevated as motifs for jewellery. The many symbolic, mythical, ceremonial and religious meanings associated with these motifs often have their origins in the properties of natural resources. There is a sliding scale from analysable characteristics and folk wisdom to spiritual or supernatural values, which should all be taken seriously in the study of the jewel, as also argued in section 4.3. and in chapter 6 on symbolism.

5.5.3 Religion

In addition to philosophy, religion is an interesting source of moral standards with respect to jewellery. One may wonder how the contemplation of jewellery is influenced by systems of religious norms and values with regard to people's outward appearance. Religion as an angle in the study of jewellery may also apply to the rich tradition of iconography, however (cf. the next chapter on symbolism).

From a western perspective such as my own, Christianity features most prominently in terms of moral standards in relation to jewellery. Multiple times, the Bible makes explicit reference to jewellery, to various forms of jewellery and to the materials from which it may be made, particularly gold, silver and precious stones. Sometimes jewellery is used as an indication of rank or a means of identification. Jewellery is in fact given all sorts of qualifications in the Bible, varying from glory, well-deserved spoils of war and other forms of reward, to punishment and damnation, when being regarded as signs of whoredom or improper profit. In addition, there are regular metaphorical references to jewellery in the Bible.

After all the positive stories about jewellery, it is also instructive perhaps to consider its moral rejection, of which there are plenty examples in the Bible. The women of Jerusalem, for example, are described in powerful detail as follows in Ezekiel 7, verse 18-21: 'They will wear robes of mourning, fear will cover them, on all faces there will be shame, on everyone's head there will be a bald spot. They shall cast their silver into the street, and their gold shall be an object of abhorrence; their silver and gold shall not be able to save them on the day of the master's wrath; they shall not be able to saturate themselves with it, nor to fill their bowels with it; for it was a stumbling block to iniquity for them. They have made of it a beautiful beauty for pride; they have made of it horrible images, their horrors: therefore will I make it an object of abomination for them. I will give it to strangers in prey, and to the wicked of the earth in prey, that they may desecrate it'.

A similar depiction can be found in Isaiah 3:18-24, where a number of specific ornaments are mentioned with which the women of Jerusalem have to part: foot rings, forehead bands, moons, earrings, bracelets, seal rings, nose rings and foot chains. (167) The story of Ohola and Ohibila in Ezekiel 23 may serve as an example of condemning jewellery in the context of whoring and as a means for immoral women to make themselves more attractive to men. (168)

Conversely, a number of positive connotations pass in review as well: jewellery in relation to pleasure and reward. (169) The appreciation of gold is well expressed in Kings in the description of the court of Solomon and the trade during his reign, even though it also suggests excesses. But as soon as gold is used for idolatry, the wrath of the Lord is released. A highly detailed description of techniques and stones can be found in the guidelines of their use by the high priest in Exodus 28, verse 15-25, a rich evocation of the arts of textile and silversmithing. (170)

Jewellery as a means of identification occurs, for instance, in the story of Isaac and Rebekah (Genesis 24:28-31). Much more complex is the story in Genesis 38 of Judah and Tamar, his daughter-in-law, who was initially married to his first son. He aroused the displeasure of the Lord and died. Then Judah let her marry his second son, but that was not a success either. Finally, she showed herself veiled to Judah, who therefore thought of her as a whore. She let him 'come unto her', on condition that he would give her a pledge: 'Thy signet ring, thy cords, and the staff that is in thy hand. Then he gave it to her, and he came to her, and she became pregnant with him'. Tamar could finally prove the fatherhood of Judah on the basis of that seal ring, the cords and the staff. She got the things she was entitled to – as well as twins.

In the Song of Songs, the author relies on jewellery and the effect of gems as a metaphor for physical attraction, even though the references to the man are perhaps more interesting, from the point of view of this study, than those to the woman.

To conclude this short treatise, I would like to cite two revealing sayings from the Bible:

There is gold, and abundance of rubies;
But the lips of knowledge are a precious jewel.
(Proverbs 20:15).

And:

Like a golden ring in a pig's snout
is a woman fair and fool.
(Proverbs 11:22).

These wisdoms come close to sayings in Dutch that I used in the introduction of my study on Dutch Jewellery in support of the Dutch resistance to showing affluence or prosperity on the body. As one of them puts it: 'gold is highly regarded, but virtue even more so'. (171) It is striking that the Old Testament contains the most flowery references to jewellery, while the New Testament rather refers to money than to gold and silver. This difference has little significance perhaps, for coins were made of gold and silver. Being a more abstract concept, money is probably easier to judge.

The Bible is a collection of religious texts, not accurate history writing. In the case of the various books in the Bible, there is a considerable discrepancy between the moment at which they are recorded and the time and the country in which the stories are situated. As far as this study is concerned, there is little or no difference between literary quotations or data from biographies and biblical texts with regard to accurate information. But the Bible's influence on western morality is much greater than that of any other text, regardless of the fact that the various books contain contradictory or at least multi-interpretable statements about decoration and gold.

The earliest history of Christianity took place within the Roman Empire, where after the arrival of the emperors, 'luxuria', or the desire for wealth, was celebrated by the nobility. The women of the Roman aristocracy in particular are attributed an important role in the imperial trade and commerce because of their capriciousness and their greed for perfumes and silk, as well as for jewellery made of gold, pearls and precious stones, all of which had to be imported. (172)

For Christian church fathers and other moral preachers, this was a welcome reason to propagate virtue and abstinence from all kinds of opulence and carnal lusts. Take the early church fathers, like Augustine, and the hermits who retreated into the desert. Gregory the Great, who was born around 504 A.D. and came from a Roman patrician family, even called the body 'that horrible garment that hangs around the soul'. Until well into the Middle Ages, this view remained valid; the body was seen as the prison of the spirit.

Le Goff inimitably formulates the following consequence: 'The height of abomination, the worst of the body and of sexuality, was the female body. From Eve to the witch of the late Middle Ages woman's body was the devil's stomping ground'. But he also explains that the life of the knight was one long eulogy to his body, that he could surrender himself with heart and soul to hunting, war and tournaments and that Charlemagne and his companions liked to bathe naked in his palace in Aachen. (173)

This cursory investigation of jewellery's reputation within Christianity, then, exposes a double morality. The sharpest edges of these ideas have worn off over the centuries. Yet within Christianity the mentality still prevails that morality is a great virtue, but that men have a right to a woman and to offspring, and that when something goes wrong in the male/female relationship, the woman is the seducer, especially thanks to all the tools to accentuate her physical charms. Moreover, the woman is an unclean and unreasonable being. In biblical iconography, evil in the world naturally has its origin in Eve, not in Adam.

In western culture, Christianity has been closely intertwined with politics and economics. Many expressions of silversmithing are permeated with Christian themes, from reliquaries and other ecclesiastical utensils to portable altars and signage. The individual rings of the successive popes will have included many a masterpiece of goldsmithing. (174) The woman as seductress with long hair and a snake as an attribute has left deep traces in the history of worldly jewellery. But the serpent as a shape for a piece of jewellery should not only be interpreted as a Christian symbol, as Geoffroy-Schneiter has shown in her research of ethnic parures. The snake that bites its tail is an ancient symbol of continuous, cyclical processes. (175)

The common approach to jewellery in western culture, whereby jewellery is identified as woman's aid in making herself seductive to men, is perfectly in keeping with Christian morality. Apparently, it may serve as a basis for condemning jewellery. At the same time, however, gold and gems are accepted in biblical texts as signs of power for men, whether a king or a high priest. This substantiates the claims in section 4.4 with regard to the basic motives for men to wear jewellery and the importance of radiating power through their ornaments.

These observations on Christianity prompt a desire to study the relationship between jewellery and religion from, for example, the angle of Hinduism, where there is much more room for sexuality and colourful decorations. In nature-oriented philosophies such as shamanism and the customs and practices of African tribes, written sources are seldom available. Many burial finds, however, unmistakably point to a correlation between philosophical views and the jewellery and other forms of clothing, ornaments and attributes that were given to the dead.

It is unfeasible to examine the relationship between jewellery and religion in the brief scope of this essay for a variety of religions. This is why I referred mainly to a number of biblical texts here. These should not be taken too literally. As in Islam, there is a discrepancy between religious texts and how they are interpreted in daily life. The observance of religious guidelines, like so many things, depends on their coordinates in space and time. And when all is said and done, differences of mentality regarding male-female relations between Christianity and Islam do not seem to be so large. (176)

Conclusions

That jewellery is not one of life's necessities and is rather intended to make life easier caused many philosophers to be critical about jewellery. A pragmatic view of jewellery and other luxury products is that they keep the economy going. In addition, philosophers have studied the mythical properties attributed to precious metals and gems and jewellery as a means of coping with earthly life or celebrating it. The philosophical approach of jewellery as a luxury product subject to constant changes may equally serve as an approach applied to fashion.

Jewellery calls for specific standards of behaviour or courtesy. This has led to customary practices in all kinds of cultures: when does one wear jewellery, which items of jewellery should one wear, how many of them is acceptable and how expensive or inexpensive should they be? There are many – frequently unwritten – rules for these various aspects that may also change over time.

As a concept, beauty is not only determined by aesthetic considerations, but also by moral norms. Being complex and relative, beauty is normally unrelated to some goal and can be dissected from all kinds of angles. Beauty can just as easily create distance as exert attraction. The fact that nature is often used as a standard for beauty is clearly expressed in jewellery, both in terms of its symbolism and choice of materials.

As far as religious norms are concerned, the Bible offers many starting points for reflection on moral standards in relation to jewellery. The double morality towards jewellery for men and women is striking. This is fully in line with the common approach to jewellery in western countries, where jewellery is seen as an aid for women to make themselves seductive for men. Because the Bible depicts women as unclean beings and as the origin of evil in the world, it is hard to link Christianity with a positive view on jewellery in general and as decorative tool for women in particular, with the exception perhaps of jewellery as religious symbol. At the same time, the predominantly negative representation of jewellery and women in the Bible has hardly proved to be an obstacle to wearing jewellery by women in most of the Christian world. That in Christian tradition one does not seem to condemn jewellery as a sign of power for male rulers and church leaders confirms the significant role of jewellery for men in the course of history.

In all eras and cultures there will have been some correlation between particular philosophical views and views on and the nature of physical adornment. In some instances, all we have left is the ornament and we have to speculate on the underlying philosophical views and social customs. Religious norms, together with moral norms from philosophy, are in line with the analysis of the underlying motives for wearing jewellery from the fields of psychology and sociology: the need for decoration as a token of pleasure in life; jewellery to break the spell of supernatural powers and of death; and, above all, jewellery as a wearable sign of the mutual relationships between people, between men and women in general, and between men and women in relation to each other. All of this underscores the need for a multidisciplinary framework for the study of jewellery.

6 Symbolism in jewellery

The symbolic values comprised in jewellery all start from human beings as point of reference. Human beings do not just have a body but also a mind, and depending their upbringing and knowledge, they are guided by all kinds of urges, such as lust, ambition, greed, goodness, sacrifice and, above all, fear. The symbolism in jewellery is rooted in the motives that underlie its wearing. Symbolism is also based on social and cultural traditions, as well as on moral standards. After having identified and addressed these motives and the various angles of approach that are necessary to gain an understanding of the social, emotional and cultural-historical aspects of the approach to jewellery, it is now possible look more closely at symbolism in jewellery. The adjective 'symbolic' is the last keyword in the definition of jewellery that needs further explanation.

From well-founded studies to informative booklets for novice collectors, there is much to be found about the symbolic values attributed to jewellery, although all this information has rarely been properly analysed. Sometimes the symbolism is hidden in an anecdote about a historical figure, but there are also complete studies devoted to amulets, talismans and mourning jewellery. A very American enumeration from the Jewellery Handbook *How to Select, Wear & Care for Jewellery* by Renée Newman includes 'expressions of love, affection and commitment, religious symbols, healing aids and political statements' as reasons for wearing jewellery. The author explains the latter meaning with the example of the jewellery of suffragettes from around 1900, which were provided with green, white and violet stones. The initial letters of these colours (G, W and V) stood for 'Give Women the Vote'. Her statement that jewellery can be used as 'portable storage of wealth and hedge against inflation' has been amply corroborated by recent economic developments in the United States. (177)

Such a list can be compared with the much better documented publication *Sieraad, Symbool, Signaal* (Jewellery, symbol, signal, 1995) by Jan Walgrave, and the listed symbolic values can be compared with each other. The more studies one involves, the longer the list becomes, but it will never be complete.

Martha Gandy Fales mentions jewellery in the introduction to her book *Jewelry in America* (1995) as one of the most enlightening sources of information on past cultures. 'It informs the beholder of basic beliefs, customs, trade patterns and artistic creativity'. After recognising that it is one of the most complex and demanding art forms to study, partly because knowledge of materials is a specialisation in its own right, she goes on to state: 'Jewellery is also the most international of arts in both substance and form, and cuts across national boundaries'. This also applies in particular to the symbolism in jewellery. Everywhere jewellery has served as a sign of love or mourning, and it has travelled all over the world as small, wearable and easily tradable objects. The range of symbolism in jewellery is endless. (178)

One of the ways to get a grip on the long list of meanings of jewellery as a wearable attribute is to link it to the different stages of people's lives. For example, jewellery for small children can be seen as a form of protection, for adolescents as a sign of reaching sexual or legal maturity, for adults as a sign of availability as a spouse, as a symbol of marriage, as a reward for childbirth, but also as a sign of infertility or rejection of sexual relations, as a sign of a social position or a religious function, as a symbol of the highest position a person has reached in life, as a warning of death and as a sign of grief. The engagement ring, the wedding ring, the beautiful gift for the first child, mourning jewellery, jewellery to commemorate an anniversary or other milestone in life, the transfer of power by means of a jewel – all such jewellery rather derives its value from symbolism than from particular decorative or material qualities.

Another and much sought-after way of interpreting the symbolism in jewellery is on the basis of the colour and physical properties of stones, and of the many meanings that have been attributed to them over the course of time. This is a common way of indexing books about gems and jewellery containing gems (see also sections 4.3 and 5.5.2). In China, jade is highly valued, based on the magical qualities attributed to this type of stone. (179) It is not easy to recognise jade, which is why every green-tinted stone in the Far East is soon called jade, if only as a sales argument. This is a general point of interest with regard to the symbolism attributed to stones: there are few people who can recognise and classify the many types of stones and who are willing to link that knowledge to knowledge about the many symbolic values that are attributed to them.

The magical is an area of endless speculation and unproven forces, as fascinating as it is questionable from a scientific point of view. However, certain effects can sometimes be analysed scientifically, such as reactions to the skin. Apart from this, the effect of (self-)suggestion should never be underestimated. Stones and other amulets or talismans can have a protective and healing effect simply because of this.

A good source for determining symbolism in jewellery is iconography, which tries to determine the meaning of signs and symbols in works of art and is part of the art historical discipline. There are all kinds of lexicons and explanatory dictionaries that can be helpful in interpreting images and naming the origin of the symbolism used in them. The wealth of information is overwhelming; the meaning of, for example, flowers and animal figures as attributes can vary enormously, depending on the time, the why and the place in the world where they were made.

An attribute is a means of identification. A well-educated art historian with a reasonable knowledge of Christianity can recognise the classical gods, church fathers, apostles and patron saints, as well as worldly rulers and key figures in history by their attributes. (180) That knowledge is developed from a western perspective. He can probably recognise the beloved and worldwide spread ornament in the form of a hand as the hand of Fatima, daughter of the prophet Muhammad. But it goes a lot further to know that this motif has a protective effect and that the five fingers symbolise the five pillars of Islam. This means that religious symbolism in widespread ornamentation can be a language that is difficult to understand in everyday life, and that cultural differences continue to play a major role in the recognition of the language of jewellery, even in an era of globalisation. (181)

Many spiritual meanings and protective functions have been assigned to animal figures. However, not every representation of an animal in an ornament is a religious symbol. It can simply be a cheerful motif or testify to a personal preference of the creator or wearer.

Still, a piece of jewellery can function as an attribute in many different ways, for example as a key to the character and social status of the wearer. This only works if, for example, the symbolism or a particular brand is known to the person among whom they are or with whom they want to come into contact. 'Être nu, c'est être sans paroles' is a statement from the Dogon in Mali. This statement not only refers to jewellery, but also to the interplay between jewellery, clothing and other body ornaments, but it is precisely in Mali that jewellery has an important part to play in this. (182)

The symbolic value of a piece of jewellery is a subject in which one can easily get lost. At this point in this essay, the main aim will be to bring some coherence to the symbolism that a piece of jewellery can contain, and in particular to look at its social, physical and personal aspects.

6.1. Power

It is already clear that power is an interesting angle for the study of jewellery, but it would be short-sighted to consider such a motive only in relation to the vertical relationships in a society. The significance of the vast majority of jewellery lies in the horizontal relationships between people. It is therefore unjustified that the vertical proportions in the historiography of jewellery have received the most attention.

Power can be seen as a bipolar concept, with self-confidence at one end of the spectrum and uncertainty or fear at the other. If there is the human urge to distinguish oneself, to express one's own personality, there is also the urge to belong to something, to conform to norms that apply within a certain group, country or time and to seek the safety of numbers. However, these two extremes cannot be linearly extended to types of jewellery. Inconspicuous jewellery, for example, can also be interpreted as signs of power and self-confidence.

Within each social group there are people who want to distinguish themselves, even if only a little bit. Small objects such as jewellery, which do not immediately catch the eye, act as excellent social and emotional indicators in the movement between people from the same social stratum of the population, because they meet each other the most. Power does not so much have to do with coercion and impressions, but with the power of one's personality and the way in which people relate to one another. The need to mark one's own identity and social position can be expressed in jewellery and accessories that are not very conspicuous, such as the marks of the freemasons. Or take a simple engagement ring: the possession of an expectant could enormously increase the position of both a boy and a girl in relation to contemporaries who had not yet made such a step.

From the sixteenth century onwards, the Netherlands has often been regarded as a country where you should always have your feet on the ground, be level-headed and avoid showing off jewellery. The upper classes in our country have seldom if ever dressed as richly as in neighbouring countries. Yet in recent decades, the work of Dutch jewellery designers has attracted international attention because of its exuberance in terms of format, use of materials and space for personal expression.

Refusing to pay much attention to one's appearance may just as well be a form of self-respect and cultural or religious snobbery.

This principle has been well studied in fashion, but with regard to jewellery it is seldom recognised and it takes a good communicator to recognise such a refusal as an expression of power. A good example was the court of Tsar Alexander I. Despite the incredible arsenal of stones available to the highest Russian nobility, for a number of years he and his czarina preferred to show themselves without any jewellery, in keeping with the ideas of the Enlightenment and the ideals from the years of the French Revolution. (183)

Large jewels as a sign of power can easily be recognised in traditional attributes such as crowns, chains, badges and rings, and necklaces with many bear teeth. Throughout history, powerful jewellery and badges have been effective indicators of the prestige that rulers of all kinds wanted to enforce. They may stand out because few or even only one person may adorn themselves with them, but they often resemble each other and within one dynasty or people these signs are often passed on from one generation to the next, with which they are also signs of conservatism and convention. For centuries the *grande parure* as a complete collection of jewels has fulfilled the same function for wives, mistresses and other favourites of great rulers. (184)

Untracht argues that almost all the decoration of the Naga warriors in India's eastern mountain regions should be interpreted as signs of power. 'In this male-dominated society, body ornament proclaimed man's superiority over real or imagined human enemies and displayed visual evidence of male supremacy over both docile and dangerous, predatory animal adversaries'. From a social point of view, the decoration of the Mughal rulers was very vertical, purely to impress. He describes the ceremony of weighing the emperor and the custom of spending his weight in gold on charity. His enumeration of jewels of Mughal rulers is impressive. (185)

Wearing jewellery was also subject to strict rules in other cultures. For more than six hundred years, Benin was the capital of a large kingdom in West Africa. The height of this empire's power was in the middle of the sixteenth century. The king was considered the connection of earthly and supernatural forces.

The highest ranks at his court received from him stiff chains of coral, which fell back into the possession of the ruler after their death. The loss of such a necklace was a mortal sin. Wide arms anklets of ivory and copper alloys were also worn as signs of rank. The cross with four equal arms, in the west usually called Maltese cross, was associated in Benin with the god Osa and was widely worn, way before any contact with Europeans. (186) This is just one example of jewellery as signs of power in a non-western culture and it is true that it is not easy to appreciate jewellery at its proper value independently of its original context.

Nowadays, social relations are so flexible that subcultures can also play the role of a cultural elite. Ironically, this often happens in protest against a cultural elite or against the norms of the social middle class. It is striking how the symbolism of punk at the beginning of the 1980s was transformed into jewellery with razor blades that only had the shape of a razor but had lost all sharpness. This means that there are not only vertical and horizontal connections in the way in which social relations affect fashion and jewellery, but also diagonal or criss-cross connections, in which case it is an open question which side serves as an example. The wave of democratisation, youth culture and the sexual revolution in the 1960s and 1970s shook up social relations considerably, and diagonal relationships have become increasingly important in fashion and music, for example, which has led to many unexpected role models. The economic problems of our time, with a growing group of super-rich people capable of absorbing financial setbacks, a middle class that is affected by them and a large group of people who are in danger of ending up in the lower layers of society, will undoubtedly also leave their mark on fashion, clothing behaviour and preferences for jewellery.

6.2 Fertility, protection and eroticism

The fact that jewellery is worn on the human body not only influences the forms of jewellery and their tactile qualities, but also has to do with the vulnerability of that body and with the sexual pleasures that can be experienced on the body.

The need for physical protection is one of the three primary motives for wearing clothes. Body style is more about mental protection; much of that decoration must have had an imploring function, which is best recognised in amulets and masks. (187) The need for protection stems from fear and the urge to survive. Jewellery may not be the first means of survival, but it has fulfilled that function, albeit usually in a disguised form, such as by wearing symbols with a mythical or religious meaning.

One of the most elementary urges of any animal species, including humans, is the urge to reproduce. Young men and young women make the reaching of sexual maturity known in many ways, more or less subtly. Even when a relationship has been perpetuated, an attempt is made to stimulate fertility by wearing jewellery with an appropriate symbolism. A very early example of such a practice can be found in a recent study by two Israeli archaeologists. They show that the transition from a hunter-gatherer existence to an agricultural society, about 11,000–14,000 years ago, has led to a preference for green stones in jewellery. From the hunter/collector period mainly jewellery consisting of beads of shells, bones, teeth, antlers and ivory has been preserved. The green probably stood for the germination and fertility of the crops. Anthropological research has shown that such beads and pendants not only served as decorations, but also as amulets. Jordanian farmers still make a direct link between the 'power' of beads and the fertility of their wives. (188)

The typical blue-green scarab from ancient Egypt and the aforementioned jewellery in the form of a snake that bites its own tail can also be mentioned here as a symbol of the cyclic nature of existence.

Hugh Tait's *7000 Years of Jewellery* contains a 1602 portrait of the Spanish Infanta Anna, painted by Juan Pantoja de la Cruz. (189) It is a wonderful example of the number of attributes with a protective function that can be given to a small and stiffly wrapped girl: various crosses and reliquaries, a bell, a pomander or perfume holder, a heart and in her hand an object with a piece of coral, which had the name that could protect children from diseases. In this case, it is clear to anyone who understood that there was a great deal of hope for that girl and that they wanted to protect her from all kinds of evils. It is very likely that children who did not belong to the class being portrayed were also given protective attributes.

Untracht also pays a lot of attention to the symbolism in jewellery and the protection of amulets and talismans against supernatural forces. He recognises this as one of the archetypal motifs for wearing ornaments to the body and describes both the positive and negative effects, because the latter should also be possible if you have confidence in the former.

Moreover, Untracht analyses the wearing of coins as a sign of prosperity, but also as a form of submission to the government by which one is governed. Mint jewellery symbolises the power of the state and thus acquires the function of amulets as a token of the protection that a state can offer. In India, they were sought after by the lower income groups, who were most dependent on the exchange value of the coins, and they were the most popular under British rule. (190) His findings show similarities with the popularity of coinage jewellery in the Netherlands as a token of loyalty to the authority of the Queen of the Netherlands and as an expression of civil self-respect (as addressed in my study on Dutch jewellery). (191)

Protection can also be sought in numbers, by wearing jewellery that belongs to one's own social group, as is so clearly expressed in regional jewellery. It is captivating to see how the forms and techniques of folk jewellery all over the world show strong similarities and yet, in each individual place, give them the certainty that they belong to a specific community and confirm their identity.
Popular jewellery such as buttons and other similar items may also create such sense of belonging.

Another aspect of jewellery that is physically related to being human is to make one's body sexually attractive. In this respect, a piece of jewellery can emit a broad spectrum of signals, varying from obvious eroticism to reliability and chastity. The sensual and erotic aspects of jewellery have already been mentioned in section 4.2.

With regard to the symbolic value of jewellery, sexuality only becomes exciting when the concept of eroticism is added. A supple necklace in the shape of a snake is experienced both as a reference and erotic. The catalogue *Erotischer Schmuck* from 1995 deals with all the clichés about sexuality and jewellery, including the statement by the artist Biggi Uhl that she sees penises and vaginas everywhere and in everything. (192) Such an outpouring is so universal and at the same time so limited that there is little point in elaborating on it. In this respect I would like to confine myself to this statement by Sigmund Freud, namely that a cigar is sometimes nothing more and nothing less than a cigar.

The point is, of course, that attraction and eroticism do not have to be directly related to physicality. Jan Walgrave states in his study *Sieraad Symbool Signaal* that the sensual qualities of jewellery have been displayed throughout history, especially in periods of decadence. (193) But as far as symbolism is concerned, the interesting work only comes to the fore under the headings of love, mourning and marriage. Take the rather literal symbolism of the heart, the hands holding each other, the arrows of Eros or the anchor.

A nice overview of romantic symbols in jewellery offers *Le bijou de sentiment* (2008) by Diana Scarisbrick. Cupids, two lines connected in a knot, forget-me-nots, clover leaves, two birds on a branch, ivy, a woman's hand with a key, swans, snakes, dogs and rabbits – all these symbols can be explained as a token of love and loyalty. Scarisbrick often performs literary quotations to explain the symbolism in these motifs. She also presents the symbolism of texts in jewellery that are formed by the first letters of the names of coloured stones (as in the aforementioned Suffragette jewels), a custom that was especially popular in the nineteenth century. (194) Then there are the medallions with the image of a loved one and double portraits that served to confirm a connection. And finally, of course, there is the ring, the confirmation par excellence of marriage. In large parts of the world, a piece of jewellery is the most important visible sign of the way in which people officially and unofficially bind together. The symbolism of the gesture – sliding the ring on each other's finger – is in many cases more erotic than the symbolism in the rings themselves.

The language of love or romance is even broader when personal points of view are taken into account, messages that are only understood by a few and sometimes even only by one other person. Beautiful examples of jewellery with a romantic symbolism are the bead cloths developed by Zulus and other South African peoples. The message is in the colour of the beads. In short, love has its own iconography.

If it is acknowledged that power and beauty can also be factors that make people attractive and that can be experienced as erotic, then the symbolism of eroticism and romantic love is interwoven with many more types of jewellery. Jewellery can act as a compensation for sexual favours. As such they can be seen as a trophy, with all its erotic implications.

Garments can cover the body or at least parts of the body, while jewellery accentuates them and attracts attention to bare parts of the body. It is very easy to link clothing to covering and decoration, and the piece of jewellery only to the latter need. However, that would be too simple. Rather, morality was presented as a psychologically motivated motif, but this norm also has a lot to do with religious and other culturally determined notions about covering the body. In general, it is already difficult to distinguish between psychological and religious motives, and that is especially true when it comes to ingrained customs. Jewellery, however, can very well be used to suggest chastity, such as a pin on a high-necked neck and the wedding ring as a signal to no longer expect attentions from the opposite sex. In many cultures, pearls stand for purity, virginity and marital fidelity – values that especially with women should be symbolised as a guarantee for pure bloodlines. And it is not surprising that many religious symbols, such as the cross or the hand of Fatima, have a moral radiance. This is symbolism, and in such signs of morality it also comes close to the third fundamental motive, namely the need for protection. The fact that it is not so much a question of protection from the cold as of the search for security within a religion or community does not detract from this underlying principle. all fundamental motives for wearing clothes have their counterpart in the world of jewellery.

6.3 Remembrance or memento

Although the underlying motifs for wearing jewellery are involved in all the symbolic meanings that jewellery can contain, there is one that covers most of the meanings in jewellery: remembrance or memento. Remembrance does not only have to do with the forms and symbolism that the maker incorporates in his jewellery, but also with the meaning that the wearer and the viewer give to it. Remembrance also stands for conventions, for forms and customs that turn out to be ineradicable; this is an inseparable aspect of the jewel as a token of power, religious conviction, social position or sign of love. Its function as memento involves three different frames of reference:

1 Conventional metaphors and references – Common at a given time and place, they may have originated in social relationships and customs or in the local flora and fauna. The question must be asked to what extent they were recognised in their own time and by whom: by broad sections of the population or only by a handful of initiates. Sometimes some of this is recorded in heraldry, folk art or religion. In the introduction to his treatise on jewellery in India, Untracht states: 'Rarely is an Indian traditional ornament simply decorative and devoid of inherent meaning or symbolic value. The ability to create and use symbols is a uniquely human characteristic. Symbols found in traditional Indian jewellery act as a metaphorical language communicated from the wearer to the viewer. (...) The highly evolved semiotic symbolism of traditional Indian jewellery may relate either to popular magic or theological metaphysics, both of which involve the general concepts, concerns, aspirations, and fears shared by the entire populace'. He refers to a general awareness of the symbolism in jewellery and other artefacts. It is interesting to note that Untracht states that this symbolism is also recognised by broad layers of the population in a very large country. Probably it exists in every culture, but it has not always been well researched and certainly not as far as the symbolism in jewellery is concerned. (195)

2 Symbolism that the maker has placed in his work – This can be done on commission, as is often the case with precious jewellery. Almost without exception, these are variants of conventional jewellery shapes. As mentioned before, the making of such pieces rarely involves taking risks. The book *Artists' Jewellery. Pre-Raphaelite to Arts and Crafts* (1989) by Charlotte Gere and Geoffrey Munn proves that a close collaboration between artist, jeweller and client can lead to interesting pieces. Work made by individual jewellery designers at the request of a client can also include very interesting pieces in terms of design, as evidenced by work by Truike Verdegaal, Ted Noten and others. (196) By interpreting existing forms, a designer may add new symbolism to a piece of jewellery.

In jewellery as a form of personal expression of the maker, symbolism can be interpreted as the sum of the visual means used to give shape to an idea. The use of colours, materials, figurative or non-figurative forms and especially the combination of these visual means can be seen as a reflection of the maker's personal experience. In the international arena in which this work is common, it is now customary to express the most intimate and personal thoughts in the work, which stretches the range of symbolic meanings indefinitely. But even if this work is based on personal experience and is presented on the basis of artistic freedom, it is still intended to be understood in one way or another, even if only by a few or a buyer who recognises something in it and can relate to it.

When jewellery is produced in series, the manufacturers and their designers have to empathise with the taste of their target group and respond to the desires with which it is living. They have to package these desires into small, wearable objects and also work a lot with symbolism.

3 Personal associations and memories of the bearer and the viewer – In addition to the two preceding types of meaning, there are personal associations and memories of the wearer and the beholder. Jewellery is often given as a gift – also as inheritance – and then it may reflect the reason for giving it or the moment at which it is received. When people buy jewellery for themselves, they are usually motivated to do so for a specific reason or particular association with the object involved.

What gives coherence to all these forms of symbolism is the persistence of conventions. Forms that have stood the test of time and that are often used, as well as forms that evoke trust and other emotions but whose original meaning is often no longer known and merely can be guessed. In her retrospective work *Sieraden van de late 18e tot de vroege 20e eeuw* (Jewellery from the late 18th to the early 20th century, 1980), L. Dewiel pays explicit attention to remembrance jewellery from the 19th century. She mentions, among other things, hair jewellery – jewellery in which hair of a loved one or deceased person is incorporated – and jewellery as souvenirs of travels, such as the Roman brooches with micro-mosaic. Dewiel presents Alexandra, the wife of Tsar Nicholas I, as a high-ranking lover of jewellery as mementoes. Alexandra had a preference for bracelets which, because of the personal memories attached to them, fulfilled the function of diaries for her; she eventually owned about five hundred of them. Her physician Martin Mandt described her as follows: The czarina preferred to alternate her outfits with her bracelets; one often sees her thinking about the five boxes in which they are stored, in order to read the richly written pages from the book of the past in her mind again. (197) Sometimes the word souvenir is literally used in jewellery. A beautiful example is a bracelet from around 1800 with letters made of diamonds on a background of blue enamel. (198)

In the Museum of Modern Art in Arnhem, a small jewellery exhibition was shown in 2008 under the title 'Irreplaceable. Jewellery and Memories'. This is a good example of an exhibition that focuses on an important aspect of jewellery, but its interpretation is not hindered by the common notion that only the 'best' pieces should be shown in a museum exhibition. The emotional aspects and the nature of the memories were suggested by simple means. (199)

There is another reason to link the concept of remembrance to jewellery. In the manufacture of new pieces, debris from the history of the profession are even literally processed on the basis of the continuous reuse of gold, stones and other materials, into whole parts of jewellery. The appreciation of authentic jewels from history, until ancient times, has always led to a lively production of forgeries. Good illustrations of historical artefacts, for example in ornamental example books, facilitated these practices. The number of forgeries in circulation can only be guessed. (200)

As far as the contemplation of jewellery is concerned, the symbolism of jewellery is a popular starting point for writers, journalists and others interested in jewellery. This could even be called a fourth frame of reference, because their own memories, background and sense of standards determine how they will think or write about this subject and this sets them apart from other wearers.

With remembrance as an important connecting factor in the symbolism of jewellery, it can be said that in addition to the primary motives for wearing jewellery, the need of people to relate their existence to those who live before, with and after them, could be seen as a primary need as well. It could be seen as an exponent of the desire for security, but this goes further and touches on questions regarding human existence. In this age of globalisation and political, economic and ecological threats, the need to reflect on one's own identity may be greater than in other times, but it is essentially something of all times. Anne Richter describes this function of jewellery as follows in the introduction to her book on jewellery from South-East Asia: 'In some Southeast Asian societies, an item of jewellery may represent the universe in microcosmic form and express complex human relations with the supernatural realm. Jewellery may also articulate links with the ancestors, and serve to define and regulate the social interactions of the living'. (201)

That jewellery is pre-eminently suited to be a memento is one of the reasons to take the history of jewellery seriously, because this aspect may also enrich other disciplines, such as cultural history or other human sciences. Literary works and sources from iconography, psychology and sociology can significantly increase our understanding of the interaction between jewellery and memory.

Conclusions

Symbolism in jewellery is an inexhaustible subject. It concerns jewellery as an attribute, as a form of protection and above all as a means of identity marking. This aspect can be approached from many different angles. Symbolism in jewellery says a lot about norms and values in a society, about trade relations and room for expressions of an artistic nature.

Power is one of those angles. It is short-sighted to focus power mainly on vertical relationships in a society and to analyse the history of jewellery by means of the most spectacular jewellery. Power and the accentuation of one's own person can also be expressed in subtle signs, which function in the mutual contact between people from the same social group and which say at least as much about their time.

With its long tradition, its combination of symbolism and conventions, and its role in our outward appearance, jewellery offers both very explicit and subtle possibilities to stake out our identity. The pursuit of physical protection and sexual connotations are symbolic aspects of jewellery that relate to the human body.

Most of the meanings associated with jewellery are tied to some form of memory or memento. This has to do with traditional symbols and conventions in wearing, with the symbolism that makers put into their work and especially with the memories that wearers attach to their jewellery items. All of this has to do with elementary human needs for identity and security. Jewellery as memento comprises a rich treasure trove of forms and artefacts, including conscious or unconscious associations triggered by a simple item such as a wedding ring. It involves a vocabulary that makers, wearers and beholders alike use and constantly enrich. This is why it is highly productive to rely on a broad spectrum of disciplines and perspectives to identify and study the role of memory in jewellery.

7 Evaluation

7.1 Five values

The definition of jewellery that served as the basis for my argument in this essay is universal. Although originally formulated in Dutch, it is not limited to any cultural, geographical or historical framework. In this study I examined the tension between the intimacy and the scope of jewellery, as well as the various symbolic meanings and temptations of individual pieces of jewellery.

The definition of a category of objects should basically be free of value judgements. My definition proved to be a useful foundation for analysing a number of prejudices – which may vary over time and from one culture to the next – echoed in many publications about jewellery. A combination of developments led to the emergence of several improper, incorrect or unproductive assumptions in the study of jewellery, including the notions that men do not actually wear jewellery, that the most important function of a piece of jewellery is to enhance the beauty of women and, above all, that valuable jewellery and masterpieces of individual designers as expressions of a financial and cultural position of power deserve the most attention (a common view in art history).

After this analysis, we can answer the question of from what it is that jewellery derives its value and, in conjunction with this, the question of which particular jewellery qualifies for serious study. (202)

Above the entrance to the noble Victoria & Albert Museum in London, a museum of great reputation for the applied arts, stands in gilded, sans-serif capitals above the Neo-Romanesque entrance: *The excellence / of every / art / must consist / in the / complete / accomplishment / of its / purpose*. This facade, designed by Aston Webb, replaced an older entrance. The construction of the facade began in 1899 and the text was one of the last parts to be made. The statement had to apply to all the disciplines collected and exhibited in this prestigious museum, including jewellery. The statement leaves nothing to be desired in terms of clarity.

A good example of a recent and equally principled approach, and this time specifically with regard to jewellery, is provided by the English specialists in the field of applied arts or crafts, Peter Dormer and Ralph Turner, in the adapted version of their standard work, *The new jewellery, trends + traditions* (1994). As the opening line reads: 'Jewellery is a decorative art and what matters is not the words that can be coined from it, but whether or not it gives pleasure to the wearer and the spectator'. With this thesis they indicate to be aware of the discourse according to which products of applied art or design can have such a visual quality that they may be called 'art'. Dormer and Turner, however, embrace another starting point: 'It should be an obvious enough point that jewellery is for wearing', even though this is 'perhaps not that obvious'. (203)

The starting point for determining the values that jewellery can represent is to be found in the purpose of wearing it. On the basis of the research reported here, it is possible to answer the question of why people wear jewellery. The most important reasons are:

- to decorate one's body as a basic need;
- to protect oneself and one's loved ones from evil of any kind;
- to keep one's wealth close to the skin and at the same time make it visible;
- to make one's identity, social status and beliefs known to others;
- to remember where one comes from and with whom one is connected.

Being an added value, jewellery should be placed in the context of all the factors that determine the outward appearance of people. It is therefore a physical, social, historical, cultural and economic phenomenon, as well as an individual and psychological phenomenon.

Based on the conclusions of this study, five different values can be assigned to pieces of jewellery as individual objects. These abstractions can easily be rendered concrete in specific examples:

- ***artistic value or visual quality***
- ***historical value***
- ***social value, jewellery as a means of identity marking***
- ***personal and emotional value***
- ***material and monetary value***

These five values are not incompatible with each other. On the contrary, even fairly small objects such as jewellery may comprise many different messages, including contradictory ones. The sum total of values expressed, then, is potentially marked by all sorts of confusing and even dubious messages, as well as a highly productive interplay amongst them.

7.2 Explanatory notes

Artistic value or visual quality – In an art historical treatise, the artistic value or visual quality of some artefact comes first, and rightly so, as argued in section 3.1. This can be determined according to a tried and tested method: art historical analysis. A piece of jewellery can just as well be judged on its art historical merits as a piece of furniture or a work of art.

Formal analysis of works of art and design will always have to start in careful observation. What is the material, the applied technique, the format, the function? What does the resulting artefact amount to? Is it in fact something? In the case of jewellery, it is always about specific expertise in materials and techniques, as well a specific insight, such as regarding proper estimations of the effect of the jewellery on a body and, if necessary, also in connection with clothing and other body decorations. In most cases it is possible to identify these various aspects quite quickly, which is followed by analysis of visual aspects such as line, form, colour, spatiality, structure, texture, rhythm in repetitive elements and, of course, the composition or arrangement of these aspects. All of these elements will also be subject to quality judgement as reflected in words such as beautiful, balanced, exciting, rich in contrast, and so on. Such qualifications are never fully objective, of course.

This is followed by analysis of content-related aspects: is there a meaning behind the object? Are there any relevant or underlying cultural or historical backgrounds? Are there other starting points? Information about the maker can be presented, as far as it is known. Does the work bear a personal signature, and if so, what does it consist of? When a great deal of information is available, the work can be situated within the development of an oeuvre. The work may also be placed in the context of its time, place of origin and specific political and social data, but other parameters may be relevant as well, such as religion, literature and other cultural expressions. With respect to jewellery, the conventional art historical gaze may be inclined to put too much emphasis on the need for innovation. At the same time, the desire to make something that is new is an elementary human drive and as such it applies to jewellery as a cultural expression as well. Furthermore, art historians will customarily address the role of the person who commissioned a work (if applicable), in particular in the case of large buildings, private homes or monumental works of art. For works produced in series or in bulk, other criteria may be applied as well, such as production-technical and market-related standards.

Subsequently, one will seek to combine the results of the formal analysis and the content analysis, as a basis for a qualitative assessment of the art historical value of a work of art. This effort is never either fully subjective or fully objective, but always somewhere in between the two, also because the systematic study of the various elements more or less automatically generates some level of objectivity. The artistic value is determined by the relationship between the design, the motives behind the creation of an object and the maker's skill and expressiveness. Sometimes the visual quality of jewellery is determined by a novelty, a product of nature or of human ability, and the creator of the jewellery has been wise enough not to drown it out.

The visual quality or artistic value of a piece of jewellery directly pertains to a basic reason for wearing jewellery: the need for decoration. This is why it is logical to consider jewellery as part of the decorative arts, regardless of developments in art history and art appreciation. A piece of jewellery is and remains a wearable ornament. The attraction of a piece may have to do with beauty, but not necessarily. Its visual quality is based on good proportions, on the right size in relation to the human body, on the temptation of colour and the immersion of the total form and all its references, while a peculiar annoyance in all of this can do miracles as well. Its visual appeal, however, may also lie in very different things, such as motifs and symbols, or in more personal concerns relevant to the beholder or wearer.

The art historical analysis of works of art and design can serve as a starting point for a value judgement on jewellery, without the accumulated prejudices that are exposed in this essay. Crucial to this are a more nuanced approach to all the social and personal values that can be attached to jewellery and more attention to traditions and signs of social coherence than has hitherto been customary in the study of jewellery.

Historical value – With the aid of art historical analysis, one cannot only identify the visual quality or artistic value of a piece of jewellery, but one can also begin to determine its historical value. After all, art history is a form of historiography. A piece of jewellery gains in historical value if its wearer is known and if, for example, data are available on how the piece of jewellery was worn. In the history of jewellery, most attention has so far been paid to the rich ornamentation of the most powerful figures in history. The changing relationships between secular and ecclesiastical power deserve extra attention in this context. In the course of the history of jewellery, religion in general – and, certainly, Christian religion – has left clear traces in jewellery design and symbolism and in the standards with regard to wearing jewellery. The hierarchies within the church have long weighed heavily and they are made visible in ornaments and attributes. Inversely, many a world ruler also decorated himself with religious symbols.

But to consider ornaments mainly as tokens of power is too one-sided an approach, one that needs to be rectified. In anthropology, ethnology or material culture studies, it is customary to differentiate jewellery according to social position, material value and other traditional or religious motives, and to refer, for example, to trade routes and the way in which materials, motives and the artefacts involved have migrated around the world. Often, attention is also paid to social status, the maker's economic position and, above all, those who purchase their work, and thus to the motives of large groups to wear jewellery within a particular society. Linking art historical analysis to the methods of ethnology or material culture, by paying serious attention to all the jewellery and fragments of jewellery ascribed to a particular time period, may provide many new insights into the history and study of western jewellery.

Jewellery is a crucial tool for people in marking their identity and presenting themselves to each other. People deploy jewellery to emphasise both their bond and their differences with others. To gain a better understanding of this cultural practice, more attention must be paid to the study of tradition and its interrelated factors, particularly regarding western jewellery, also as a way to move beyond the current preoccupation with individuality. This applies just as much to historical pieces of jewellery as to contemporary works.

Research in art history tends to focus on work by the great masters as basic standard for dating and situating the work of the lesser gods as well. This approach can also be seen regarding jewellery, whereby particular pieces of jewellery are easily dismissed as being not so precious, of lesser value or even as fake. The latter qualification, I believe, is a misconception that has been a quiet characteristic of the overall approach to jewellery so far. Every object considered a piece of jewellery is 'real', whether it is made of shells, scraps of textile or white gold with diamonds and sapphires. Accordingly, even fake jewellery, as an imitation of its valuable counterpart, is real jewellery. (204)

As historical artefacts, jewellery made of any material can be a key to a better understanding of the time and culture to which they bear witness. Why do we consider certain historical pieces as characteristic for some region, social group, culture or time-frame? This is only possible if they contain something that at the time had a broader validity than the individual tastes of certain ladies or gentlemen, no matter how leading their position may have been. The creators of this jewellery must somehow have touched on something that was in keeping with larger developments of which more people wanted to be part.

Social value, jewellery as a means of identity marking. – This pertains to the value of jewellery as a social factor and as a means of identity marking. So far, this value has not been sufficiently addressed in the literature on jewellery. Most of the critical conclusions from my research are directly or indirectly concerned with this social dimension of jewellery.

On the basis of all the characteristics and meanings of jewellery reviewed so far, it can be said that the human body defines the kind of jewellery we wear. Yet physical inconvenience is not always a decisive factor. Wearing heavy jewellery may be uncomfortable or even painful, but the same can be true of applying body-linked decorations, a laborious hairstyle or certain garments. The most important criterion, then, is that people want to wear a particular piece of jewellery. A piece of jewellery has value when it appeals to a specific desire to wear it to which people also attach a particular value, which potentially is recognised by others and perhaps even shared by others.

In order to determine the social value of a piece of jewellery, several underlying motives for its wearing are potentially relevant as well, such as the need for decoration or its rejection, the search for protection, the manifestation of power, and above all, the accentuation of one's identity and compliance with the norms of the groups to which one wishes to belong. These primary motives cover an entire spectrum of values and these are rarely mutually exclusive. The basic angles for interpreting these various meanings are derived from sociology, psychology, anthropology, philosophy and religion, but cultural expressions from the worlds of film, theatre and literature, theatre and film may be invoked as well.

A great quality of jewellery is that it can be used to emphasise one's identity and play a role in mutual relationships between people, both in horizontal as well as vertical and diagonal social relationships. A piece of jewellery can also be deployed to challenge or undermine existing social relationships. It shares this quality with clothing, fashion and body-linked decorations which have been studied more intensively than jewellery, and these studies may be consulted to see if they can contribute to determining the social values of jewellery. In this age of globalization, the issue of identity has become subject to fierce debates, but jewellery has always served as an identity marker.

The maker of a piece of jewellery provides it with a more or less artistic identity of its own, but, as mentioned above, in a more figurative sense a wearer can make or break a piece. As such, its identity can be looked at as a negotiation between maker and wearer, while it should also be understood in the context of social, cultural and historical developments. Conventions thereby play a crucial role. One of the conclusions of this research is that, when studying jewellery, more attention should be paid to the constants and that one should not only focus on innovation. In addition, in terms of shape, size, colour, and other aspects, a piece of jewellery should always be held up against its relationship to the human body, which, in principle, is also a constant.

The social value of jewellery lies in its symbolic value and the way in which people use jewellery, clothing, hairstyles and other forms of decoration to determine their outward appearance. But this symbolism can also be inward-looking and rather relate to the personal and emotional values that people attach to their jewellery. These two sides are not mutually exclusive; on the contrary, they can reinforce each other.

On closer inspection, social aspects of jewellery actually belong to the art historical analysis of objects, as is true of emotional values. But so far, too much emphasis has been placed on jewellery's monetary value, artistic quality, as well as on the jewel as part of the history of style and as historical artefact or *petit histoire*.

Two major criteria regarding the social value of jewellery are validity and accuracy. Validity means that a symbolic value is recognised and shared. Accuracy goes even further: as with the historical value of a piece of jewellery, its social value can be accurately expressed in a way that it can serve as a key to analysing social and historical developments. Some jewellery items, understood as an ensemble of meanings, may well reflect particular broader developments and even serve as accurate embodiments of them, if not symbols. Regardless of whether people shape their time or are being shaped by it, it is important to understood that everything is being shaped, a construction. Accuracy in the social and symbolic value of a piece of jewellery means that a piece of jewellery can be a concentrated form to convey a message or evoke a feeling. A piece of jewellery can create clarity and make lucid statements about complex social processes, all the more so because it is a wearable and fairly small object. This can be done in a single piece, but also be a characteristic of whole category of items generated at a particular time. In the latter case, it is relevant to ask – as common in art history – who was the first to create it and, subsequently, who made it possible for so many people to wear such a piece of jewellery.

The meanings contained in jewellery are so diverse that it is impossible to list them all, yet it is possible to classify them in groups. But, obviously, some meanings will outweigh others, and there are also despicable meanings that can be harmful or even damaging to people. That is why the quality of a meaning counts in determining the social value of a piece of jewellery, for example when involving social or political issues worth fighting for. From a historical point of view, however, it is interesting and important to study manifestations of a despicable mentality.

Personal and emotional value – These values are easiest to define as a category, as well as most difficult to subject to a value judgement. As subjective, personal and emotional norms, they quickly withdraw from quantifiable values, but that doesn't make them any less important. The best source of insight into personal and emotional values that can be associated with jewellery is literature and, for recent times, also film, television and other media.

This subjectivity is partly a matter of time. Fifty years or more after the creation of a piece of jewellery, such subjective values are usually lost in oblivion, unless they are linked not only to a personal memory but also to a fact of historical importance. In addition, new emotional values can be attached to a piece of jewellery. One of the qualities that deserves special attention in the emotional valuation of a piece of jewellery is its role as a simple expression of pleasure in a decorative accent. In this respect, basic jewellery such as beaded necklaces or smooth bracelets have the great quality that they can easily be fitted into how people dress and behave. This also has to do with the tactile qualities of such jewellery. Such simple pieces are given little or no attention in publications about jewellery, and when they are mentioned at all, they are often vilified. The pearl necklace, for example, is a favourite target for individual designers from the gallery circuit. But it is also a cornerstone of the jewellery trade and has been one for centuries, in the Netherlands and elsewhere. (205)

Such archetypical forms of jewellery and universal decorations, such as natural and geometric forms, should never be overlooked when considering jewellery. Nor should they, as cheerful accents in people's overall appearance, be despised at all. Simplicity and a certain neutrality can prove their worth on personal grounds, but also from a social point of view. The need to belong to something (larger) is often far greater than the urge to be an exception. This much is evident from the indestructible popularity of these age-old symbols of social cohesion. Simple jewellery also offers all kinds of possibilities for some distinction, even if this is only in the clasp of a necklace or in a small engraving on the inside of a smooth gold ring or bracelet.

In contrast to this equally elementary and universal social need for affirmation, there is the unmistakable quality of the romanticism of jewellery: a piece of jewellery can very well symbolise something of which one knows that one will never own it, but this is precisely why it is so seductive. This concerns the unattainable, in a material sense, or the elusive, in a figurative sense.

This applies to the temptation of the grande parure, including the tiara, which we will never have the opportunity to wear but which we would still like to own. This applies to the protection and magic sought after in religious and mythical symbols or to the glass slipper from Cinderella's fairy tale, which fits no one but her. The romance of the jewel is also found in exotic ornaments, which have travelled the world as a small and wearable part of a culture and which one can wear without really being able to grasp its meaning. Sometimes the unattainable in a piece of jewellery still seems to be almost within reach and that makes some pieces very valuable from a personal point of view.

As a memento, jewellery represents all the emotional values and personal memories kept alive by it. A piece of jewellery can symbolise the happiness of a moment or the memory of a whole life, and one does not have to weigh more than the other. The range of emotions and experiences that can be bundled in a piece of jewellery is endless. Again, this is often about continuity in the profession, about conventions that can be given new meanings, but which essentially are unchangeable.

Material and monetary value – Despite its ambiguities, monetary or financial value is an unavoidable and interesting aspect of the valuation of jewellery. In practice, this value, measured by the precious metal and precious stones used, is usually the first point of reference when considering a piece of jewellery. Jewel lery has even functioned as money. But because the range of materials for jewellery is much greater than these raw materials, because there are many more and very different values that can be attributed to all these materials and especially because all these different material values constitute the sum total of the four preceding aspects of jewellery, this is the last to be considered.

Judging jewellery purely by its market value would be appropriate perhaps in a society completely determined by the status of its economy and the value of its money. From this point of view, jewellery can be seen as a symbol of the human need for luxury and appearance, and as a nest egg for bad times. Yet this would amount to a one-sided approach to jewellery, suitable at best for jewellery made of precious metal and/or precious stones.

Establishing the market value does not seem to be a problem for this expensive category. In principle, this is the day's rate of the metal and/or stones applied, or the so-called 'scrap value'. A piece of jewellery is placed on the scales, the precious metal is weighed, the stones are valued and especially for diamonds this is done very precisely on the 4 c's: carat, clarity, cut and colour, which refer to weight, clarity, polish and colour intensity. (206) The sum is the scrap value, which provides a perfect appraisal of the material value of a piece of jewellery. However, this is an approach that will hardly satisfy lovers of jewellery and, moreover, it is inadequate. A jewel with a historical value and a well-designed piece of a renowned jeweller's house will yield much more than the scrap value. And there are also jewellery items to which people are so attached that they would never want to sell them. (207)

No matter how intangible many of the values that can be attributed to a piece of jewellery may be, a piece of jewellery is always a material object. Jewellery can be made of a wide array of raw materials. Often, they are also realised with respectable craftsmanship. In the course of the long history of jewellery, all kinds of meanings have been attributed to these raw materials. Many books on jewellery elaborate on medicinal values and mythical qualities attributed to stones or animal materials. This craftsmanship may have gained mythical proportions, for example in the Greek god Hephaistos, who was called Vulcan in the Roman world of gods. In many religions, silversmiths have their patron gods, such as Saint Eligius in Christianity. The names of great silversmiths from history are also used as quality standards, such as Benvenuto Cellini and René Lalique.

As regards the material and financial aspects of jewellery, it is important to devote more attention to jewellery as consumer product, as argued in section 5.4.4. From a western perspective, it is worthwhile to study jewellery as an economic factor in non-western countries, where jewellery features more often as a means of exchange, which underlines the importance of jewellery within a social group or culture. This also includes excesses such as child labour, degrading labour conditions in gold mines and the corruption and war violence fuelled by the trade in blood diamonds.

Jewels are tangible objects and the material quality should not only be linked to the financial value of the materials used, but should also be involved in all the meanings and forces that creators and wearers have attributed to these materials. One does not have to believe in magic and spirits to admit that whole nations do assign spiritual powers or a protective effect to materials and symbols. The values attributed to the material aspects of jewellery range from pure magic to subtle and diverse forms of sensorial pleasure. (208) All tactile qualities are best judged in natura, and when this is not possible, they can still be judged from many different perspectives.

7.3 Quality assessment

Frans Leidelmeijer, the renowned Dutch specialist in Art Nouveau and Art Deco, once told me that quality will always prevail. (209) After all, one will never throw away any good pieces. If they are sold for little money, there is always another owner who trades them for more, until they end up in a top collection. This may be true, but in practice, interesting jewellery of little material value, but which may have been meaningful when it was made, will actually slip through the cracks of this commercial network.

Of all the bead necklaces shown at the exhibition 'The Woman' in 1913, not a single documented specimen has been found, not even on the basis of Marjan Groot's thorough research of sources for her *Vrouwen in de vormgeving 1880–1940* (Women in design 1880–1940). However, such bead necklaces do have a historical value, are typical of their time and are probably well designed and worn with pleasure. Pieces in precious metal tend to be marked, but other jewellery, such as bead necklaces, is generally not. This means that the first owner may have been aware of the qualities of a piece in financial, cultural and emotional terms, but that this knowledge is bound to vanish at one point.

Quality is not a one-dimensional, universal or timeless concept. When making a quality judgement about a piece of jewellery, you have to deal with a number of dimensions of the concept of quality that are related to the five values that can be attributed to the piece of jewellery. They are also dependent on the specific purpose of such judgement. The quality to which Leidelmeijer referred was probably the type of quality he was looking for as an art dealer. Any quality judgement will be subject to preconceptions. In my argument, I have uncovered a number of them with regard to jewellery and its wearing. What is the best way to neutralise the corruptive effect of this?

7.3.1 Rehabilitation of 'inconspicuous' jewellery

The most important condition for making a nuanced quality judgement is that the gaps in the historiography of a piece of jewellery must first be filled in. As far as historical material is concerned, it is of great importance that the social status of historical jewellery is better differentiated in vertical, horizontal and diagonal relationships, and that not only upper-class forms of adornment are considered, but also those of other social groups. Throughout my discourse, as will be clear, social values associated with jewellery play an important role.

When it comes to the study and presentation of historical pieces in a museum context, for example, preference will always be given to well-designed pieces. But as soon as the social status of jewellery is taken into consideration, it proves to be incredibly interesting to consider these commonly small items on the basis of all sorts of other values they comprise and that are not always easily noticed.

As an object of study, jewellery is vulnerable because it is usually possible to encounter modest and even unsightly specimens everywhere in everyday life. This means that their intimacy can be violated, especially in our time, in which immodesty seems to have become the norm and the private domain is under pressure. As a result, such jewellery can easily be condemned on the basis of all kinds of arbitrary criteria, such as its financial value, its design or the way in which it is worn. It can cause moments of discomfort for the wearer, but, more importantly, pieces that may seem insignificant at first glance can still represent beautiful meanings.

When jewellery is considered purely from a traditional and elitist art historical point of view, the inconspicuous pieces tend to be swiftly dismissed, despite all the traditions and emotional values they potentially represent. Pieces that are immediately noticeable in everyday life can be seen as expressions of a desire for validity and confirmation of a cultural or social status, but they may just as well show a large dose of elementary decorative desire or simply pleasure in life. Precisely because jewellery is so close to people's skin and can be linked to all kinds of personal and emotional values, they are vulnerable to being misjudged and misinterpreted.

Unobtrusive pieces in terms of design can sometimes have a great social, historical or religious value. Take rosaries or other prayer cords: simple beaded necklaces that form a tangible connection between the earthly and the sublime. Moreover, it is not productive for the study of jewellery simply to replace financial value as highest standard by cultural and artistic value, and to approach all jewellery from this elitist perspective. Thus one remains trapped in vertical relationships, while quality may well be found in all kinds of other aspects.

7.3.2 More attention for conventions and the role of the wearer

Many in art history and criticism will initially focus on the maker and the time in which a piece of jewellery was made. The drawback of this take is that the value of a piece will immediately be linked to the strong works representative of a certain period, causing changes in time to become the most important criterion. But many pieces of jewellery are in fact meant to stand the test of time on other grounds. An important characteristic of jewellery is that, in principle, it is about sustainable products: they are not thrown away, except for the more transient and ephemeral ornaments. They are made or purchased at some point to symbolise some private concern, but in most cases they will have a broader validity. Another approach to jewellery is to take this sustainability into account and to pay more attention to the continuity and recognisability of the design and all its symbolism.

It is questionable whether there will ever be a proper balance between the two approaches. Without wanting to limit the attention and appreciation for the makers, it is also time to look more closely and less prejudiced at the role of the wearer and especially the number of wearers in studying jewellery. Jewellery is a means for people to express their identity, and this applies as much to men as it does to women. Moreover, it also applies to children, regardless of whether they themselves express a need for it or whether they are a vehicle for the identity imposed on them by their parents. The current approach to jewellery as a means of emphasising individuality should, as a far too one-sided approach, be replaced by an approach with more attention to traditions and to jewellery as a sign of social, political and religious coherence. It is of crucial importance that jewellery is examined in the context of cultural, social, economic and, for example, medical developments. Memento serving as one of the important functions of jewellery, individual items must also be tested against traditions and the longitudinal waves that characterise many cultural developments.

7.3.3 A matter of numbers

When studying jewellery and other utilitarian objects, one should determine when they were made, for whom they were intended and whether they developed into a much-imitated fashion, which may certainly be called a quality. It is a big difference, especially in our day and age, whether a product needs to find a single person to buy it, a group of people, or a mass of people. In the latter case, success depends on a correct assessment of the general developments in fashion and taste, finding an effective form for it and being able to produce and market it at the right price. Timing is of crucial importance. By anticipating the direction of the interest of the general public correctly but being a bit too early in bringing a product on the market, one will get stuck with unsold products and the competitors, who are just in time, will earn all the profits. In this part of the market, trend sensitivity and commercial insight are golden.

For a proper study of jewellery, it is therefore necessary to determine when dealing with a particular ring or bracelet whether it is produced as a unique piece, as part of a small series or as a bulk item. If this is normally not a large problem regarding contemporary work, it may be more difficult regarding historical pieces. How do you know if a certain brooch is a unique piece or part of a series? Although technical issues, such as whether or not moulds were used in their production, may provide a partial answer, this does not say much yet about the quantity produced and the popularity of such a piece or type of jewellery. Sometimes company archives that have been preserved are useful in this context.

For many periods in the history of jewellery it is not possible to establish what was popular at a certain time, because both the jewellery itself and the data on this mass market product are missing. It is very well possible that jewellery items which are currently shown as unique pieces in a museum were hardly considered special in their own time. But such pieces can still be worth studying, and they may even be highly representative for the time to which they belong on the basis of their broad acceptance. More attention for jewellery as consumer product in both the past and the present will broaden the overall level of scholarship on jewellery and, accordingly, increase our understanding.

When determining the quality of a piece of jewellery, numbers always come into play. Jewellery is mostly understood as involving unique pieces that can accentuate the physical and personality of the individual wearer. Most jewellery was probably made in series, potentially involving imitations of older models, and produced mechanically or industrially (in the case of work from the nineteenth and twentieth centuries). Attention to numbers is not only useful to recognise exceptional quality in design, but also to identify dominant conventions and traditions within the jewellery trade. Such patterns of what is most common may serve as a key to insights into fields beyond the world of art and design. Linking insights from various disciplines can in turn provide more knowledge about the meanings of such ornaments.

In the contemporary study of jewellery, the intimate has been elevated to the norm, which more or less directly pertains to the buyers' or wearers' need to accentuate the uniqueness of their personality through a piece of jewellery. But this should not become a retroactive criterion on the basis of which the entire history of jewellery is analysed and described. Artistic quality can be defined reasonably well on the basis of an art historical analysis, but numbers are also necessary to recognise exceptional qualities in the design of a piece of jewellery. Connoisseurs have been trained to look with their eyes at overcrowded display windows of jewellers, antique dealers, trade fair stands or display cases of auction houses, hoping to spot anything 'interesting' about the design of a piece of jewellery. In other words: quantity helps to highlight the special.

Eloquent words by David Hume, from *The Standards of Taste* (1757), are relevant here: 'It is impossible to continue in the practice of contemplating any order of beauty, without being frequently obliged to form comparisons between the several species and degrees of excellence, and estimating their proportions to each other. A man, who has had no opportunity of comparing the different kinds of beauty, is indeed totally unqualified to pronounce an opinion with regard to any object presented to him. By comparison alone we fix the epithets of praise or blame, and learn how to assign the due degree of each.' (210) This view agrees with the perspective of art historian Kenneth Clark in his nice attempt to analyse what a masterpiece is. As he put it in the first sentence of his lecture 'What Is a Masterpiece?', published in 1979: 'Although we may disagree about a theory, the impact of a masterpiece is something about which there is an astonishing degree of unanimity.' (211) The ultimate consequence of Hume's thesis is that as long as there are still clear gaps in the study and historiography of jewellery, no pieces should be dismissed as unimportant.

There are several reasons why it is always useful to try to gain a comprehensive overview of a field as whole, from the reprehensible through the insignificant and the boring middle note to the visual highlights. This is relevant first of all because one needs the ordinary in order to be able to situate the exceptional. Secondly, it is also useful because of the clarifying aspect and the opportunities for linking data and insights to other areas of research. Moreover, according to the law of action and reaction, forms of jewellery neglected for a long time may suddenly return to the spotlight, and then it is certainly a benefit to know their origin. The most important reason, however, is that beautiful meanings can also be contained in insignificant pieces.

7.3.4 Art is not a quality standard

One of the art historical issues relevant to the study of jewellery is the confusion that has arisen in recent decades about the concept of art in relation to jewellery and, above all, about the improper way in which the concept of art has been elevated to a standard of quality. It is undeniable that the dividing lines between the visual and the applied arts or design from the 1960s onwards have been fought as hard as any Balkan border. Artists, scholars and critics from the Netherlands have made a considerable contribution to this by emphatically naming the 'idea' or 'concept' behind the design of a product as a crucial factor in its assessment. This shifted the discussion from decorative to content-related aspects, such as the symbolism in the work and the personal expression of the maker. This was a clever tactic that has continued to cause a stir in recent decades.

Supported by the boom in international interest in products, especially from the work of Dutch furniture designers, and lured by the rapidly rising prices paid for unique products and small series, in line with the proceeds of the work of a select group of artists, the same discussion has recently flared up again. (212) The motivation may be slightly different from a few decades ago, but the underlying principle remains the same, namely that the term 'art' is used as a quality standard.

The view that jewellery should not be considered part of the domain of the fine arts has its origin in art historical traditions. Of course, these traditions may be discarded, but what is gained then? That everything will be called 'art'? Not until the current notions are adjusted as to what is visual art will products of applied art also be called, in short, 'art'. This may take a long time, but until then, the jewellery made by designers and intended to be worn remains just that: jewellery. If they make autonomous work, organise happenings or make installations, they can present their work as fine art and measure themselves against the standards within that discipline. In fact, the same logic applies to jewellery made by visual artists: their jewellery is jewellery, period. This does not yet turn these artists into designers, and their jewellery simply has to be judged as jewellery. (213)

The somewhat uncomfortable symbiosis between the material value of jewellery and the 'artistic' value is not only about fascination with the financial value of gold and precious stones, but also about exemplary functions within a society. It is about both attraction and rejection of luxury goods. The world of jewellery shares this schizophrenia somewhat with the world of fashion, but not with the fine arts. The quality of the paint used by a painter is seldom included in a description of his work. A beautiful piece of marble and a solid weight of bronze represent a material value, but the appreciation of a work of art is in principle independent of its material value, with Damien Hirst's diamond-encrusted skull as the exception that confirms the rule. (214) This is only one of the reasons why the contemplation of jewellery cannot be included in its entirety in the contemplation of art, while it can benefit greatly from recent developments in the study of fashion.

This whole discussion does not at all detract from the fact that a piece of jewellery is intended to be worn on the body, as a form of decoration. This means that a piece of jewellery must be considered to be an item of applied arts or design. Jewellery with an outspoken artistic charge can claim its own domain within the jewellery trade, but that does not mean that it automatically belongs in the domain of the visual arts as well. In short, the concept of art cannot be used as a quality standard. The artistic value and the visual qualities of jewellery can be analysed and rewarded on the basis of standards of its own.

Even though it would be wrong to disqualify pieces of jewellery in advance from what is currently the jewellery tradition as cultural heritage, it is now possible, after having established the five core values, to articulate several overarching criteria on the basis of which a judgement on quality can be made. I would like to derive these criteria from the study of literature. In section 6.3 on remembrance and memento, I discussed literature as a highly useful key to a better understanding of all the values comprised in a piece of jewellery, especially a bundling of memories and with respect to emotional and social aspects.

Two American literary scholars, René Wellek and Austin Warren, courageously attempted in 1949 to develop a general theory of literature, which is still highly regarded within the field of literary studies. In the 'Evaluation' chapter of their *Theory of Literature*, they first state that a value judgement must be based on the nature and purpose of what one wants to judge, in accordance with the quote on the facade of the Victoria & Albert Museum in London. It must do what it is supposed to do, even when involving grand notions such as art or ethics.

They also support the principle of comprehensiveness: 'Our criterion is inclusiveness: "imaginative integratio" and "amount (and diversity) of material integrated"'. Fortunately, the latter is not a reference to the fact that, in the case of jewellery, you always end up with the amount of gold and number of stones used, as Wellek and Warren continue their argument as follows: 'By diversity of materials, we may mean particular ideas, characters, types of social and psychological experience'. This statement can easily be extended to the five most important values of jewellery. (215)

Quality in jewellery can be found in the concentration and interplay of the five different values that can be attributed to jewellery. It is not only about validity, accuracy or symbolism in itself, but also about the way in which they confirm and reinforce each other. And it is not only about comprehensiveness in the sense of 'the more the better', but also about effectiveness. A social value, for example, gains in strength when involving an inexpensive piece of jewellery that has been or can be distributed more widely.

In their evaluation, Wellek and Warren also make a distinction between 'easy' and 'difficult' beauty, a distinction that they trace back to the eighteenth-century discussion about 'the beautiful and the sublime', in which the sublime stands for the 'difficult', which may be regarded as true greatness. The same distinction can be applied to jewellery, with simple charm and familiar forms and materials on the one hand, and the challenge of bold statements on the other. These two extremes, as argued by Wellek and Warren, should also have a more complex dimension expressing a sense of size and validity.

The world of unique, single items, i.e. the jewellery of designers who convey their innermost drive in their work, could be seen as such a stronghold, a territory of their own which they defend at all costs. But the problem here is rather that there are too few people who want to enter that territory, who feel at home there and who are willing to present themselves with all their cultural baggage as role models for other social groups. Nor is it true that other designers and producers are pushing for their ideas to be commercialised. The value of this type of work lies in the exceptional nature of this kind of artefact and in the way in which its creators develop a sustained oeuvre. This should be taken into account in any reflection on jewellery.

However, jewellery from independent designers may be subject to the aforementioned criteria as much as any other piece of jewellery or type of jewellery. The above argument shows that the sublime in jewellery must be sought in the accurate symbolization of what drives people in their lives, not in isolated, self-proclaimed territories. In his analysis of the masterpiece in the visual arts, Kenneth Clark identifies the artist's empathy as a decisive factor: 'The artist must be deeply involved in the understanding of his fellow men'. (216) This invariably applies to the masterpieces of jewellery.

There is a strong tendency to place the highest value on the sublime, but the wearer's greatest pleasure lies more in jewellery as a memento, in the affirmation of oneself and in the simple pleasure of ornament or decoration. It is the designers who focus on a wider audience and align their ideas with other developments in their time who are best able to realise a general validity in their work. These may even be pieces that, regardless of their maker's intention, have become a symbol for an event, a conception, a development in the visual arts or, for example, in fashion. (217)

In my opinion, quality is only real if a piece of jewellery meets the criteria of comprehensiveness and accuracy – if it is not only well-designed and has a certain degree of representativeness for a time or style, but also stands for a view or a specific function of jewellery and thus provides a starting point for the wearer to link his or her own identity and emotions to it. Such values also count for pieces which no longer betray their beauty or the sublime or which may never have had these traits.

Another criterion that I would like to derive from the study of Wellek and Warren is the principle of reciprocity: that one treats things in the same way as one wants to be treated oneself. (218) I would argue, based on this principle, that if one is willing to make jewellery the subject of serious study, one must make clear which qualities one is looking for. This may be monetary or financial value, design or other art historical qualities, or aspects linked to social relations or political claims, but it may just as well be an integral part of a fashion image. A piece of jewellery can derive its value from the fact that it accentuates an attractive part of the body, and that personal associations can thereby play a role. But even if one is looking for some cutting edge or the sublime, the bar should never be set so high that jewellery becomes disconnected from its elementary functions and that one neglects the universal forms and the underlying motives for wearing it, because that is where all the qualities of jewellery can be found.

The various criteria elaborated in this chapter played a role in the selection of the jewellery described and depicted in my study of Dutch jewellery in the twentieth century. But two qualifications are relevant here. First, for the period from 1900 to 1967 there was usually not much to choose from, due to a lack of available pieces and written sources. Secondly, I could only render explicit these considerations with regard to a value judgement about jewellery on the basis of the research for this essay and the conclusions drawn from it. In retrospect, however, it can be concluded that they were decisive for my study's organisation and the choices I made, namely by highlighting as many sides of Dutch jewellery as possible, by providing a context for this and by making the choice of depicted pieces on the basis of both artistic and historical, social, emotional and material values and the way in which these clarify and reinforce each other. As such my study on Dutch jewellery in the twentieth century contains examples of all the values and combinations of values mentioned and explained in this chapter.

8 Conclusion

8.1 Multidisciplinary approach

The aim of this research was to create a theoretical framework for the study of jewellery. This must be a multidisciplinary framework. Jewellery derives its value from a wide variety of characteristics, and their proper study requires insights from a wide range of disciplines in order to arrive at a scholarly, substantiated approach and, in its wake, a deeper understanding.

This discourse has shown that art history is an appropriate basis for the study of jewellery. But it was also argued that input from other disciplines is extremely welcome. For a sound and valid basis of the study of jewellery, it is useful to draw insights from general historiography, psychology, sociology, ethnography, material culture, fashion history and the theory of fashion, medicine, economics, political science and theology.

The specific knowledge of the jewellery profession – such as of the many materials used and their locations (including gemmology), the high quality techniques of goldsmithing and the simple skills such as stringing a good bead necklace, and the laws of hallmarking and the system of marks – have always been part of the study of jewellery and of formulating quality judgements. As with the study of other artefacts, there is an intrinsic tension between scientific or contemplative disciplines and the professional knowledge of their creators and specialists. But this expertise is also part of the package of useful components for the study of jewellery.

The theoretical framework for the contemplation of jewellery presented here is broad – at first sight perhaps too broad. Yet the dangers of benevolent amateurism do not seem to outweigh an overly one-sided approach to jewellery. The other and equally essential conclusion that can be drawn from the above argument is that, in order to consider jewellery, one must first define the subject and distil the crucial questions from it, such as the question of why people wear jewellery, how they wear it and what values can be attributed to jewellery on these grounds – values that include jewellery as a means of identity marking and a sign of social mobility. One does not have to be an accomplished psychologist, sociologist, economist or political scientist in order to have the necessary basis for the study of jewellery. The wisdom in applying this multidisciplinary framework lies in recognising the limitations of the art historical framework, in making use of studies from related disciplines that provide sound overviews and in calling on the specific expertise of experts if further insight is required. Partly on the basis of this follow-up research, this working method can be recognised as having structured the research for my study on Dutch jewellery in the twentieth century.

Another option, which I consider to be the model for the twenty-first century, is the effective cooperation of several people with different backgrounds. It is essential to build one's skills and insights, no matter how specialised they may be, and to use that knowledge to ask the right questions and to enter into a dialogue with other sources of knowledge and insight.

This plea for a multidisciplinary framework for the study of jewellery with art history as the starting point can also serve as a model for the study of other areas of design. The need to include consumer responses to products and the habits of wider segments of the population in this process is also becoming increasingly apparent in the study of graphic design, interiors and furniture and, for example, utilitarian ceramics. This constitutes a rift with the attention traditionally paid to the artistic masterpieces that form the backbone of art history as discipline. The study of fashion is at the forefront of this and informed my argument in useful ways.

This principle is also in line with a much broader development in our time. In just about all academic branches, processes of specialisation have emerged in the course of the last century that have led to in-depth research and interesting insights. This has resulted, however, in an endless archipelago of small islands, on which a handful of specialists all want to be king. One could link this development in science to the process of individualisation, which is described in my study on Dutch jewellery both in a general sense and in a specific sense with regard to the design of this jewellery. Many newspaper articles and scientific publications of the past ten to twenty years have highlighted the need to open up specialisms and to strive to link insights and to make interrelationships. (219)

This brings me to the point of cross-pollination. The advantage of a multidisciplinary approach to jewellery may also be that it offers points of departure with regard to the study of general history, of human interactions, economic processes and religious views – in short, all disciplines that can make an important contribution to a meaningful theoretical framework for jewellery. Such interferences have been used both in archaeology and in the study of material culture. Why, then, should this not be the case for research into other cultural expressions? (220)

Another conclusion from this argument could be that, on the basis of the many points of view covered, one can opt to go in any direction with the study of jewellery. This has happened and why not let it happen – jewellery can take a punch. A personal approach and even an approach that is questionable from a political or moral point of view can still produce new facts and insights. It would be useful, however, if the reader of studies on jewellery are explicitly informed of such approach, rather than that it has to looked for in between the lines.

The final point that must be made in response to this plea for a multidisciplinary approach to jewellery is that art history has indeed provided a wonderful basis for considering jewellery as a strong and ineradicable cultural phenomenon, because this discipline is based on the undivided pleasure in the study of independent objects. The fact that jewellery is not one of the priorities within this discipline does not detract from this. The direct contact with jewellery also gives rise to the right questions regarding the making, wearing and evaluation of jewellery. Art history also provides a historical framework for the history of jewellery and offers a frame of reference for other expressions of culture. All in all, art history constitutes an indispensable basis for understanding the scope of jewellery as a cultural phenomenon, including all its material, social and philosophical implications. And as a true lover of jewellery as a bundle of ornamental and symbolic values, I will forever deeply respect the artistic qualities of artefacts and the fascinating interrelated historical developments, as I was first trained to do during my study of art history.

8.2 The next phase

One of the inevitable paradoxes of a historical discipline is that one always approaches the past from the present. With the results of this essay, the history of jewellery as a cultural heritage can be rewritten, this time on the basis of better differentiated norms and values.

This means that it is high time to shake up the valuable work of my predecessors, to examine it and to reorganise it, based on the combination of partly old and partly new insights from various scientific disciplines. The pitfalls for the approach to jewellery include overly subjective prejudices about the wearing of jewellery, as well as the one-sided focus on the 'most beautiful' examples that history has produced and the equally one-sided focus on the process of innovation, both of which are characteristic of art history as a discipline. Moreover, there is always the danger that a beholder may quickly lose himself in the overwhelming number of manifestations of jewellery, without recognising the constants, the social conventions and the importance of the long traditions in them.

I am aware that also my study marks a moment in the long history of jewellery and stems from circumstances and developments in the present time. In this respect, this contribution to the contemplation of jewellery can be compared to that of the generation of viewers who placed jewellery on a pedestal and also condemned it as belonging exclusively to the domain of women. The aim of this research is to take the contemplation of jewellery to the next level, partly on the basis of the many valuable sub-studies on jewellery that have appeared in recent decades. This phase is characterised by a critical examination of the premises for the study of jewellery with the aid of contemporary insights in the field of the human sciences, the economy, medical insights and changing morals. In short, a reflection on the developments in our own time. This has already happened in fashion and is also in line with the study of material culture. This plea for a multidisciplinary approach to jewellery offers all kinds of starting points for the presentation of jewellery in exhibitions. Angles of incidence from other disciplines can be made visible. This can be done with the aid of other utilitarian objects, such as garments and accessories, with the aid of works of art and other images of people wearing jewellery, or, for example, by showing historical documents, providing social data or information about the symbolism in a piece of jewellery and how it came about. Displaying jewellery is about creating a context in which the quality and scope of the presented piece of jewellery becomes visible, as well as the reasons for displaying it at that moment.

This implies discontinuation of the current approach to jewellery. From the perspective of developing notions in art history, jewellery is usually exhibited as separate objects. In museum installations, jewellery is almost without exception presented as separate objects. One is lucky if a portrait is exhibited in the neighbourhood where one can see how such a piece of jewellery was worn. The same isolation characterises the contemplation and presentation of contemporary work by independent jewellery designers who show their work mainly within the cultural sector. The way of presenting that is customary in the fine arts has so far been the norm. The jewellery is presented on a background that is as neutral as possible, preferably far apart, in order to make each individual piece come into its own. In presentations and museum exhibits by ethnographers, on the other hand, it is customary to show the jewellery in a context, with information about how it was worn and how it relates to other utensils from the environment of the peoples concerned. This reveals some of the basic principles of anthropology, ethnology and material culture as applied to jewellery: jewellery serves as a material link within a culture and as a sign of recognition within social relations.

The assessments that can be made on the basis of this research with regard to the study of historical pieces can also be made for contemporary work. When the five most important values of jewellery are taken into account in the classification of jewellery, which is based on the current system of distribution and interrelated media, it is possible to generate enlightening insights. Jewellery has a very strong material value. Jewellery items have long featured as welcome starting points for individual memories and emotions, but they only become really interesting when their expensive materials are well designed or when they function as a beacon of relevant social phenomena. Jewellery as an expression of contemporary culture does not have the exclusive right to artistic quality, as this may as well be found in fashion jewellery and high jewellery. Fashion jewellery is often dismissed as fake jewellery, but it is a much broader phenomenon. Not all antique pieces are interesting from a historical point of view; they are rather valuable as a personal memento, as a vehicle for emotions or as a means of identity marking. In the case of wearable signs of a social message, the question of the social value is superfluous, but in principle this question can be examined and assessed better and in a more nuanced way in all categories. This is true even in the case of ethnic jewellery, which originates from a partly or largely unfamiliar culture whose deeper symbolic values are only known within the culture itself or by a handful of specialists. The most important criteria in making such considerations involve the principles of comprehensiveness and accuracy, i.e., the question of whether the various values are coherent and whether they reinforce each other.

By juxtaposing the above criteria for making value judgements about jewellery with the current division of groups within the jewellery profession, new and more differentiated value patterns may come into view. Yet the situation is slightly more complicated perhaps. First, the available historical materials must be assessed, with much more attention for the various social and symbolic values of the piece of jewellery. Moreover, more fundamental research needs to be done into decoration of the less privileged in society, especially in western countries and cultures. But the greatest challenge pertains to the tackling of a number of obvious prejudices in the study of jewellery, simply because this takes time. This is why adjusting an already shaky classification as discussed in section 2.2 is hardly the first concern. The various classifications on practical grounds, as mentioned in that same section, are likely to be useful for at least some time to come.

It is all about a new framework for the study of jewellery as a versatile and meaningful cultural expression. The framework developed in this essay offers a way of looking at the concept of jewellery in all its aspects in order to do justice to it. This text not only deepens and underpins the considerations made in the research for may study on Dutch jewellery in the twentieth century; it has resulted in an independent and purely theoretical framework for the study of jewellery in all its manifestations. Both the scope and the intimacy of all forms and meanings that jewellery can have are integrated in a manner of investigation and in a number of coherent perspectives and criteria for making value judgements on jewellery.

In the next phase, this approach may productively be linked to more developed research proposals and serve as a guideline for the study of contemporary jewellery.

As far as such contemporary study of jewellery is concerned, a few more conclusions can be drawn on the basis of this essay. In this day and age, full of political and economic threats, energy scarcity and ideological confusion with regard to social norms and values, the interest in etiquette books is reviving and designers of all kinds are interested in traditional forms and matching behaviour. Fashion and jewellery are once again being used as means in the struggle for a better social position, just as in the 1930 and 1940s, the years of economic crisis and war. The achievements of the cultural revolution of the 1960s and 1970s, on the other hand, as well as the ideas of Modernism, are now subject to critical questions. All of this means that incentives for new developments can come from all angles, from the most intimate thoughts of individual makers to rebellious behaviour within subcultures. And equally from designers with a clear sense of fashion and taste development, who have put their talents at the service of commerce. Frankly, the latter currently have a pretty good chance of being regarded as an indicator of their time within our capitalist society, in particular when taking into account the massive scale of modern production and communication technologies.

It is in this configuration that the contributions of individual jewellery designers to their profession are so valuable. An interesting question here is how precisely they deal with the conventions in their profession and with jewellery as a means of identity marking. Nowadays there are many more or less ironic references to the traditional cornerstones of the jewellery profession to be found.

Jewellery is an archetypical phenomenon and it is so close to men and women and all their various pleasures that it will survive every development and temporary fad while also reflecting those in one way or another. In all times people have been seduced by wearable ornaments, by their shapes, materials, their technique and symbolism, also in times of war and disaster. But the automatic answer to the question of whether jewellery can make someone happy takes almost without exception the form of denial: jewellery is mere display of vanity or betrays a penchant for luxuries – there are other things that make people happy. This, too, is a prejudice that should finally be put into perspective. The crux of jewellery is that it is a catalyst of desires and fears, of emotions, sexual drives, social relationships and the need for identity – in short: of everything that drives humans in their lives. Anyone who is aware of the incredible number of decorative and symbolic values embodied in jewellery in its long history, and of the basic motives behind the wearing of jewellery, will always be able, on the basis of reciprocity, to find a confirmation of their own identity and their own desires in these small objects, and thus to find something that makes them happy as well. And in line with my argument for a multidisciplinary framework for the study of jewellery – with reference to the study of fashion – it can be said that even those who feel most comfortable by not wearing jewellery and who refuse to immerse themselves in it still represent a remarkable fact for the study of jewellery. (221)

1 Hughes 1966, p. 9: 'Jewellery has influenced human affairs and expressed human nature: its small size belies its great significance.'

2 Hughes 1966, p. 7: 'Their appeal is universal but their impact is confidential.'

3 Unger 2004, p. 7. In the introduction to the book, I only indicated the following about my approach: 'Within the discipline of art history, the history of style offers a useful guideline for the treatment of a subject such as jewellery, involving ornaments par excellence. Internationally, this is the most common approach, which allows for comparisons with other forms of applied and visual arts. In this seemingly ephemeral subject, the broad lines of traditional historiography offered a valuable hold. For me, this was still too limited a framework, however, and gratefully I made use of related disciplines such as iconography, Dutch history (...) and the history and sociology of fashion and adornment, while I also relied on a tried and tested means: critically looking at the artefacts themselves'. This approach was rendered concrete in the structure of my six chapters, each of which deals with a period from the twentieth century. Each chapter begins with a broad and multidisciplinary study plus a more general-historical and sociological account of the specific Dutch context. With regard to international developments in jewellery and fashion, I made extensive use of fashion history, which was originally part of art history, but has meanwhile evolved into an independent multidisciplinary discipline.

4 In histories of jewellery, great emphasis is put on precious jewellery, on practices of adornment of those in power and on the wealthy upper class. The history of style serves as chief tradition for outlining a more specific historical context, while artistic qualities are mentioned in particular in the case of jewellery from the nineteenth and twentieth century. Developments in fashion and clothing are mainly used as a context for highlighting changes in style. Such approach falls short, however, when addressing cultural artefacts from the Netherlands in the 20th century, in particular when discussing jewellery against the backdrop of the wave of democratisation in the 1960s and 1970s or the ensemble of transformations referred to as 'the cultural revolution', which includes changes in youth culture, feminism and sexual morals. I elaborate these issues in this essay, but I also did so in *Het Nederlandse sieraad in de 20ste eeuw.*

5 See section 7.1 below. See also Dormer 1994, pp. 7, 14; and Weber 2004, p. 11: 'No other artistic statement – with the exception of fashion – is so closely connected with man as jewellery. (...) Jewellery is always related to the body, and this is an essential obstacle to consider it as a work of art without any doubt'.

6 For a number of surveys on jewellery to support this point, see:

- Hammes 1944. The 'Hammes', which is the Dutch standard work on the technique of goldsmithing from 1944, is very precise in the description of all raw materials and techniques, but contains no definitions of the various end products. Maybe this is too much to ask from such a technical work, but in more contemplative publications, such as the next one listed below, the situation is different.
- Flower 1967. This book, originally from 1951, was called unique at the time because it was the first book which presented a historical framework for jewellery from the Victorian era. It relies heavily on the developments in fashion. The introduction does not contain a definition; the only claim made there is that jewellery, like any other form of decoration, reflects the tastes and circumstances of the time in which it is created.
- Evans 1970. Joan Evans was a renowned art historian who published texts on jewellery since the early 1920s. The first edition of this thorough history of jewellery is from 1953. Since then it has served as a model for many art historical treatises on jewellery. The foreword to the second edition of 1970 states that interest in nineteenth century jewellery in particular has increased sharply since the publication of the first edition. The two opening sentences of the first chapter come close to a definition: 'Jewel-

lery is one of the oldest of the decorative arts. It answers to the deep human love of intrinsically beautiful materials, to the deep human wish for bodily beautification, and to the superstitious need for reinforcing human powers by things that seem to a savage more lasting and more mysterious than man'.

- Giltay 1961. Starts with some remarks about jewellery in general. No definition.
- Gans 1961. Dives into jewellery history right away.
- Hughes 1968 (1963). Calls his book 'the first serious effort to record what has happened to jewellery in the western world in the past seventy-five years'. No definition.
- Hughes 1966. No definition, but an informative introduction.
- Gregorietti 1970. Nice introduction about vanity and prehistory. No definition.
- Tait 1976. In the first edition, which still has the character of an exhibition catalogue, he opens as follows: 'Jewellery was man's answer to the profound human need for self-adornment and, consequently, is one of the oldest forms of decorative art'. This author does not spend a single word on all the possible meanings of jewellery, even though it is precisely in this book that he offers insight into these meanings, with the help of the many curators who worked at the British Museum in London. Yet he does not provide a satisfactory definition.
- Dewiel 1980 (1979). Opens her overview of jewellery from the late eighteenth to the early twentieth century rather randomly, it seems, by discussing jewellery from Greece.
- Cartlidge 1985. Good introduction, arguing that 'jewellery is a quite extraordinary artifact; it is not essential for survival like food, shelter or clothing; yet it has existed since time immemorial and is found, in one form or another, in every civilization from the most primitive to the highly sophisticated'.
- Phillips 1996. Starts with antiquity. No definition. For the revised edition, published in response to the new layout of the jewellery study collection in the Victoria & Albert Museum in May 2008, she wrote a new introduction on materials and techniques, but she did not add a definition.

- Bennett 1996. *Understanding Jewellery* is a nice title, but the authors do not give a definition, not even an introduction; they start with discussing gems.
- Weber, 2004. No definition, but a generous introduction on 'Jewellery as a cultural and social phenomenon', pp. 10–11.

7 Like antique dealer Nico Kruimel, who always talked about 'that cramped and stiff Dutch work', while showing me beautiful French and English jewellery. Quote from a letter to the author by artist/designer Arnold van Geuns, a member of 'duo Ravage': 'I hope I'm not hurting you when saying that in general Dutch jewellery does not make me very happy. But I have to admit that in your beautiful book you give it a very interesting and fascinating treatment'.

8 Cf. Unger 2006; Unger 2005; Unger 2008; Lindemann 2008; Ahl 2008, pp. 36-44. Since 2005, valuable symposia on the theory of jewellery have been organised annually by the FH Trier, Fachbereich Gestaltung, Idar-Oberstein, under the title 'SchmuckDenken'.

9 Unger 2004, p. 543. Stones were often the starting point for the design of a jewel. See also section 5.4.2.

10 M.H. Gans, author of the standard work *Jewellery and People* (1961), uses the French word bijou as a synonym for both high jewellery and jewellery. Because his book is mainly about precious jewellery and he focuses especially on diamonds, the distinction between high jewellery and jewellery did not play a role for him. The current meaning of 'bijou' in Dutch is 'kleinood' (small valuable item); translated from French it means 'gem' 'jewel', 'trinket'. The use of the word bijou by Gans was possibly tied to the fact that in the Netherlands the upper classes would still converse in French among themselves. In her useful booklet on jewellery from the same year, Giltay-Nijssen also sometimes uses the word bijou as an equivalent of jewellery and jewel, for example when she refers to French examples and publications (cf. p. 92).

11 Walgrave 1995, p. 18.

12 Unger 2006.

13 Richter 2000, p. 7.

14 See e.g. Hansmann 1966, chapter 'Tier und Mensch', pp. 77-116.

15 Richter 2000, pp. 10-11; Edwards 2003; Spiering 2008.

16 See Hughes 1972, chapter 'Discoveries', pp. 195-210; Edwards 2003; Spiering 2008/2. The most informative and concise publication on the archaeology of jewellery is Jack Ogden, *Ancient Jewellery*, 1992.

17 As far as jewellery in the western world is concerned, Gerhard Eggert is the exception that confirms the rule (discussed in more detail in section 3.1). Within anthropology it is customary to use social differentiations in the study of clothing and ornaments. From a field of study such as material culture new research is to be expected. In the Netherlands, A.J. Schuurman has done pioneering work in this area. See section 5.1.3.

18 Paul Derrez, for example, refers to this classification as a stepping stone for defining art jeweller or author's jewellery: 'it is made by one „author" who decides the concept and the design'. On the other hand, jewellery that is 'shiny, glittering, easy-to-wear' is sold through jewellers and department stores. He elaborates on the fashion market, and he also mentions 'alternative' silversmiths and jewellery from non-western countries. Astfalck 2005, pp. 11-13.

19 Unger 2004. Regional jewellery: pp. 506-509; 'entourage ring': pp. 345-347; influences from the Dutch East Indies: pp. 172-179, ethnic: pp. 506-509.

20 Ogden 1992, pp. 8-17.

21 There are painters who are very precise in depicting jewellery in their portraits. Nicholas Hilliard (1547-1619) and Robert Peake (?1551-1619) are known to have been trained as goldsmiths at first, as I found out during a visit to an exhibition on English portraiture in the Tate Britain. I suspect that this was the case for more painters from this period. In any case, the professions of goldsmith and portrait painter were not far apart socially and they served similar clients. I have always appreciated the publication *Jewellery in America* 1600-1900 by Martha Gandy Fales from

1995 because she has included many portraits as a reference for the jewellery she discovered, including rather insignificant images of ordinary American citizens.

22 Evans 1970, p. 9, p. 181. In her epilogue she adds: 'It is not easy to see a future for the art of jewellery; it may even be considered that as an art it has no future. For all the centuries of recorded time it has existed as an art in which style and fashion were set by the taste of an aristocracy; bourgeois jewellery, peasant jewellery and jewellery in less precious materials such as we now call costume jewellery, all imitated court fashions.' She further states that this source of inspiration no longer works because since 1918 relatively few court jewels have been made and since 1939 almost none at all. Evans 1970, p. 183. One should also consider in this light her remark about her own time as a period of strict functionalism (see 3.3 below). In *Het Nederlandse sieraad*, I mentioned the jewels of the three Dutch queens of the twentieth century only if they were important for developments in the jewellery trade or if they marked a major moment in history or expressed a particular mentality.

23 Eggert 1988, p. 10. In her book on Victorian jewellery, Margaret Flower distinguishes between 'primary jewellery' and 'secondary jewellery'. The second group includes jewellery that is less expensive than large jewellery, novelty jewellery (jewellery that belongs to a new fashion), regional jewellery and jewellery from the Arts & Crafts movement. Flower 1967, pp. 7, 8. In later works on the history of jewellery, authors did not adopt this accurate classification, but fell back on the knowledgeable if elitist approach to jewellery as presented by Joan Evans in her 1953 book.

24 Cf. section 7.1.

25 One of the most beautiful, the 'Grüne Gewölbe' in Dresden, is once again open to the public after several extensive restorations. Other examples can be found in Der Residenz in Munich, the Topkapi Palace in Istanbul, the Hermitage in St. Petersburg and The Tower in London. Due to the use of materials and the elevated social status of the jewels, such treasuries do not provide a good frame of reference for jewellery from the second half of the twentieth century and beyond.

26 Waarborg 1997, pp. 5-16.

27 Flower 1967 [1951] , p. 33.

28 See 5.1.2.

29 In addition to members of royal families and the high nobility, wealthy industrialists and other entrepreneurs, especially the most important courtesans or grandes horizontales, also belonged to this clientele.

30 The main sources are: Bennett 1996, Cerval 1998, Duncan 1994, Vever 2001 and Snowman 2002.

31 M.H. Gans was a partner of Premsela and Hamburger in Amsterdam. David Bennett and Daniela Mascetti are employees of Sotheby's.

32 Big 2007, pp. 217-232. As far as jewellery designers are concerned, she treats Lily de Fremery-Gull, Jo Buekers, Conelia Vos, Nel van der Chijs, Maud Smit and Joanna Brom, amongst others, whose work is also discussed in *Het Nederlandse sieraad*. Groot refers to a number of sources that I did not consult for that study. This suggests that there are still good starting points for further research into Dutch jewellery and its subareas.

33 The numbers and management also played a role. In terms of professional practice, there were more male goldsmiths who had their own studios for a longer period of time (decades) than women active in this profession.

34 Evans 1970, p. 39. If this remark suggests pride, it also suggest bitterness, especially in relation to how she defines her era and how from the end of the 19th century she saw no future for jewellery as pinnacle of refinement and goldsmithing art.

35 A number of designers from the United States have a special position in the development of Modernism, with their work from the 1940s and 1950s. The work of Margaret de la Patta, Irena Brynner and Earl Pardon looks very modern and is poorly known in Europe. It is depicted in a Canadian exhibition catalogue that sheds a different light on what can be called modern. Cf. the exhibition catalogue on *What modern was*, pp. 101, 159-160, 221, 286.

A new study devoted to North American jewellery from this period, which also offers a discussion of principles such as production versus uniqueness, is Marbeth Schon, *Modernist Jewellery* 1930-1960 from 2004. She refers to the work of these generations of jewellery designers as 'modernist'.

36 Most of this jewellery, such as that by François Hugo, was made by goldsmiths. These items are translations into gold of sketches or details from paintings by visual artists. See Hugo 2001. Alexander Calder's jewellery, on the other hand, has the immediacy and sparkle that also characterises his smaller sculptures. He also took into account the wearer, initially his own wife. In addition, he has made many pieces of jewellery especially for friends. See Rower 2007; exhibition catalogue *Calder Intime*; exhibition catalogue *Nur für ihre Frauen*. In my opinion, the exhibition catalogue *Bijoux sculptures* contains some more interesting jewellery by artists such as Lucio Fontana, Anish Kapoor, Man Ray, Robert Rauschenberg and Bernar Venet. They are interesting, wearable objects, rather than images with a pin on their backside. I have also included a number of items of jewellery by Dutch artists in *Het Nederlandse sieraad*, but only if they represented a particular quality as jewellery and, consequently, could rightfully claim a role for themselves within jewellery as a field.

37 Unger 2005, pp. 19-22.

38 I already commented on this development in 1987, in a text for the magazine *Bijvoorbeeld* (For example), with the title 'Sieraad komt niet los uit bedenkelijke driehoeksverhouding'. See Unger 1987. See also section 7.3.

39 Astfalck 2005, p. 12.

40 Exhibition catalogue *Sieradiën*, no page numbering

41 Exhibition catalogue *Des Wahnsinns fette Beute*, pp. 13, 26-28. His full title is 'Prof. Dr. Florian Hufnagl, Leitender Sammlungsdirektor *Die Neue Sammlung*, Staatliches Museum für angewandte Kunst/Design in der Pinakothek der Moderne, München'. The subject of this book is the work of the students trained by Otto Künzli as jewellery designers at the prestigious 'Akademie der Bildenden Künste' in Munich, a focal point of contemporary jewellery design.

42 Ibid., pp. 29-35.

43 Ibid., p. 34.

44 Van Zijl 2005, p. 91. It is no wonder, then, that on this point I was criticised by her for the approach I have taken in *Het Nederlandse sieraad*: 'The boundaries between the two manifestations of jewellery, visual art object or user object, are not always sharply defined. Nevertheless, in my opinion, it is a methodological error on the part of M. Unger that she does not want to make this distinction in her publication *Het Nederlandse sieraad in de twintigste eeuw* (Dutch Jewellery in the 20th Century). She mixes the history of designer's jewellery with a historical overview of everything that was worn as jewellery in the Netherlands in the 20th century. The last subject is incredibly fascinating and the overview contains a wealth of information, but its conclusions are less valuable because she compares apples and oranges.' Although Van Zijl makes clear which of my views she does not share, it is a methodological error, in my view, to label Gijs Bakker's jewellery, which given its form and content is clearly intended to be worn, as 'objects of fine art'.

45 Li Edelkoort, a leading trend watcher and prognosticator, assumes in *The Future is Handmade. The Survival and Innovation of Crafts* from 2003 (p. 69) that the contrast between craft, industry, design and art will become irrelevant: 'I believe that we will see the day when the industrial will carry the soul of the crafted, while arts and crafts will sustain itself through the discovery and acceptance of virtual discoveries. There will come a day when the two fields will merge and become an indiscernible whole.' It will take some time before this will be a reality for jewellery as a field.

46 This I established during my research, and I checked it in bibliographies in surveys of jewellery. The bibliography of *Flower* (1967), originally from 1951, is short and divided into three parts:

I. Jewellery and precious stones

II. Fashion and costume

III. Exhibitions and the arts

This division reflects the fact that for her ground-breaking work on Victorian jewellery she still depended heavily on professional publications and costume history, and for the latter on the insights and collection of Doris Langley Moore. The bibliography in Evans (1970) is the most extensive. The reissue of 1970 includes a number of titles published after the first publication in 1953. Nevertheless, it is clear that the many articles and other publications from before 1950 are mainly professional publications or art historical studies on a specific topic (such as a legacy, an interesting expansion of a museum collection, or one portrait or one piece of jewellery). General books on jewellery from after 1960, which were often intended as an introduction to the phenomenon of jewellery, usually have short bibliographies. Almost without exception they refer to the work of Evans.

47 Staal 2006, pp. 113-116.

48 I have asked myself the question whether the human body could be a slightly too strict a limitation for the concept of jewellery. There are also jewels for dogs, cats and horses. But animals don't put them on themselves; it is people who see their pet or mount as an extension of their own ornamental urge and as a sign for their financial prosperity. In principle it is possible for human jewellery to be worn by animals. In *Het Nederlandse sieraad* on p. 492 there is an image of a white poodle with jewellery from The Gem Kingdom. However, this rare and fascinating excursion into the presentation of jewellery is no reason to include bodies other than those of human beings in the definition of jewellery as independent objects with a decorative and symbolic effect. Jewellery is and will remain a human affair.

49 Tait 2006, p. 167.

50 Gregorietti 1969, p. 305. This author arrives at the same conclusion: 'Forms too, such as necklaces, bracelets, rings and earrings, are very much the same as those used in antiquity'. He even states that this also applies to techniques: 'A survey of the history of approximately five thousand years of jewellery reveals that from the point of view of the workmanship, ancient jewels do not differ substantially from modern ones.' He then mentions a few exceptions, such as the cutting of diamonds.

51 Ted Polhemus, 'Text 1' in: Exhibition catalogue *Les Fleurs du Mal*, n.p.

52 Unger 2004, pp. 515-519.

53 See, amongst others, Deighton 1987, pp. 63-64.

54 Broby-Johansen 1968, p. 8.

55 Nijland 1997. Evert Nijland is an example of a young Dutch jewellery designer who was clearly inspired by portraits and, in particular, nudes from the Renaissance.

56 Bacon 1638, pp. 131-133, 199-200; Le Goff 2006, p. 449; Untracht 1997, p. 339.

57 Much has been written about the relationship between the effects of stones and the signs of the zodiac, from scientific treatises to smooth sales arguments for ornaments as appropriate gift. Such connections are made in various cultures; however, clarity and unambiguous meanings are hard to find.

58 Questions that are difficult to answer here are whether they can take over the role of a magnetiser and whether a magnetiser really belongs in the health care sector.

59 Hughes 1966, p. 36. In his introduction to this handy pocket with the compact title *Jewellery* from 1966, he describes the purpose of jewellery as follows: 'Their aim is to enhance the wearer's glamour, and that may mean to make her look richer, nicer, bigger, finer, more alluring, more colourful, or more overwhelming. Glamour is an elusive quality, but the world hangs upon it. The jewellery mystique cannot be summarised, but without jewels women would certainly have less allure; indeed throughout history and before, women have actually felt underdressed without some ornament in gold, silver or stones'. Not a word about jewellery for men. Another strong remark can be found in the chapter 'Fashion' on p. 94: 'to understand jewels, one must understand women, and know the difference between art and fashion'. But the second chapter in *Jewellery* is about 'chieftains, kings and commoners'. On p. 26 he mentions Louis XIV of France as probably the last man to wear extensive jewellery as a political tool. However, he also mentions several major jewellery wearers, such as Frederick II in Berlin and August the Strong in Dresden, both from the second half of the eighteenth century, and the Persian shah, who ruled in the decades after the Second World War. This is related to the other important point of view in all of Hughes' publications: the importance of stones and the value of jewellery. These rulers loved stones and had the most beautiful specimens at their disposal to emphasise their elevated status.

60 Giltay 1961, pp. 24, 100. On p. 92 she quotes another statement by Fouquet. In translation: 'A jewel is the unexpected chord, striking but logical, sounding right on time in the symphony of femininity. No details, no floral lines, but a short ceremony, a richness that does not overwhelm'. See also Dewiel 1980. Dewiel describes the history of jewellery from the late eighteenth century to the beginning of the twentieth century. On p. 14 she spends very few words on jewellery for men. This must be due both to the timeframe she describes and to the moment at which she was writing: the late 1970s.

61 Michael 2006, pp. 10-11. Untracht is also very explicit on this point in his book about traditional jewellery in India, in many places. See also section 6.1 on power.

62 Giltay 1961, p. 44.

63 Exhibition catalogue *De ideale man*, pp. 14-15.

64 Tait 2006, p. 213. See also the portrait of Infanta Anna discussed in paragraph 7.2.

65 Unger 2004, pp. 515-519.

66 Ross 2008, p. 6. Robert Ross, in his recent study *Clothing. A Global History* from 2008, gives answers to the question of what clothing is for: 'The Germans describe the use of clothing as Schutz, Scham und Schmuck', without saying which Germans he means. In his conclusions on p. 171 he says more about this: 'The gendered aspects of clothing thus emphasise one, perhaps two, of clothing's prime functions. Modesty – Scham – and to a lesser extent ornament – Schmuck – are more clearly related to the question of identity and gender construction than is the protection against the elements – Schutz – which clothing also provides. Nevertheless, as this book has shown, none of these are absolutes. All have been interpreted in a multitude of different ways over the course of the last few centuries. In this way they have been used to mark the ever-shifting identities of the world as they have been developed'.

67 Broby-Johansen 1968, pp. 6-8.

68 Laver 1969, pp. 1-13 ('Modesty and its Foes').

69 Brandt 2006, p. 398.

70 Bell 1976, pp. 25-56. In this book Bell leans so heavily on the theory of Veblen that at the end he adds an entire chapter to make clear where he deviates from his great example. According to him, Veblen offered no explanation for the fact that fashion could also be very simple. This is a good point, at first sight, but with regard to both fashion and clothing, simplicity can be very expensive and require a lot of upkeep.

71 This starting point forms the basis of Gerhard Eggert's research into jewellery worn by the wealthy middle classes. See Eggert 1988, p. 10.

72 Hofstede 2000, p. 68. The vast majority of people in this world live in societies in which the interests of the group prevail over the interests of the individual. Schuurman emphasises this point in the conclusions of his research of ownership of valuable objects in the Zaan region around 1860. In order to show prosperity, he states that people consciously or unconsciously opt for a form that is understandable to their peers at times. The desire to belong to a group means, on the one hand, that one conforms to the rules of conduct that such a group applies in order to oppose itself collectively against others; on the other hand, one can afford variations in order to distinguish oneself from fellow group members. Schuurman 1986, p. 240.

73 Gregorietti 1969, p. 305. The transition from medieval society to the Renaissance, marked in terms of jewellery by the great golden chains of the wealthy bourgeoisie, is one of the periods of social change to which Eggert devotes a great deal of attention.

74 Giltay 1961, p. 27.

75 Scarisbrick 2007, pp. 108-111, 196, 209, 229, 235, 239, 242.

76 Fales 1995, p. 83-97.

77 In addition to etiquette books from the United States, literature is the best source for understanding what American standards meant for social positions and how the highest positions should behave. Henry James, Edith Wharton and F. Scott Fitzgerald in particular are very explicit about jewellery as a characterisation of individuals and as an indicator of social relations. In Tender is the Night by Scott Fitzgerald from 1939 there is a passage in which the protagonist notices two young men sitting on the beach of Saint Tropez reading a book about etiquette. 'Planning to mix with the quality' is his friend's comment. Scott Fitzgerald 1973, p. 86.

78 This phenomenon is the crux of the well-known story by Guy de Maupassant titled 'La Parure'. Maupassant 1959, pp. 443-462. The trade in counterfeit jewellery was not limited to fashion jewellery. The issue of fake jewellery will be discussed in section 5.4.3.

79 Giltay 1961, p. 61. Margaret Flower quotes gorgeous statements from the first half of the nineteenth century about the rules for wearing jewellery, including: 'Young ladies should never wear rings on their fingers, unless they desire to seem older'. Flower 1967, p. 6.

80 White-tinted jewellery was very popular in all western countries at the end of the nineteenth and the beginning of the twentieth century and was produced everywhere. It had the additional advantage that it could also be worn during periods of mourning. As discussed in *Het Nederlandse sieraad*, jewellery with diamonds and pearls and set in white metal is called 'white goods'. This was a lucrative and striking category of jewellery, certainly in the Netherlands, when the diamond cutting and trading industry was still an integral part of Dutch culture and economy. Unger 2004, pp. 20, 29, 54, 92, 117, 154-155, 159, 163, 192.

81 Geoffroy-Schneiter 2001, p. 16.

82 Unger 2004, pp. 80-87. See also Schuurman 1986 and Schuurman 1990.

83 Broby-Johansen 1968, p. 13

84 Ibid., p. 5. The following very humane and tolerant statement from Broby-Johansen's introduction can also serve as a model for my fascination with jewellery: 'The history of dress is full of deception and self-delusion, deliberate mistakes and unconscious mistakes, the calculated and uncalculated in a long and illogical record of human folly. In short, it is simply the history of mankind'.

85 Ibid. 'The history of dress cannot be treated as a conducted tour in which wheels revolve and carry both author and reader to a predetermined destination. The reader must be a pedestrian and use his legs; he must halt continually to adjust his bearings and change his point of view, sometimes to regard woman from the man's angle and at other times vice versa'.

86 Like Robert Brain, *The Decorated Body* (1979). In his introduction, this anthropologist also directly includes blindness for one's own practices in condemning body decorations in other cultures. He made a division of types of body decorations. Bernard Rudofsky approaches extreme body deformities and associated beauty ideals in *The Unfashionable Human Body* (1971) from psychology, sociology and anthropology. From the outset, he mixes western and non-western notions, thus fighting western prejudices and inhibitions. A recent and multifaceted study is the catalogue Medicine Man, based on Henry Solomon Wellcome's incredible collection of body related objects. It is an edition of the British Museum Press in London from 2003. See also section 4.2.

87 Geoffroy-Schneiter 2001, p. 15

88 Schuurman 1986, Schuurman 1990. In his contribution to Aards Geluk (1997), J.J. Voskuil gave jewellery a place in his study 'Boedelbeschrijvingen als bron voor de kennis van groepsvorming en groepgedrag: Maasland in de negentiende eeuw' (pp. 179-200). Thera Wijsenbeek-Olthuis did the same in her article 'Urban decay and cultural patterns' (Wijsenbeek-Olthuis 2001, p. 222).

89 Untracht 1997, pp. 172-186.

90 Vreeland 1980 p. 203.

91 Brand 2006, e.g. pp. 11-12, 15.

92 See also e.g. Fouchard 2005, pp. 47-51: 'Le moteur de la mode, c'est le désir.'

93 Polhemus 1978, p. 19.

94 See for example Unger 1994, catalogue for the project on Fashion and Jewellery, organised in 1993.

95 Brand 2007, in particular the texts of J. Teunissen, 'Waarom accessoires het modebeeld bepalen' (Why accessories determine the fashion image), pp. 10-23; M. Unger, 'De taal van het sieraad' (The language of jewellery), pp. 66-77; and M. Vos, 'Het modesieraad' (Fashion jewellery), pp. 178-183.

96 However, this meaning can also be attributed to taste, as the ninth meaning given for this word in *Van Dale* (dictionary of the Dutch language) indicates: 'wat volgens de heersende opvatting goed staat, verfijning of voornaamheid tekent' (that which, according to the prevailing view, looks good, characterises sophistication or distinction).

97 Teunissen 2005. Essentially, this distinction between fashion and clothing may also be made with regard to jewellery: jewellery as an expression of developments and desires from one's own time, as well as jewellery that is somewhat separate from it and more in keeping with traditions and, for example, with customs in subgroups within a society. However, this is not entirely true. Fashionable clothing is a consumer good and jewellery, with the exception of typical fashion accents, is rather intended to last for a long time and possibly to be passed on to future generations as a memento or identity marker of traditions important within a family or a social group.

98 Ibid., p. 71.

99 Giltay 1961, p. 9.

100 The first publication in 1976 also served as a catalogue for an exhibition at the British Museum. In the following publications from 1986 and 2006, the information from the original book has been incorporated into the running text.

101 Brand 2006, pp. 404-405.

102 Lurie 1981, p. 4. See also Polhemus 1978, Fashion as a language system, pp. 17-19. In my opinion, however, one should be careful to consider jewellery as a language. Although it is true that the many manifestations, the symbolism and the personal meanings that people connect with jewellery amount to a substantial vocabulary that can be dealt with in many different ways, the habit of calling everything that is image a language is mainly based on semantics and ignores the power of language to make sharp distinctions or formulate clear questions. This makes me reluctant to call jewellery explicitly a language. In the study of jewellery as a universal cultural expression, important characteristics of a language can be recognised, as a way to get a handle on the diversity of objective and subjective values that people attach to jewellery.

103 Flügel 1950, p. 7; Broby-Johansen 1968, p. 21. Both refer to Herbert Spencer as the one who recorded it, but who is probably not the original author.

104 Scarisbrick 2008, pp. 9, 57.

105 Exhibition catalogue *Het Versierde Ego* (The Decorated Ego), p. 20. At that time, motifs for jewellery were also derived from esotericism and theosophy. See e.g. the winged brooch of Frans Zwollo sr. in Unger 2004, pp. 30-31.

106 Dahl 1988, p. 35.

107 Tomasi 2001, p. 127.

108 Tolstoy 2001, p. 8.

109 Márquez 2008, pp. 55-56.

110 Némirovsky 2007, p. 36.

111 Bordewijk 1954, pp. 9, 27-28.

112 Wharton 1987, pp. 212-213.

113 De Maupassant 1959, pp. 405-412.

114 Simenon 1961, pp. 72-73.

115 Scott Fitzgerald 1974, p. 172.

116 Hill 2001, p. 4.

117 Shakespeare 1990. p. 223; Abkoude 2002, pp. 199-200.

118 Conan Doyle 1976, pp. 153-154.

119 Carvajal 2008. The news that more than twenty people involved in these spectacular jewel-thefts were arrested also appeared in the columns of the *International Herald Tribune* of 23 June on p. 4. That the real world and the world of literature reality often go hand in hand is shown by a short and unsigned report in *Trouw* (12 November 2008, p. 6). The report mentions a robbery of a late-night shop, in which one of the robbers also tried to steal the shop owner's precious necklace. During the struggle, the robber's gun went off, killing the owner.

120 Koeprin 2002, p. 95.

121 Zweig 1951, pp. 419, 435.

122 Initially I collected these literary fragments for a book about the work of the Dutch jewellery designer P. Sajet (to be published in 2009).

123 This is a reassuring thought when purchasing jewellery. Jewellery can even be considered as travel insurance. I own a fairly heavy chain of 22-carat gold that I often take with me when I travel, in the safe expectation that I will always get home, should something happen to me along the way. A friend of Jewish descent once bought a pair of rings with good diamonds with the idea that they may come in handy in the event she has to escape some dire situation. There is a name for that: flight diamonds.

124 The studies of Annemarie Moors are interesting in this respect. Moors has described the function of gold jewellery owned by women in the Middle East: 'On the one hand, gold jewellery is an important economic resource, an investment good; on the other hand, as it is worn as jewellery and as such displayed on the body, it is also a form of adornment. Gold jewellery as a material asset invites a discussion about the central place of gold in the world economy and the international monetary system, as well as about local manifestations of gendered property ownership. Wearing jewellery brings to the fore how women employ bodily adornments in negotiations about status and in the construction of identities. Gold jewellery then connects what is often seen as separate: the monetary system and notions of personhood, economy and culture, investments and adornments. Investigating the multiple meaning of gold jewellery also invites a discussion about how women are implicated in processes of globalization, as wearing and owning gold jewellery in the Middle East is by and large a woman's affair'. In her essay, Jansen also mentions several times that jewellery is still seen as an investment in many countries around the Mediterranean and in the Middle East, but that this is less and less the case in the Netherlands, partly because of the insurance costs.

125 Tait 1976, p. 20. Weber-Stöber 2004, p. 20; Hughes 1968, p. 61: 'In pre-war India banking was neither customary nor practical, so you kept your wealth at home, and quite simply you wore your bank balance. (...) Just as in early Europe, so in recent India it was the goldsmiths who served as bankers, and it was not artistic passion but simply surplus money that created the finest jewels. Alas for the craft, sophisticated countries now prefer the stock certificate in a filing cabinet to the bangle on a beautiful wrist'.

126 Hughes 1966, p. 20. Hughes first sums up the treasures that rulers such as Philip the Good, Jean de Berry and Charles the Bald wore in the form of jewellery during important meetings. Le Goff states that the wealth laws, which were introduced at the end of the thirteenth century, particularly in France and Italy, were undoubtedly related to the economic crisis which then arose. The question of whether gold is safer than money and credit is a recurring theme in the economy. Le Goff 2006, p. 483. See also Eggert 1988, pp. 11-14.

127 Spence 2007; Mons 2008, Dijkstra 2008; Menkes 2008. The short article by Menkes is about new attempts to create a standard for the chain of responsibilities within the diamond trade, from the mines to the jeweller. The author of an article in NRC Handelsblad (10/11 November 2007) is optimistic about international cooperation aimed at banning 'blood diamonds' from global trade. See Janssen 2007. In my opinion, this does not mean that they will soon disappear from circulation.

128 Basically, items of precious metal have to be marked, for instance with maker's marks, grade marks and, possibly, importer marks and weight marks. Large items may also be marked by year letter designations, but this mainly applies to silverware. The rule for items of precious metal is that an item may be ascribed to a specific maker with certainty only on the basis of assaying or documentation in the shape of drawings, photographs or explicit texts.

129 Heller 1992.

130 Unger 2004, p. 289.

131 See e.g. Hughes 1966, p. 90.

132 Jansen 1997, pp. 108-109: 'White gold is an excellent expression of the ambivalence of the Dutch towards jewellery. It is more expensive and stylish, but at the same time less conspicuous. It shines less, it looks cool, and because it looks so much like silver it looks more modest and cheaper than yellow gold. Just like platinum, it offers the possibility of 'understatement'. It takes a connoisseur's look to distinguish it from silver, and whoever owns that look indicates that they belong (or want to belong) to the same group'. In the period she refers to, the late 1960s and 1970s, white gold and platinum were also very popular in other countries. Moor 2001, p. 16: 'Beginning in the 1960s a new type of gold jewellery had appeared on the market, "Italian gold". These were smaller, but more exclusive pieces of jewellery, imported from Italy. They were often referred to as "small pieces" and consisted of a large variety of nicely made necklaces, bracelets, pendants, rings, earrings and so on. Because it was only 18-carat gold and thus had a greater hardness, it could be worked into a much wider variety of models and fashions. With labor costs much higher and more additional costs, such as import duties, this Italian gold was less valuable as a source of economic security and investment; when selling it, women would incur a considerable loss. Italian gold became first popular amongst the upper classes. For these women gold had always been more a statement about status than a source of economic security. The option of selling their gold did not concern them much; gold jewellery was to them not primarily an economic resource, but represented particular events and embodied specific social relations. In these circles wearing Italian gold coincided with new notions about marriage arrangements and dower registrations'.

133 Sennett 2008, p. 7.

134 Tait 1976, p. 12.

135 In *Het Nederlandse sieraad* I paid little attention to sketches and drawings. First of all because the aim was to map out developments in jewellery covering the entire twentieth century, but documentary material on ornaments and engravings of jewellery was no longer published at one point. Secondly, because there was hardly any material for comparison between drawings and executed pieces. At the same time, it is also true that the little documentation preserved on work by particular designers revealed that the actual design process often took place in the material itself. This certainly applied to the work of leading goldsmiths such as Archibald Dumbar and Chris Steenbergen, of whom I was able to study archival material. I discussed cases in my study only when drawings were truly instrumental in the creative process, for example because designer and maker were not one and the same person, for instance in the collaboration between Matthieu Lauweriks and Frans Zwollo sr. (Unger 2004, pp. 110-114). In the case of Emmy van Leersum, drawings would mostly feature as a starting point in her work and these are mentioned as such (Unger 2004, pp. 368-374).

136 Unger 2004, pp. 520-527. For an earlier publication on re-use of materials, see my catalogue Materiaal. Stof voor vormgeving (Material. Fabric for design) from 1992.

137 McDonough 2002.

138 Mulder 2009.

139 Tait 2006, p. 21.

140 Brentjens, 1998, n.p.; Reinewald 2006.

141 Arjen Ribbens describes on 4 February 2009 a recipe for a modern ring by Ted Noten as a first: 'You take the inner tube of a scooter tyre, a piggy bank found on Marktplaats and a pearl necklace from your grandmother. You group these three objects into a small installation, of which you have a three-dimensional scan made. Using modern software on your computer, you can subsequently „print" greatly reduced titanium copies. That's it! The rings are ready'. Ribbens 2009. In other fields, this technique has been used for several years.

142 De Maupassant 1959, pp. 443-462.

143 Hammes 1944, pp. 468, 469. The Netherlands has never been at the forefront of the production of fashion jewellery, neither in the twentieth century nor in the centuries before. Still, interesting jewellery has been made within the framework of fashion and has been dealt with in several chapters in my study on Dutch jewellery. This concerns both the beloved bead necklaces from the period 1910 - ca. 1932, a necklace with fake pearls by fashion designer Frank Govers from around 1970, and the work of The Gem Kingdom from the 1990s. See Unger 2004, pp. 172, 356, 357 and 492-494.

144 Unger 2004, pp. 239, 252.

145 Hughes 1968, p. 8. However, valuable pieces also have a limited chance of surviving the times unscathed: 'magnificent pieces are regarded more as financial investments than as objects of beauty, and the only value of which one may be reasonably sure fifty or a hundred years hence is de residual mineral worth of the metal and stones. Art and craftmanship have very little effect on second hand prices'.

146 Unger 2004, 'De mythe van de modernen' (The myth of the modern), pp. 359-368.

147 Hue-Williams 2001, pp. 12-13. She calls this 'provenance'. She also introduces the Factor X: 'The overall appreciation of the beauty of a jewel will always be a subjective matter, influenced by individual sentiment and style. This is as it should be: buying a jewel is the most personal of purchases and the individual is the best judge of the worth of a particular piece to him or her'.

148 The first auction was held on Thursday 19 June 2008, the second on Tuesday 16 December, the third on Monday 15 June 2009.

149 Schuurman 1997, p. 26; Schuurman 1990, pp. 19-23.

150 Le Goff is a good example of this approach. He has done ground-breaking research, but he also had to admit that in the

Middle Ages, for example, the peasant families formed a community that was silently ignored and about which hardly anything is known. Le Goff 2006 p. 385.

151 Jansen has provided figures for jewellery ownership by Dutch families for the year 1997 (from Statistics Netherlands, or CBS). In particular, the figure of 18,200 guilders for average jewellery holdings of higher income groups appears to be very low. This may be due to the fact that I deal a lot with people who are interested in jewellery, design and fashion. It can also be proof of my suspicion that the possession of jewellery in the Netherlands nowadays avoids any form of inventory, on the basis of inheritance tax and other forms of registration that increase the risk of theft. Schuurman observed that amongst the bourgeoisie and the wealthier farmers of the Zaan region around 1860 the possession of 'preciosa' amounted to more than ten percent of their ownership of consumer goods, and that they also owned comparatively more preciosa when their wealth increased. He deduced these percentages from estate descriptions, figures that are not directly comparable with the figures that Jansen had at his disposal. Schuurman 1986, pp. 220-221.

152 Unger 2004, pp. 240-253. This is a smaller-scale study for which I uncovered a great deal of material. This demonstrated the importance of political and economic perspectives in the study of jewellery and provided insight into a category of jewellery that was worn by broad segments of the population.

153 More 1964 [1518], pp. 85-86.

154 Eco 2007, p. 264. Eco quotes Kant as follows from 'The dispassionate Pleasure of Beauty', *The Critique of Judgement* I, 1, II, 1790: 'This definition of Beauty can be derived from the preceding definition of it as an object of pleasure apart from any interest. For that which makes us conscious that our feeling of pleasure is independent of any interest can only be evaluated this way. It must contain grounds for pleasure for everyone. For, since (pleasure) is not based on some inclination of the subject (or any other premeditated interest) and since he who judges feels entirely free with regard to his appreciation of the object, he cannot explain his pleasure on the basis of any personal conditions'. As a criterion for beauty, Kant presented an unselfish subjective pleasure, a criterion that has been adopted by many a spectator after him.

155 Mazumdar 2008.

156 Schuurman 1997, p. 26 (note 9).

157 Mandeville 2008; Groot 2008; Tolstoy 2001, p. 8.

158 G. Lipovetsky, *Le Bonheur Paradoxal*, Paris 2006. Translation in: Brand 2007, pp. 25-41.

159 Sources included Haeften 1936 and Groskamp ten Have 1939.

160 For the effect, see the beautiful photo books on ethnic decoration, such as Africa Adorned by Angela Fisher, and the explanations they give for this ostentatious decoration: 'Although they vary in the amount they travel, all these tribes have a minimum of material possessions, as they must be able to pack up easily and travel light when necessary (...). Instead, the creativity of these people has been directed towards beautifying and adorning themselves'. See Fisher 1994, pp. 13-14.

161 Boudier-Bakker 1931, p. 408.

162 Jansen 1997, p. 116; Moors 2002; Geoffroy-Schneiter 2001, p. 26.

163 Mabille 2001. This is also a recurring subject in literature. See e.g. Zweig 1951, p. 435.

164 Warhol 2007, p. 67.

165 Hojer 1997. Ludwig I emphasised this moral norm, but he himself had extramarital relationships, which attracted a great deal of attention and caused him many problems during his reign. The singer and dancer Lola Montez, his most famous mistress, is also part of his gallery of beauty.

166 As far as the philosophical question concerning objective and subjective beauty is concerned, the approach of Eco and my own approach in *Het Nederlandse sieraad* correspond to the principle of reciprocity (cf. section 7.4). Reciprocity or the possibility of cross-pollination is also one of the reasons why a multidisciplinary framework for the study of jewellery makes sense, see section 8.1.

167 'And the Lord said, Because the daughters of Zion are dilapidated, and walk around with stretched necks and beckoning eyes, because they walk with a tripping gait and let her foot rings ring, then the Lord will make the skull of Zion's daughters scabby, and the Lord will expose her nakedness. In that day the Lord shall take away the sparkle of the foot rings, the forehead bands, moons, earrings, bracelets, veils, headscarves, footchains, girdles, scent bottles, magic potions, signet rings, nose rings, feastcloths, shawls, bags, hand mirrors, undergarments, headdresses and overgarments. Then, instead of the smell of balm, there shall be filth, instead of a girdle, a rope, instead of the baldness of the hair, instead of a gown of mourning, a mark of burning instead of beauty'.

168 Verse 2-3. These daughters of one mother committed illicit sexual acts in Egypt: 'There her bosom was touched and her virgin breasts were caressed' (Ohala and Ohibila are metaphors for Samaria and Jerusalem). And verse 42-44: 'They put bracelets on her arms and put an elegant crown on their heads. Then I thought, "Does this wilted woman commit adultery? Will they even commit adultery with her?" They went to her like a whore, so they went to Ohola and Ohiliba'.

169 Ezekiel 16:10-12. 'I clothed thee with a colourfully embroidered garment, shod thee with the most precious leather, wrapped thee in a fine linen headscarf, and paid thee tribute in silk. I adorned you with jewellery, put bracelets on your arms and a chain around your neck. I gave you a ring for the nose, earrings for your ears and an ornamental crown on the head'. Actually, the order is not entirely correct, because this description of the jewel as glory serves as the run-up to the abovementioned punishment of the women of Jerusalem.

170 'Thou shalt make a breastplate of judgment, skilful work. In the same way as the ephod thou shalt make it, of gold, blue, red, scarlet, and twined fine linen shalt thou make it. It shall be square, double, a span long, and a span wide. And thou shalt fill it with bricks, four rows of stones: a row of red jasper, chrysolite, and malachite, the first row; the second row, haematite, lasurite, and praseme; the third row: Amber, agate, and amethyst; the fourth row: turquoise, chrysopazzah, and nephrite. Surrounded by gold, they shall be encased in their settlements. And the stones according to the names of the children of Israel shall be twelve in number according to their names: as engravings shall they be for the twelve tribes, each by his name. And thou shalt make wreathen chains upon the breastplate, wickerwork of pure gold. And thou shalt make upon the breastplate two rings of gold, and put the two rings at the end of the breastplate. And thou shalt put the two braided chains of gold in the two rings of the breastplate. The two other ends of the two braided chains thou shalt put upon the two sockets of the ephod in the front'. The subsequent guidance is also very precise. Some of the stones have been found in the area of present-day Israel, but some probably also had to be imported. For the original quote (in Dutch) I used my high school bible in the new translation from 1954. In other translations, however, other stones are mentioned.

171 Unger 2004, p. 8. What I naturally like about this research is that, in these proverbs, reason is just a little more important than delighting in gold and corals.

172 The exhibition catalogue *Luxury & Decadence* offers information about this, including many statements from the time. This is the Dutch version of a travelling exhibition with publications in various languages.

173 Le Goff 2006 pp. 478-479; the quote is in the English translation indeed. See also: Le Goff 1992, p. 83.

174 Giltay 1961, p. 97. Provides a neat description of the papal ring or fisherman's ring.

175 See e.g. Giltay 1961, p. 37; Bennett & Mascetti 1996, pp. 116-119 and 128-129; Geoffroy-Schneiter 2001, p. 25; Möller 2004, p. 100.

176 A good starting point for studying the relationship between jewellery and religion in different cultures is Tait 2006 [1986]. The quality of this publication lies in the combination of insights from very different cultures. Untracht 1997 offers a lot of information about the symbolism of Hinduism and other religions in India.

177 Newman 2007, p. 1.

178 Fales 1995, pp. 11-12.

179 Tait 2006, pp. 197-198; Su Tong, 2006. p. 13. A secondary effect of the magical powers of stones is that they can produce wonderful stories. The idea that opals bring misfortune is fed by Sir Walter Scott's novel *Anne of Geierstein*, which caused the turnover in opals around 1900 to plummet. See e.g. Cavey 1992, p. 62.

180 See e.g. Walgrave 1995, p. 16. Jan Walgrave offers a brief overview of the backgrounds and meanings used in jewellery. He refers to sixteenth century Christian and secular emblemata, to the second half of the nineteenth century and to symbolism around 1900. He concludes: 'The symbolic value of jewellery is one of the historical achievements of our culture, so it is good to preserve this treasure of information that has been built up by generations'. I agree; conventions in the symbolic language of form can have an incredible power and continue to work into our time. Whether people are aware of the original meaning or not does not even matter.

181 Speaking of cultural confusion: I own a Hindu ornament with an image of the god Ganesha, who has an elephant's snout. It hangs from a chain and falls high up against the neck. Once I was asked by someone politely and in earnest if that was my family crest.

182 Geoffroy-Schneiter 2001, p. 40. See also paragraph 7.2.

183 Michael 2006, pp. 45-53.

184 Gregorietti, 1969, p. 13. Although this author does not give a definition of jewellery in his survey of the history of jewellery over the centuries, his opening sentences are very strong: 'The story of jewellery is as old as human vanity. Even in earliest times, though scarcely yet in a position to organise his society, man found a pretext for satisfying its narcissism by creating hierarchies which required signs of rank. These badges were usually precious objects or, if of low intrinsic value, objects enriched by the craftsmanship of particularly talented individuals.'

185 Untracht 1997, pp. 55, 343-345.

186 Tait 2006, p. 177.

187 Tait 2006, pp. 194-197; Hansmann 1966.

188 Spiering 2008.

189 Tait 2006, p. 213.

190 Untracht 1997, pp. 88-140. 'Coins as amuletic jewellery', pp. 120-124.

191 Unger 2004, pp. 70-75, 240-250.

192 Exhibition catalogue Erotischer Schmuck, Ludwig 1995, p. 41.

193 Walgrave 1995, p. 20. By the way, this is already a shift in emphasis from sexual to sensual.

194 Scarisbrick 2008, pp. 284-287. Amongst other things, she shows two bracelets of Empress Josephine of France, which have the names of her children on it. In Victorian England, jewellery with such sentimental symbolism was very popular, and it can still be found in large numbers in antique shops and, for example, in sales guides for collectors of jewellery. A popular text in colour stones for rings and other jewellery was 'd-e-a-r-e-s-t'. See also Tait 2006, pp. 185-188; Fales 1995, pp. 28-31. Fales devotes a number of pages to jewellery as a symbol of love in eighteenth century America.

195 Untracht 1997, p. 15. In *Het Nederlandse sieraad* a number of such generally recognizable motifs are mentioned and depicted, such as the charms in the form of windmills (fig. 219 on p. 307). In Loekie Metz's bracelet on p. 298 (fig. 211) and p. 300, a Dutch farmer and farmer's wife are easily identified. The 'Old Dutch' jewellery described on pp. 528-535, both inside and outside the Netherlands, appeals to something specific about Dutch culture, in this case seventeenth century painting.

196 Unger 2004, pp. 499-513.

197 Dewiel 1980, pp. 13-14, 26-30.

198 Scarisbrick 2008, p. 337.

199 It was a graduation project of Maaike Feitsma for the master's programme in Fashion in Arnhem. This young guest curator explained 'Remembrance' as a characteristic of jewel-lery as follows: 'Wearers often have an intimate bond with their jewellery, because it embodies precious memories of people, places and events. The wearer cherishes and loves this piece of jewellery. Not only because of its material or artistic value, but because the object managed to capture a particular memory and its accompanying emotions. The inimitable value of memory is central to this exhibition. This is why it is not only jewellery by designers that derives its inspiration from memory. Everyday jewellery that may not be of great artistic or material value is also put on a pedestal. After all, no piece of jewellery represents a value as matchless as an object to which the wearer has pledged his heart'.

200 Ogden1992, pp. 9-17; Unger 2004, pp. 520-527.

201 Richter 2000. p. 7. This point is in line with Lipovetsky's argument about luxury. See also section 5.5.1.

202 The term 'jewel' (sieraad) is also used figuratively in Dutch and as an indication of value, being something that enhances the beauty of something or of the whole to which it belongs, of its surroundings, or as something to be proud of. This does not apply here.

203 Dormer 1994, p. 7, 14.

204 The same point fascinated Henry David Thoreau. See *The Heart of Thoreau's Journals*, London, 1961, pp. 179-180: 'I hear the neighbors complain sometimes about the peddlers selling their help false jewellery, as if they themselves wore true jewellery; but if their help pay as much for it as they did for theirs, then it is just as true jewellery as theirs, just as becoming to them and no more; for unfortunately it is the cost of the article and not the merits of the wearer that is considered. The money is just as well spent, and perhaps better earned. I don't care how much false jewellery the 207 peddlers sell, nor how much of the eggs which you steal are rotten. What, pray, is true jewellery? The hardened tear of a dis- eased clam, murdered in its old age. Is that fair play? If not, it is no jewel. The mistress wears this in her ear, while her help has one made of paste which you cannot tell from it. False jewellery! You know of any shop where true jewellery can be bought? I always look askance at a jeweller and wonder what church he can belong to'.

205 Unger 2004. A description of the pearl necklace as a proud possession of Dutch ladies can be found on pp. 32-33. In the chapter 'The myth of the moderns', pp. 359-401, the pearl necklace is described as a negative benchmark for a new generation of jewellery designers.

206 Hue-Williams 2001; p. 9. Möller 2004, p. 15.

207 That is why, as a viewer, you never get to see certain jewellery, such as inherited items that were made and bought as a result of a marriage or birth. That was a difficult point in the research for *Het Nederlandse sieraad*. I couldn't get to a lot of work because it's stored in the safes of wealthy families. Take Jan and Eloy Brom's jewellery from the Utrecht studio that in the first decades of the twentieth century produced the most beautiful church work in the Netherlands and also deployed their craftsmanship and sense of refinement for making jewellery. Most of these items are in the hands of wealthy, Catholic families. If these pieces may occasionally be cleaned, they are never released into the market.

208 See among others the recipes of Francis Bacon in paragraph 4.3.

209 His remark concerned an unnoticed piece by Bert Nienhuis, who in his white colour scheme also slightly deviated from the already known pieces.

210 Quoted in Eco 2007, p. 245. Hume is talking about the search for beauty, and about beauty as a relative value. See also paragraph 5.5.3.

211 Clark 1979, p. 9.

212 In recent years, for example, the term 'art design' has been introduced to refer to this category of products. The term 'DesignArt' is also buzzing around; during the prestigious Frieze Art Fair in London in 2008, selected products of design were presented under this denominator. The reason for this is the current economy and the status of a handful of artists and designers who can put a price tag on their work of which they never have dared to dream. Anyone who is able to present his or her products in such a way that the superrich pay a lot of money for them, seizes that opportunity. As an expression of short-term thinking, however, the whole discussion around the proposition that the best products of design, including jewellery, should actually be labelled as art, does not yield anything substantial. Rather, it may be called a narrowminded form of opportunism reflective of the times. The global financial crisis, which manifested itself in the last months of 2008, will once again change the framework conditions for the purchase of contemporary jewellery. See Rawsthorn 2008; Smallenburg 2008/2.

213 Gerard Lakke already wrote in 1988 in a text for *Bijvoorbeeld* about 'artist-design': 'And this brings us to the root of the problem. With the tendency for autonomous artists to make design products, there is a danger that such one-off design work will attract more attention than the work of professional designers due to the status of the visual artist, regardless of the quality. Today, free artists are still held in higher esteem than designers. (...) When it comes to applied art, different criteria and norms apply than in the visual arts. Of course, it is nice and even welcome that artists explore the world beyond their field of expertise, but it is also necessary to consider their achievements there in the right proportions'. *Bijvoorbeeld* 1 (1988), pp. 4-9, quote p. 9; Huyghen 2008, pp. 334-335.

214 Dijk 2008; Smallenburg 2008/2.

215 Wellek 1980, chapter 'Evaluation', pp. 238-252; quotes on p. 245.

216 Clark 1979, p. 17.

217 See also section 8.2.

218 Wellek 1980, chapter 'Evaluation', p. 238-252. This principle was also mentioned when I addressed the concept of beauty in section 5.5.1.

219 Consider the Nobel Price for scientific disciplines. In recent years they mainly went to two or three people who often carry out research in different parts of the world, who shared and combined their insights and who thus managed to realise a breakthrough in their field of expertise.

220 Given its multidisciplinary approach, *Het Nederlandse sieraad* offers many points of departure for further research of other areas of design and also for research in other disciplines. This is also evident from Marjan Groot's study of the role of women in design between 1880 and 1940.

221 See José Teunissen's statement about people who avoid any form of fashion in section 5.2.1.

Abkoude 2002
Chr. van Abkoude, *Kruimeltje*, Alkmaar 2002 [1923].
Ahl 2008
Z. Ahl and P. Ernkvist, *Crafted form, continuation, praxis and reflection*, Stockholm 2008.
Arnold 2003
K. Arnold, D. Olsen, Gh. Lawrence et al., *Medicine Man*, London 2003.
Astfalck 2005
J. Astfalck, C. Broadhead and P. Derrez, *New directions in jewellery*, London 2005.
Bacon 1638
F. Bacon, The Right Honorable Francis Lord Verulam, Viscount S. Alban. *The History of Life and Death, With Observations Natural and Experimentall for the Prolonging of LIFE*, London 1683.
Barthes 1961
Roland Barthes, 'Des joyaux aux bijoux' in: *Oeuvres complètes* (vol. 1), Paris, 2002 [1961], pp. 1089-1093.
Bell 1976
Q. Bell, *On Human Finery*. New edition revised and enlarged, London 1967/2 [1955/1].
Bennett 1996
D. Bennett and D. Mascetti, *Understanding Jewellery*, Woodbridge, Suffolk 1996 [1989/1].
Bijbel 1954
Bijbel. Nieuwe vertaling in opdracht van het Nederlands Bijbelgenootschap, Amsterdam 1954.
Bordewijk 1954
F. Bordewijk, *Mevrouw en meneer Richebois. Twintig korte verhalen*, The Hague 1954.
Boudier-Bakker 1931
I. Boudier-Bakker, *De klop op de deur*. Amsterdamse familie-roman, n.y. [1931].
Brain 1979
Robert Brain, *The Decorated Body*, London 1979.
Brand 2006
J. Brand and J. Teunissen, *De macht van de mode. Over ontwerp en betekenis*, Arnhem 2006.
Brand 2007
J. Brand and J. Teunissen, *Mode en accessoires*, Arnhem 2007.
Brentjens 1998
Y. Brentjens, *Gijs Bakker*, Amsterdam 1998.

Broby-Johansen 1968

R. Broby-Johansen, *Body and Clothes. An Illustrated History of Costume*, London 1968 [1966].

Cartlidge 1985

B. Cartlidge, *Twentieth-Century Jewellery*, New York 1985.

Carvajal 2008

D. Carvajal, 'The brazen return for the Pink Panthers? Gang's global trail glitters with jewels', in: *International Herald Tribune*, 13-14 December, 2008, pp. 1-8.

Cavey 1994

C. Cavey, *Edelstenen & Juwelen*, Lisse 1994 [1992].

Cellini 1969

B. Cellini, *Het leven van Benvenuto Cellini*, Amsterdam 1969 [1728].

Cerval 1998

M. de Cerval, Ch. Bizot et al., Dictionnaire international du Bijoux, Paris 1998.

Citroen 1967

K.A. Citroen, *Taal en Teken* (public lecture given at the University of Amsterdam on Tuesday, 29 November 1966), Assen 1967.

Citroen 1985

K.A. Citroen, *Valse zilvermerken in Nederland*, Lochem 1985/2.

Clark 1979

K. Clark, *What is a masterpiece?*, London 1979.

Conan Doyle 1976

A. Conan Doyle, *The Great Adventures of Sherlock Holmes*, New York 1976.

Dahl 1988

Roald Dahl, *Georgy Porgy. More Tales of the Unexpected*, London 1988 [1960].

Deighton 1987

Len Deighton, *Winter. A Berlin Family 1899-1945*, London 1987.

Dewiel 1980

L. Dewiel, *Sieraden van de late 18e tot de vroege 20e eeuw*, Utrecht/Antwerp 1980 [1979].

Dijk 2008
M. v. Dijk, 'Die schedel is immoreel', in: *Trouw*, Tuesday 29 October 2008 (Verdieping), p. 6.
Dijkstra 2008
F. Dijkstra, 'Verhagen: Pak Mugabe z'n diamanten af', in: *Trouw*, 9 December 2008, p. 10.
Dormer 1994
P. Dormer and R. Turner, *The new jewellery. Trends + traditions*, London 1994 [1986].
Drutt 1995
H.W. Drutt English and P. Dormer, *Jewellery of our Time. Art, Ornament and Obsession*, London 1995.
Duncan 1994
A. Duncan, *The Paris Salons 1895-1914* (Volume I: Jewellery. The Designers A-K, Volume II: Jewellery. The Designers I-Z), Woodbridge, Suffolk 1994.
Eco 2007
U. Eco, *History of Beauty*, New York 2007 [2004].
Edwards 2003
M. Edwards, De Scythen in Siberië, meesters in goud, in: *National Geographic*, June 2003, pp. 92-109.
Eggert 1988
G. Eggert, *Generations of Jewellery from the 15th through the 20th century*, West Chester, Pennsylvania, 1988 [1984].
Eliëns 1997
T.M. Eliëns, M. Groot and F. Leidelmeijer, *Kunstnijverheid in Nederland 1880-1940*, Bussum 1997.
Elsevier Stokmans
M. Elsevier Stokmans, *Bijoux ethniques: Afrique, Asie et Îles du Pacifique*, Paris 2002.
Evans 1970
J. Evans, *A History of Jewellery 1100-1870*, London 1970 [1953].
Exhibition catalogue *Bijoux sculptures*
Exhibition catalogue *Bijoux sulptures*, La Piscine, musée d'art et d'industrie André Diligent, Roubaix 2008.
Exhibition catalogue *Calder Intime*
Exhibition catalogue *Calder Intime*, Musée des Arts Décoratifs Parijs, 1989.

Exhibition catalogue *De ideale man*
Exhibition catalogue *De ideale man. Man in de mode*, Gemeentemuseum Den Haag, 2008.

Exhibition catalogue *Des Wahnsinns fette Beute*
Exhibition catalogue *Des Wahnsinns fette Beute. Schmuck an der Akademie der Bildenden Künste München: Die Klasse Künzli, 01.03. – 18.05.2008*, Die Neue Sammlung, München 2008.

Exhibition catalogue *Design What modern was*
Exhibition catalogue *Design 1935-1965: What modern was*, Le Musée des Arts Decoratifs de Montréal, 1991.

Exhibition catalogue *Erotischer Schmuck*
Exhibition catalogue *Erotischer Schmuck*, Erotic Art Museum, Hamburg 1995.

Exhibition catalogue *Het Versierde Ego*
Exhibition catalogue *Het Versierde Ego*. Het kunstjuweel in de 20ste eeuw, Koningin Fabiolazaal, Antwerp 2000.

Exhibition catalogue *Jewellery Redefined*
Exhibition catalogue *Jewellery Redefined*, British Crafts Centre, London 1982.

Exhibition catalogue *Les Fleurs du Mal*
Exhibition catalogue *Les Fleurs du Mal* – Florian Ladstätter, Museum of Applied Arts Vienna, Vienna 2007.

Exhibition catalogue *Luxe & Decadentie*
Exhibition catalogue *Luxe & Decadentie*. Leven aan de Romeinse goudkust, Museum het Valkhof, Nijmegen 2008.

Exhibition catalogue *Nur für ihre Frauen*
Exhibition catalogue *Nur für ihre Frauen*. Schmuck von Karl Schmidt-Rottluff, Emil Nolde, Erich Heckel und Ernst Ludwig Kirchner, Stiftung Moritzburg, Halle 2003.

Exhibition catalogue *Sieradiën*
Exhibition catalogue *Sieradiën... een noodzakelijke zotheid*, Rotterdam 2006 .

Exhibition catalogue *Trauerschmuck*
Exhibition catalogue *Trauerschmuck vom Barock bis zum Art Déco*, Museum für Sepulkralkultur, Kassel 1995.

Fales 1995
M.G. Fales, *Jewellery in America 1600-1900*, Woodbridge, Suffolk 1995.

Feitsma 2008
M. Feitsma and F. de Vries, *Tijdschrift beeldanalyse visie concept product*, Arnhem 2008.
Fisher 1994
A. Fisher, *Africa Adorned*, London 1994 [1984].
Flower 1967
M. Flower, *Victorian Jewellery*, London 1967 [1951].
Flügel 1950
J.C. Flügel, *The Psychology of Clothes*, London 1950 [1930].
Fouchard 2005
G. Fouchard, *La Mode*, Paris 2005.
Frei 2003
U-B. Frei and F. Bühler, *Der Rosenkranz. Andacht – Geschichte – Kunst*, Bern 2003.
Fullée 1990
C. Fullée, *Bijoux du 20ème siècle*, London 1990.
Gans 1961
M.H. Gans, *Juwelen en mensen. De Geschiedenis van het bijou van 1400 tot 1900, voornamelijk naar Nederlandse bronnen*, Amsterdam 1961.
Geoffroy-Schneiter 2001
B. Geoffroy-Schneiter, *Parures ethniques. Le culte de la beauté*, Paris 2001.
Gere 1989
Ch. Gere and G.C. Munn, *Artists' Jewellery. Pre Raphaelite to Arts and Crafts*, Woodbridge, Suffolk 1989.
Giltay 1961
L. Giltay-Nijssen, *Juwelen*, Bussum 1961.
Goetz 2008
A. Goetz and C. Joannis, *Bijoux*, Musée du Louvre, Paris 2008.
Le Goff 1992
J. Le Goff, *The Medieval Imagination*, Chicago and London 1992 [1988].
Le Goff 2006
J. Le Goff, *De cultuur van middeleeuws Europa*, Amsterdam 2006 [1984].
Gregorietti 1970
G. Gregorietti, *Jewellery through the ages*, London 1970 [1969].
Grönig 1997
K. Grönig, *Decorated Skin. A World Survey of Body Art*, London 1997.

Groot 2008
G. Groot, 'Wij zijn allen Gekko's geworden. Bernard Mandevilles "Fabel van de bijen" over maatschappelijke ondeugd vertaald', in: *NRC Handelsblad*, 26 September 2008 (Books), p. 7.

Groot 2007
M. Groot, *Vrouwen in de vormgeving in Nederland 1880-1940*, Rotterdam 2007.

Groskamp-ten Have 1939
A. Groskamp-ten Have, *Hoe hoort het eigenlijk?*, Amsterdam, n.y. [1939].

Haeften 1936
O. van Haeften, *Manieren. Wenken voor wie zich correct willen gedragen*, Amsterdam 1936.

Hall 1993
J. Hall, *Hall's Iconografisch Handboek. Onderwerpen, symbolen en motieven in de beeldende kunst*, Leiden 1993.

Hammes 1944
J. Hammes, *Goud, zilver, edelstenen*, Amsterdam 1944 [1943].

Hansmann 1966
L. Hansmann and L. Kriss-Rettenbeck, *Amulett und Talisman. Erscheinungsform und Geschichte*, Munich 1966.

Heller 1992
C.B. Heller, *Jugendstil. Kunst um 1900*, Darmstadt 1992.

Henny 1986
A. Henny, *Geld tussen zekerheid en risico. De rol van het goud in de geschiedenis*, Zeist 1986.

Hill 2001
Tobias Hill, *The Love of Stones*, London 2001.

Hinks 1975
P. Hinks, *Nineteenth Century Jewellery*, London 1975.

Hofstede 2000
G. Hofstede, *Allemaal andersdenkenden. Omgaan met cultuurverschillen*, Amsterdam 2000 [1991].

Hojer 1997
G. Hojer, *Die Schönheitsgalerie König Ludwigs I*, Regensburg 1997.

Hue-Williams 2001
S. Hue-Williams, *Christie's Guide to Jewellery*, New York 2004.

Hughes 1966
G. Hughes, *Jewellery*, London 1966.

Hughes 1968
G. Hughes, *Modern Jewellery. An International Survey 1890-1967*, New York 1968 [1963].
Hughes 1984
G. Hughes, *The Art of Jewellery. A Survey of Craft and Creation*, New York 1984 [1972].
Hugo 2001
P. Hugo, J. Peignot, G. Picon et al. *Bijoux d'artistes/Artists' jewels*, Aix-en-Provence 2001.
Huibers
J. Huibers, *Twee eeuwen sieraden. Leerboek van De Vakschool*, n.p. and n.y.
Huygen 2007
F. Huygen, *Visies op vormgeving. Het Nederlands ontwerpen in teksten*. Part 1 (1874-1940), Rotterdam 2007.
Huygen 2008
F. Huygen, *Visies op vormgeving. Het Nederlands ontwerpen in teksten*. Part 2 (1944-2000), Rotterdam 2008.
Impelluso 2005
L. Impelluso, *De natuur en haar symbolen*, Gent/Amsterdam 2005 [2003].
Jansen 1997
W. Jansen, 'Waar is het goud gebleven? Sieraden en identiteit', in: *Ons Soort Mensen. Levensstijlen in Nederland*, Nijmegen 1997.
Janssen 2007
R. Janssen, 'De bloeddiamant is uitgebannen. Diamanten worden nauwelijks meer gebruikt voor financiering van oorlogen', in: *NRC Handelsblad*, 10 and 11 November 2007, p. 23.
Kant 1790
I. Kant, *Critik der Urtheilskraft*, 1790
Klep 1997
P.M.M. Klep, J.Th. Lindblad, A.J. Schuurman et al., *Aards geluk. De Nederlanders en hun spullen 1550-1850*, Amsterdam 1997.
Koeprin 2002
A. Koeprin, *Olesja en Vera. Twee liefdesverhalen*, Amsterdam 2002.
Lakke 1988
G. Lakke, 'Kunstenaarsdesign', in: *Bijvoorbeeld*, nr. 1 1988, pp. 4-9.
Lanel 1944
L. Lanel, *L'orfèvrerie*, Paris 1944.

Laver 1937
J. Laver, *Taste and Fashion. From the French Revolution until today*, London 1937.

Laver 1969
J. Laver, *Modesty in Dress. An Inquiry into the Fundamentals of Fashion*, London 1969.

Lindemann 2008
J. Lindemann, *12. Erfurter Schmucksymposium*, Erfurt 2008.

Lugt 1997
R. van der Lugt, D. Watkins and K. van Zoomeren, *Onno Boekhoudt, Why not jewellery?*, Groningen 1997.

Lurie 1981
A. Lurie, *The Language of Clothes*, New York 1981.

Mabille 2001
G. Mabille, *Les Diamants de la Couronne*, Paris, Gallimard 2001.

Malaguzzi 2008
S. Malaguzzi, *Bijoux, pierres et objets précieux*, Paris 2008 [Italy 2007].

Mandeville 2008
B. Mandeville, *De fabel van de bijen* (Collected works, part III), Rotterdam 2008.

Márquez 2008
G.G. Márquez, *Liefde in tijden van cholera*, Amsterdam 2008 [1986].

De Maupassant 1959
G. de Maupassant, *Contes et nouvelles*, Paris 1959.

Mazumdar 2008
Pravu Mazumdar, *Preferring not to die: Some reflections on jewellery and death* (lecture at symposium 'Siamo Qui/We are here'), Florence, 17 April 2008.

McDonough 2002
W. McDonough and M. Braungart, *Cradle to Cradle. Remaking the Way We Make Things*, New York 2002.

Melikian 2009
S. Melikian, 'The connoisseurs take back control of the market', in: *International Herald Tribune*, 10-11 January 2009, p. 10.

Menkes 2008
S. Menkes, 'Jewellery sets responsible standards', in: *International Herald Tribune*, 9 December 2008 (Style), p. 10.

Michael 2006
Prince Michael of Greece, *Jewels of the Tsars. The Romanovs & Imperial Russia*, London 2006.

Möller 2004
R. Möller, *Schmuck. Fakten Preise Trends*, Berlin 2004.

Mons 2008
G. Mons, 'Het goud wordt duur betaald', in: *Trouw*, 21 August 2008 (Verdieping), p. 5.

Moors 2003/1
A. Moors, 'Women's gold: shifting styles in embodying family relations', in: Beshara Doumani (ed.), *Family History in Middle Eastern Studies. Household, Property, and Gender*, New York 2003, pp. 101-119.

Moors 2003/2
A. Moors, 'Gendered globalization: the multiple meanings of gold', in: *Nour* 2003, pp. 58-64.

More 1964
St. Thomas More, *Utopia*, New Haven and London 1964 [1518].

Mulder 2009
R. Mulder, 'Miljoenen aan goud verdwijnen uit crematoria', in: *NRC Handelsblad*, 13 januari 2009, p. 10.

Müller 2006
F. Müller, *Les Paruriers. Bijoux de la Haute Couture*, Brussels 2006.

Munn 1984
G.D. Munn, Castellani and Guiliano, *Revivalist Jewellers of the Nineteenth Century*, London 1984 [1983].

Némirovsky 2007
Irène Némirovsky, *Le Bal*, 2007 [1930].

Newman 2007
R. Newman, *How to select, wear & care for jewellery*, Los Angeles 2007.

Nijland 1997
E. Nijland, *Pendants*, Amsterdam 1997.

Ogden 1992
J. Ogden, *Ancient Jewellery*, London 1992.

Peesch 1983
R. Peesch, *The Ornament in European Folk Art*, New York/London 1983.

Phillips 1996
C. Phillips, *Jewellery from Antiquity to the Present*, London 1996.

Polhemus 1978
T. Polhemus and L. Proctor, *Fashion and Anti-Fashion. An Anthropology of Clothing and Adornment*, London 1987.

Rawsthorn 2008
A. Rawsthorn, 'Limited-edition furniture is feeling the crunch. The critical question for the "design-art" market is how damaging the current slump will be', in: *International Herald Tribune*, 1 December 2008, p. 6.

Reinewald 2006
C. Reinewald, 'Computersieraden', in: *Tableau* 6 (December 2006/ January 2007), pp. 84-89.

Ribbens 2009
A. Ribbens, 'Ambacht domineert de designbeurs Rotterdam', in: *NRC Handelsblad*, 4 February 2009, p. 9.

Richter 2000
Anne Richter, *The Jewellery of Southeast Asia*, London 2000.

Ross 2008
R. Ross, *Clothing: A Global History, or, The Imperialists' New Clothes*, Cambridge UK 2008.

Rower 2007
A.S. Rower, M. Rosenthal and J. Adlin, *Calder Jewellery*, New York 2007.

Rudofsky 1974
B. Rudofsky, *The Unfashionable Human Body*, New York 1974 [1971].

Scarisbrick 2007
D. Scarisbrick, Ch. Vachaudez and J. Walgrave, *Schitterend Europa. Juwelen uit Europese vorstenhuizen*, Brussels 2007.

Scarisbrick 2008
D. Scarisbrick, *le grand frisson. le bijoux de sentiment de la Renaissance à nos jours*, Paris 2008.

Schon 2004
M. Schon, *Modernist Jewellery 1930-1960. The Wearable Art Movement*, Atglen 2004.

Schuurman 1986
A. J. Schuurman, 'Het bezit van preciosa in de Zaanstreek rond 1860. Een reconstructie van leefstijlen', in: *AAG Bijdragen* 28 (1986), pp. 217-244.

Schuurman 1990
A.J. Schuurman, *Materiële cultuur en levensstijl. Een onderzoek naar de taal der dingen op het Nederlandse platteland in de 19e eeuw: de Zaanstreek, Oost-Groningen, Oost-Brabant*, Wageningen 1990.

Schuurman 1997
A.J. Schuurman, *Aards geluk. De Nederlanders en hun spullen 1550-1850*, Amsterdam 1997.

Scott Fitzgerald 1973
F. Scott Fitzgerald, *Tender is the Night*, London 1973 [1939].

Scott Fitzgerald 1974
F. Scott Fitzgerald, *The Beautiful and Damned*, Harmondsworth 1974 [1922].

Sennett 2008
R. Sennett, *The Craftsman*, London 2008.

Shakespeare 1990
W. Shakespeare, *The Complete Works of William Shakespeare*, London 1990.

Simenon 1961
G. Simenon, *Maigret en de moord op de Quai des Orfèvres*, Utrecht 1961.

Simon Thomas 1996
M. Simon Thomas, *De leer van het ornament. Versieren volgens voorschrift 1850-1930*, Amsterdam 1996.

Simon Thomas 2008
M. Simon Thomas, *Goed in vorm. Honderd jaar ontwerpen in Nederland*, Rotterdam 2008.

Smallenburg 2008/1
S. Smallenburg, 'Design als kunst? Het is echt gewoon maar een bankje', in: *NRC Handelsblad*, 5 September 2008 (Cultural Supplement), p. 16.

Smallenburg 2008/2
S. Smallenburg, 'Schedel Hirst is fabelachtig', in: *NRC Handelsblad*, 1-2 November 2008 (Art), p. 7.

Snowman 2002
K. Snowman, *Maîtres Joaillers*, London 2002 [1990].

Spence 2007
C. Spence, 'The hidden cost of a pecious stone', in: *International Herald Tribune*, 27 December 2007, p. 5.

Spiering 2008/1
H. Spiering, 'Groene-kralenmode in prehistorie. Nieuw symbool van vruchtbaarheid aan het begin van de landbouw', in: *NRC Handelsblad*, 17 June 2008.

Spiering 2008/2
H. Spiering, '12.000 jaar oud graf van vrouwelijke sjamaan ontdekt', in: *NRC Handelsblad*, 8-9 November 2008 (Science), p. 5.

Staal 2006
G. Staal and Ted Noten, *CH2=C(CH3)C(=O)OCH3. Enclosures and other TN's*, Rotterdam 2006.

Su Tong 2006
Su Tong, *Mijn leven als keizer*, Breda 2006 [1992].

Tait 1976
H. Tait, *Jewellery through 7000 years*, London 1976.

Tait 2006
H. Tait, *7000 Years of Jewellery*, London 2006 [1986].

Teunissen 2005
J. Teunissen, 'Het culturele emancipatieproces van de mode', in: *Morf* 4 (2006), pp. 70-80.

Thoreau 1961
H.D. Thoreau, *The Heart of Thoreau's Journals*, London 1961.

Tolstoy 2001
L.N. Tolstoy, *De Kreuzersonate. Verzamelde werken – verhalen en novellen*, Amsterdam 2001 [1891].

Tomasi 2001
G. Tomasi di Lampedusa, *Il gattopardo / De tijgerkat*, Amsterdam 2001 [1958].

Trommius 1982
A. Trommius, *Nederlandse concordantie van de bijbel. Verantwoording uit 1690*, Kampen 1982.

Unger 1987
M. Unger, 'Sieraad komt niet los uit bedenkelijke driehoeksverhouding', in: *Bijvoorbeeld* 1 (1987), pp. 34-38.

Unger 1992
M. Unger, *Materiaal, stof voor vormgeving*, Amsterdam 1992.

Unger 1994
M. Unger and G. Staal, *Mode en Sieraad* (exhibition catalogue/supplement Bijvoorbeeld 2), Amsterdam 1994.

Unger 2004
M. Unger, *Het Nederlandse sieraad in de 20ste eeuw*, Bussum 2004.

Unger 2005
M. Unger, *Unlimited. Presenting jewellery out of the box*, Amsterdam 2005.

Unger 2006
M. Unger, 'Wat niet verandert', in: *Morf* 2 (2006), pp. 133-143.

Unger 2008
M. Unger, 'Afscheid', in: *Morf* 9 (2008), pp. 6-17.

Untracht 1997
O. Untracht, *Traditional Jewellery of India*, London/New York 1997.
Veblen 1899
Th. Veblen, *The Theory of the Leisure Class*, New York 1899.
Vever 2001
H. Vever, *French Jewellery of the Nineteenth Century*, London 2001 [1906-08].
Voet 1982
E. Voet jr., *Nederlandse goud- en zilvermerken* (10th edition, edited by P.W. Voet), Leiden 1982.
Vreeland 1980
D. Vreeland, *Allure*, New York 1980.
Waarborg 1997
Waarborg Platina, Goud en Zilver NV. Nederlandse verantwoordelijkheidstekens sinds 1797, Gouda 1997.
Walgrave 1995
J. Walgrave, H. De Decker, P. Westerkamp and D. Meigen, *Sieraad, Symbool, Signaal*, Antwerp 1995.
Warhol 2007
A. Warhol, *The Philosophy of Andy Warhol. From A to B and Back Again*, London 2007 [1975].
Weber 2004
Chr. Weber-Stöber, *Schnellkurs Schmuck*, Cologne 2004.
Wellek 1980
R. Wellek and A. Warren, *Theory of Literature*, New York 1980 [1949].
Wharton 1987
Edith Wharton, *The Custom of the Country*, London 1987 [1913].
Van Zijl 2005
Ida van Zijl, *Gijs Bakker and jewelry*, Stuttgart 2005.
Zweig 1951
S. Zweig, *Maria Stuart*, Frankfurt am Main 1951.

Summary

Jewellery in context - A multidisciplinary framework for the study of jewellery

After having worked with jewellery and jewellers in many different capacities, and after having written many texts on these subjects, including a hefty book on Dutch jewellery design in the 20th century, the subject of jewellery has been approached once again in this thesis and this time from scratch. As an art historian and design critic, I wanted to analyse the many different attitudes towards jewellery.

Many books on jewellery have failed to provide a definition of jewellery. Their authors, it seems, did not see a need for defining as common a subject as jewellery. At the same time, however, this allowed them to write whatever they wanted on this matter. They could choose to illustrate their claims with examples from a multitude of pieces that are still with us today, or from the many different ways in which jewellery has been depicted in the course of history. In the Dutch language, there are two words for jewellery: 'sieraad' for all sorts of adornment of the body, and 'juweel' for pieces of adornment in precious metals and with stones. In German, French and Italian, there are in fact similar distinctions in terminology.

This thesis, after defining its subject, focuses on an analysis of the diverging aspects of jewellery as a worldwide phenomenon. This comprehensive approach starts from the view that all human fears and desires have somehow materialised in objects of human adornment. Specifically, my analysis aims at developing a sound theoretical framework for the study of jewellery, the main aim of this thesis.

People have always treated precious jewellery seriously because of its economic value. Today the study of jewellery is a sub-category of the study of the applied arts, which in turn is a sub-category of the discipline of history of art and architecture. In Chapter 3, I disentangle the blessings and shortcomings of the art historians' approach to jewellery. If art history is not a very old discipline, the study of jewellery as a subject in its own right within this framework took off only in the 1950s and 1960s. The history of jewellery as a worldwide phenomenon can be traced back, after recent archaeological findings, some 100,000 years. Due to this discrepancy, perhaps, the study of jewellery has been blemished with many misconceptions and stereotypes, for example the notion that jewellery is meant to beautify women only, and not meant for men as well. Although the obsession of many authors with only the most precious and refined jewels made for wealthy and powerful figures can be considered a matter of taste, it has certainly reduced the social dimension of jewellery to mere proof of envy or naked display of power. The argument in this chapter also underscores that the art history approach to jewellery has largely been dominated by Western attitudes

Next, the relationship between jewellery and the human body is explored in chapter 4. Jewellery is made by human beings, but, just as important, it is worn on the human body. The wearer can give his or her own meaning and even a certain quality to a piece, without altering it. In the study of jewellery, one should carefully address the triad of maker, wearer and onlooker. The basic shapes of pieces of jewellery such as rings, bracelets and necklaces have been remarkably constant, throughout the world as well as across the centuries of which pieces have survived.

Chapter 5 is devoted to the analysis of various disciplinary lines of approach: psychology, sociology, anthropology and material culture; fashion history, with emphasis on recent developments in fashion theory; literature, economics and moral attitudes based on religion, philosophy and distinctive notions of beauty. The economy of jewellery is discussed in terms of the legal, material and technical aspects specific to jewellery. Many of the reflective points of view from the various disciplines are useful for the general study of jewellery, even if so far most authors have paid little attention to them. Exceptions are mostly found in specialised studies and in studies of adornment in non-Western cultures, which discuss interesting social functions and distinctions, as well as relevant ritual values.

The symbolic meaning of jewellery is an infinite theme when considered as a multilayered and many-cultured phenomenon with a history longer than that of any other artefact, except weapons. In chapter 6, I have systemised this symbolism somewhat by distinguishing three main categories: power, fertility and sexuality, and remembrance or memento. In many publications from the last decades, the focus has been on aspects and forms of jewellery that are considered new, while the backbone of jewellery making is rather the continuity of its symbolic shapes and meanings. Jewels are first of all signs of coherence in a society; people recognise them as signs of distinction only from a certain cultural perspective. What is fascinating indeed is the endless way makers and wearers have been able to vary on jewellery over time.

The results of this research are summed up in chapter 7, where I evaluate the values and functions that can be ascribed to jewellery, and the way they relate to each other. By distinguishing between artistic or cultural values, historical value or jewellery as sign in social relationships, emotional or personal values and the unavoidable issue of the economic value of jewellery, this thesis develops a set of standards that can serve as a model for the study of many more subjects within the crafts, applied arts and design.

Finally, my conclusion is quite straightforward: I argue for the need to combine many different points of view and to balance them in sensible ways as the basis for a new theoretical framework for the study of jewellery. In this respect it is appropriate to advance the discipline of art history. After all, the careful material, aesthetic, cultural and historical analysis of objects, which forms the basis of this discipline, is equally crucial in the study of jewellery. In addition, specific knowledge of materials and techniques is needed.

The title of this thesis, Jewellery in context, reflects a multidisciplinary approach. Among other things, such an approach has particular implications for the presentation of jewellery, and even more so for the historical research of this subject. Especially in the Western world, it is important to address the adornments of the not so happy few and the many layers of the upper and middle classes. In this respect, there is much to be learned from anthrpology and the study of material culture.

Of course, with my background you never work completely from scratch; inevitably you bring in a lot of things you have seen and read, and, in the case of jewellery, also things you have worn yourself. This becomes clear in particular in the notes and the bibliography. In the process of writing this thesis all my own notions about jewellery, my assumptions and my experiences in wearing it, have been pushed around and around. My travels to different continents have also contributed to this dynamic. In the end, however, all these notions and experiences have found their way into the theoretical and multi-disciplinary framework for the study of jewellery.

Curriculum vitae

Marianne de Boer, born February 11, 1946.
1964 HBS-b (Higher Civic School),
1964–1967 School of Applied Arts in Amsterdam,
Industrial design department (not completed).
In 1968 married to Gerard Unger.
Works and publishes under the name Marjan Unger.
1974–1987 Art history at the University of Amsterdam, specialising in modern art, fashion and textile design, architecture, industrial archaeology and art history of China and Japan.
Lecturerships at the Amsterdam Fashion Academy, Academy of Visual Arts in Rotterdam and the Gerrit Rietveld Academy in Amsterdam.
Has numerous publications and lectures to her name and has been member of many juries and advisory committees.
1980–1989 Editor-in-Chief of *Bijvoorbeeld*, design magazine.
1991–1993 Director of Dutch Form.
1995–2006 Head of the Department of Free Design at the Sandberg Institute, the post-academic courses associated with the Gerrit Rietveld Academy in Amsterdam.
2002 organisation of *Zonder wrijving geen glans*, exhibition about Dutch jewellery from the 20th century in the Central Museum in Utrecht.
2004 the book *Het Nederlandse sieraad in de 20e eeuw* published in Bussum.
2004–2008 editor-in-chief of *Morf*, design magazine aimed at design students at Dutch academies, colleges and universities.

Cooperation and co-publishers

This English translation of Marjan Unger's dissertation has been realised on the initiative of Theo Smeets in cooperation with Chequita Nahar, Suzanne van Leeuwen, Wolfgang Lösche and Dirk Allgaier. It has been made possible by the generous support of the following project partners:

Gesellschaft für Goldschmiedekunst e.V.
Deutsches Goldschmiedehaus Hanau

JAKOB BENGEL
INDUSTRIEDENKMAL

Handwerkskammer
für München und Oberbayern
Galerie Handwerk

Maastricht Academy
of Fine Arts and Design
MAFAD
ZUYD

RIJKS MUSEUM

Trier University
of Applied Sciences
Gemstones
and Jewellery
HOCHSCHULE TRIER
IDAR-OBERSTEIN

and the following co-publishers:

Akademie der Bildenden Künste Nürnberg
Association for Contemporary Jewellery
Atelier Ted Noten
Beppe Kessler
Birmingham School of Jewellery
Claudia Stebler
Clodagh Molloy
CODA Museum
Current Obsession
Dr. Karin Findeis
Estonian Academy of Arts
Felieke van der Leest
Françoise van den Bosch foundation
Fred Brom, Steltman Juwelier
Galeria Alice Floriano
Galerie Door
Galerie Marzee
Galerie Ra
Galerie Spektrum
Gerrit Rietveld Academy
Gijs Bakker
Goldschmiedeschule mit Uhrmacherschule, Pforzheim
Grupo Broca
hedendaagsesieraden.nl
Iris Bodemer
Jewellery Association Aura
Klimt02
Kun Zhang
Lucerne University of Applied Sciences and Arts
Lucy Sarneel
Makiko Akiyama
Michelle Stewart
Monika Brugger
Nedda El-Asmar
New Craft Object Design, University of Applied Arts Düsseldorf
PIN – Associação Portuguesa de Joalharia Contemporânia
PXL-MAD School of arts, Hasselt
Rae Mearkle
RHOK Academy Brussels
Saimaa University of Applied Sciences, Fine arts
Saskia Kolff
Sienna Patti
SIERAAD, International Jewellery Art Fair
Tabea Reulecke
The Finnish Jewelry Art Association
Truike Verdegaal
Ute Eitzenhöfer

Colophon

www.arnoldsche.com

Author	Marjan Unger
Design	Gerard Unger
Translation	Ton Brouwers
Editing and lay-out	Theo Smeets
Proof reading	Oranna Kammann

Printet by logo Print, Metzingen on Salzer EOS 1.3 Vol. 90 g/qm.

Bibliographic information published by the Deutsche Nationalbibliothek: The Deutsche Nationalbibliothek lists this publication in the Deutsche Nationalbibliografie; detailed bibliographic data are available on the internet at www.dnb.de.

The original text of this dissertation is available on the internet at openaccess.leidenuniv.nl/handle/1887/15121.

ISBN 978-3-89790-579-5

Made in Europe, 2019